PLATO'S MODERN ENEMIES
AND THE THEORY OF
NATURAL LAW

PLATO'S MODERN ENEMIES
AND THE THEORY OF
NATURAL LAW

BY JOHN WILD

THE UNIVERSITY OF CHICAGO PRESS

THE UNIVERSITY OF CHICAGO PRESS, CHICAGO 37
Cambridge University Press, London, N.W. 1, England

TO CATHERINE

PREFACE

THIS book has grown gradually from courses on the philosophy of Plato which I have given at Harvard during the last ten years when the interest in classical philosophy has been steadily growing. In this interval of time many anti-Platonic tracts have appeared bringing serious charges against Plato, both as a man and as a thinker, which I have discussed with my students. Their reaction has deeply interested me. Most of them at first have accepted these charges as cogent and convincing, but then, after gaining more familiarity with the *Dialogues*, have found them less convincing. This has often led them to inquire concerning the reasons for this barrier which now seems to be separating my generation and theirs from a sympathetic and intelligent appreciation of that seminal Socratic literature from which so much that is best in our Western tradition has grown. This pattern of response has been widespread. It has led me to believe that there is perhaps now a need for the presentation of another side, an answer to these charges, an explanation of some of the misunderstandings on which they are based. This book is an attempt to meet this need.

The nucleus from which it grew was a lecture delivered before the Philhellenic Society of the University of Washington in 1950. Since that time I have been greatly aided by conversations with my friend, Professor Ronald Levinson of the University of Maine, whose forthcoming book on Plato will be a monumental contribution to classical scholarship. I am also very grateful to Professor W. C. Greene of the Classics Department of Harvard for his criticisms of my manuscript. Neither of them of course is responsible for any of the opinions I have expressed.

I wish to thank the editors of *Ethics* and of the *Journal of Philosophy* for their permission to use the substance of two articles published in these periodicals ("Natural Law and Modern Ethical Theory," *Ethics*, October, 1952, and "Tendency: The

Ontological Ground of Ethics," *Journal of Philosophy*, July 3, 1952) in writing chapters seven and eight, and the Clark Fund of Harvard University for its financial aid.

I wish finally to express my thanks to my daughter Cynthia for her clerical assistance.

J. W.

CAMBRIDGE, MASSACHUSETTS
January 14, 1953

TABLE OF CONTENTS

PART II. THE THEORY OF NATURAL LAW

INTRODUCTION

Pᴌᴀᴛᴏ's profound and lasting interest in moral and political problems can hardly be subject to any reasonable
doubt. His early dialogues are concerned primarily with
the analysis of moral virtues and with the basic issues raised
by the life and death of his teacher Socrates, the moralist. The
greatest work of his middle period, the *Republic*, is a study of
individual and social justice in which he attempts not only to
express the moral philosophy of Socrates, but also to develop
its epistemological and metaphysical implications as well—
something which Socrates himself had never done in a systematic way. One cannot commit himself to a practical philosophy
without also becoming committed to certain principles concerning the nature of human knowledge and the universe. Plato
was committed to the moral principles which had guided the
life of Socrates. In his written dialogues, he tried first of all to
keep alive the thought and the spirit of Socrates—to undo the
work of the hemlock, to suggest to the reader by protreptic
questioning and argument the basic and inescapable importance
of this moral spirit; and finally, as his own peculiar contribution,
to work out its broader philosophical presuppositions. The primary moral interest was maintained throughout the whole
period of Plato's life.

This is clearly indicated by the *Philebus*, a moral treatise devoted to the criticism of hedonism and the delineation of the
good for man, which was written in his late maturity. It is
finally confirmed by the nature of that ambitious but unfinished
project to which Plato seems to have devoted the last years of
his life.[1] This was to include the account of a practical version
of ideal society sketched in the *Republic*, which might be
realized in the future (the *Laws*); a survey of human history
down to Plato's time; a sketch of the early prehistory of man;
and finally, an imaginative and philosophical account of the
origin of the world (the *Timaeus*). Only the first and last parts
of this project were ever completed, though a fragment of the
third has come down to us as the *Critias*, and a part of the

second is found in the *Laws* (Book III). We could hardly expect a surer confirmation of the sustained practical orientation of Plato's thought as a whole. Living his mature life after the Peloponnesian War in a period of culture collapse, aroused by the person of Socrates, he devoted his intellectual energies to the task of formulating an intelligible conception of the ideal human life and of the ideal human community in which men like Socrates might actually feel at home. Guided by this natural norm, in many of his dialogues he diagnosed the intellectual and moral errors of the great Age of Pericles which lay at the root of the cultural catastrophes and decay of his own time. In others, like the *Republic* and the *Laws*, he attempted to paint pictures of a better state in which these evils might be corrected.

Plato's moral and social philosophy has had a deep effect on the intellectual history of the West, and here and there it has played a certain subordinate role in the shaping of historic life and institutions. But the practical orientation of his thought as a whole has often not been sharply focused. Each period tends to find itself in Plato and to ignore what it is not. Thus, the modern era of post-Cartesian philosophy has focused its attention on problems of epistemology. Indeed for the consistent idealist, being is mental being, and philosophy is hardly distinguished from the theory of knowledge. Hence, it is not remarkable that throughout this period idealistic interpreters of Plato have emphasized the theory of ideas and have been far less interested in his moral philosophy. So far as they have dealt with this, they have tended to dilute its peculiar features and to merge it with more familiar modern doctrines, such as Kantianism or utilitarianism, though, as a matter of fact, Platonic ethics is radically opposed to both.

In recent times, however, perhaps as a result of the moral chaos and political tensions of our period, there has been a renewed interest in moral philosophy, and more especially in the moral philosophy of Plato. Many such studies have appeared in the English-speaking world during recent years; in 1934 *The Platonic Legend* by Warner Fite, in 1937 *Plato Today* by R. H. S. Crossman, in 1940 *The Genesis of Plato's Thought* by A. D.

Winspear, and finally in 1946 *The Open Society and Its Enemies* by K. R. Popper. Many more articles and reviews in technical journals could also be mentioned. These studies recognize moral philosophy as an essential strand in Plato's thought. This is sound. They also agree that Plato's social and political conceptions are relevant to the burning problems of our own time. Unlike the nineteenth-century writers, who had not yet witnessed unmistakable symptoms of social barbarism and decay and who, therefore, viewed Plato's bitter attacks on tyranny with antiquarian detachment, these authors have observed manifest social corruption. Hence, they have no difficulty in understanding the issues with which Plato is concerned, and they all attempt to relate his doctrines to the problems now confronting us. This is also sound. The similarity between the condition of Hellenic civilization in Plato's time and that of our Western civilization today is striking.

But there are other phases of this revival of interest in Plato's moral philosophy which are more dubious. All the authors whom we have noted are anti-Fascist and prodemocratic in their points of view. This is sound; Plato also bitterly opposed tyranny. But he opposed it for definite reasons—which he carefully formulated on the basis of an intelligible position—quite different from those of the individualistic, utilitarian, Marxist, and positivistic writers we have referred to. They have been so impressed by these differences, which indeed are very basic, as to infer that since Plato is philosophically opposed to them, he must be politically opposed to them as well. Hence, though they differ from one another in many important respects, they all agree that Plato, if he were alive today, would take his stand with totalitarianism and dictatorship against the forces of "liberalism," "progress," and "democracy."

According to Fite, "In the *Republic* we have a social and political theory, unique in the history of thought, for devotion to the leisure-class ideal."[2] Plato has no understanding of personal freedom and democracy. "Of personality, of individuality, as I have pointed out—and much less of any species of 'democracy' —he has not the slightest appreciation."[3] Plato has no concern for the value and dignity of the individual. According to Win-

spear, Plato is a reactionary aristocrat opposed to every manifestation of social progress. According to Crossman, Plato is a
fanatical dogmatist who believes he has discovered a final truth
which must destroy all actual freedom. ". . . He turned the
Socratic belief in reason into a dogmatic and authoritarian
code."[4] His philosophy is a defense of tyranny; if employed for
"worthy" ends, he would approve of the sort of murder and
violence which has been used to support dictatorship in Germany and Russia.[5] According to Popper, "Plato's political pro-
gram, far from being morally superior to totalitarianism, is
fundamentally identical with it."[6] He is the classic enemy of
freedom and democracy who even "tried to implicate Socrates
in his grandiose attempt to construct the theory of the ar-
rested society."[7]

The manifest rationalism of Plato's moral philosophy and his
hatred of tyranny under any form, which strikes the eye of even
the most superficial reader, would seem to make these charges
somewhat questionable. Nevertheless, they are accepted by a
wide variety of authors and teachers representing many divergent positions. In countless courses on government and philosophy in universities of England and the United States and
throughout the English-speaking world, Plato is now generally
used as an example of authoritarian and Fascist ideology. In
a recent presidential address to the Pacific Division of the
American Philosophical Association, the president referred to
Plato's *Republic* as "that original philosophical charter of
Fascism."[8] Many of those who repeat such charges do so without offering any verifying references or careful argument. And
so the doctrine spreads even more rapidly without the need for
controversy or debate. Those who make these statements claim
to stand for "reason," "scientific method," and "the freedom
of opinion," so it would seem as if they ought to welcome a
critical examination of this widely accepted theory. But whatever their view may be, I believe that the time has come for an
unprejudiced examination. Was Plato really a Fascist, a defender of dictatorship and tyranny?

In the light of our cultural history, this question is a matter
of some importance. Plato's influence on Western thought has
been so decisive and so constant that it is hard to imagine what

our intellectual heritage would have been without the goading, stimulating power of his writings. From the fourth century B.C. down to the present time, they have awakened the minds of countless readers with the questioning spirit of Socrates and have elicited and sustained a trust in the rational faculties of man and a hope for philosophic wisdom. Are these the seeds of dogmatism and tyranny? Are we to be persuaded that from these seeds of Platonic rationalism has sprung the awful fruit of modern totalitarianism and mass despotism? Are we to assist in the nurture of a generation brought up to despise this literature as the breeding ground for tribal provincialism and ruthless power politics? Many voices are now urging us to these conclusions. I suggest that we should not yield to them, at least without examination, and in the following pages I propose to attempt such an investigation.

First of all, in Part I let us consider the most serious charges that have been brought against Plato by modern "progressive" writers. Was he an irrational dogmatist, a militarist, a totalitarian, a racialist, a propagandist for the closed society, and finally an implacable enemy of modern "democracy"? If, as we believe, these charges arise from certain misconceptions of the nature of Platonic moral philosophy, let us then turn to this doctrine and attempt to clarify it by comparison and contrast with the views of its modern opponents. What are the grounds of Plato's opposition to tyranny, and how do they differ from those of modern "democratic" philosophers?

These grounds are based on the conception later referred to by the term *natural law*, a notion completely strange to the atmosphere of modern ethical and political thought, but acutely relevant to contemporary social problems and once again beginning to receive some attention from disciplined minds. So in Part II of this study we shall investigate the nature, history, and classical origins of this theory.

Having systematically examined the nature of moral realism and natural-law philosophy, and having learned something of its origin and history in Western thought, we should then be able to judge of its significance for us. Hence, in Part III we shall try to bring this realistic philosophy to bear on certain basic problems of contemporary ethics.

PART I
PLATO'S MODERN ENEMIES

CHAPTER ONE

PLATO AS AN ENEMY OF FREEDOM
AND THE OPEN SOCIETY

I<small>T WOULD</small> be impossible to find a single category which would adequately characterize the modern enemies of Plato. Their name is legion, and they speak from positions which cover the whole spectrum of modern political thought. The Communist attacks Plato as a bourgeois idealist, while Western liberals have often attacked him as a Communist. The four most influential recent treatises, which we have already mentioned and to which we shall refer in this discussion, represent a wide variety of views. Warner Fite is an individualist, Winspear a Marxist (though not of the most extreme and consistent type), Crossman a Socialist member of the British Labor party, and Popper a self-styled utilitarian with strong sympathies for modern positivist thought. Similar charges against Plato have been made from very different points of view by Reinhold Niebuhr, the Neo-orthodox theologian, and Arnold Toynbee, the philosopher of history.

Nevertheless, there are certain attitudes which they all hold in common. They share an acute sense of progressive modernity, of speaking for this present world. Hence, we must think of this as a modern attack. They also share a deep sympathy for equalitarianism and democracy, though they would doubtless define this latter term in divergent ways. They all agree that Plato is an enemy of freedom and the open society, a defender of political reaction and even tyranny. As we have already noted, they are the most articulate exponents of similar views widely held throughout the English-speaking world.

We shall now break down these broad charges into their distinct components and examine them one by one. We shall take note of the major charges urged by all the authors on our list, but shall focus our attention on the contents of K. R. Popper's *The Open Society and Its Enemies*, which is by far the most extreme and pretentious anti-Platonic tract to be penned in recent times. Our aim will be to achieve a fair appraisal of these basic charges, not to defend Plato at any cost. Where we find certain criticisms to be justified, we shall candidly so state them. No author is infallible. In our opinion, Plato's political doctrines, as they are found in the texts available to us, are certainly not free from error. But where we find criticisms based on misunderstanding, we shall point them out, together with our reasons.

Section I. PLATO AS AN IRRATIONAL DOGMATIST

Plato leaves us in no doubt as to where he stands as a moral thinker. Not only does he develop a clearly articulated system of moral principles based upon a coherent view of the nature of man, but he also gives us a moving picture of Socrates, the concrete embodiment of his ethical principles, the moral man in action. In contrast to influential modern views which base moral value on arbitrary preference or self-imposed maxims, Plato's ethics is founded on the nature of man and the nature of things. Modern ethical discussion is abstract and theoretical, remaining aloof from any concrete consideration of the moral virtues and the exigencies of everyday life. Plato's ethics embraces a description of the human virtues in the concrete, as well as a more abstract attempt to found them on the laws of human nature.

To the modern mind this conveys an impression of overweening dogmatism, one of the commonest charges made against Plato by almost all of his modern enemies. Thus, Popper believes that Plato's ethical system, with its anthropological and metaphysical substratum, is a dogmatic authoritarianism which blasphemes the memory of his doubting master.[1] Socrates was associated with "the Great Generation" of Athenian liberals and democrats, "which lived in Athens just before and during the Peloponnesian War."[2] Of this great generation, which included Pericles, Democritus, Gorgias, Antiphon, and Antisthenes, Socrates was "perhaps the greatest of all."[3] He held firmly to a "creed of individualism," believing in "the human individual as an end in himself."[4] Philosophically speaking, however, his attitude was purely "agnostic,"[5] and he kept away from metaphysical theories.[6] The essence of Socratic teaching is philosophical ignorance. He was skeptical of all such learning, "whether it was that of the philosophers of the past or of the learned men of his own generation."[7] This antiphilosophical philosophy of Socrates, according to Popper, "is the true scientific spirit."[8] "The Spirit of Science is that of Socrates."[9]

In answer to this, we may point out that in the *Apology*, which Popper accepts as an accurate historical account of the trial, Socrates clearly expresses several basic convictions of a positive nature. First, there is a divine being higher than man, possessing a wisdom compared to which human wisdom is as nothing;[10] second, vice and injustice, evils of the soul, are worse than sickness and death, evils of the body,[11] which implies that man is a composite of body and soul and that the soul is more important than the body; third, tending the soul is more important than tending the body;[12] fourth, virtue depends primarily on knowledge;[13] and fifth, it is not so evil to suffer injustice as to do it.[14]

It is true that at the time of his trial Socrates does not develop and elaborate these basic doctrines. But he does clearly state them, which shows that it is absurd to regard him merely as an "agnostic." Science today means primarily the discipline of physics and the study of quantitative structure. Socrates says explicitly in the *Apology* that he has no interest in such physical theories.[15] Cautious doubters with no positive philosophical convictions do not live the Socratic life or die the Socratic death. Significant questions do not arise at random. They result from accepted principles and certain incomplete but definite answers. Socrates certainly held such principles, if Plato's account of him is at all trustworthy. Among them were included the five we have mentioned. The whole Platonic ethics and metaphysics is rooted in these principles. If this is dogmatism, then Socrates also was a dogmatist—and, indeed, so is anyone with any moral principles at all—for any ethics must be grounded ultimately in some view of the nature of man and of the world in which he lives.

Warner Fite also accuses Plato of dogmatism[16] and gives this charge a peculiar moral twist. According to him, Plato is haunted by scenes of debauchery, and his one moral idea is that of self-restraint.[17] As to the first inference concerning Plato's debauchery, we must pass this over, as there is no relevant evidence.

Concerning the negativism of Plato's ethics, a point often urged in connection with the *Phaedo*,[18] we may refer to the texts, which offer decisive evidence. When the *Phaedo* is read carefully, it will be found that the most extreme ascetic passages[19] are marked by important qualifying phrases. Thus, the philosopher will have "*the least possible* communion with the body."[20] Those who are materialistically minded will scorn this life of reason and virtue, the only true life of man, as a living death.[21] But it is the uncontrolled pursuit of physical objects and physical pleasures which buries the soul in a bodily tomb.[22] Thus, Niebuhr is quite wrong in suggesting that the classical view of man is a "dualism" which identifies "the body with evil" and assumes "the essential goodness of mind or spirit."[23] Genuine human life requires the restraint of such pursuits so that the higher rational phases of human nature may exercise their proper functions of free activity and rational control. This is also the consistent teaching of the *Republic*,[24] the *Philebus*,[25] and the *Laws*.[26] Plato never urges self-restraint as an end in itself. The good for man is the full realization of human nature, including especially the acts of reason and deliberate choice.

The most extreme version of this attack on Plato as a dogmatist is to be found in Crossman.[27] The greatest of all the errors committed by Plato is his view that philosophy can "discover what is right and just."[28] Platonism is thus a dogmatic philosophy. "Asserting the existence of absolute truth, it succeeded in giving to a dying order and an outworn social structure the trappings of eternal verity."[29] Any such assertion of philosophic truth must lead to tyranny. ". . . Plato was forced to destroy that freedom without which reason must die. . . ."[30]

Are we then to believe that freedom is nourished upon ignorance? The obvious reply to this commonly repeated charge is a reference to the distinction implied throughout the whole of Plato's works between freedom and anarchy, and the closely related distinction between knowledge and opinion, which lies at the root of Platonic philosophy.

Erroneous opinion, which thinks it knows when it does not know, is, of course, an enemy of freedom since it breeds false authoritarianism and tyranny. But sound insight and the respect for truth, far from being inimical to human freedom, are necessary conditions for its exercise, without which it evaporates into anarchy, the mother of tyranny. How are we to distinguish between sound knowledge and opinion? The confirmed philosophical skeptic, of course, cannot do so. For him, all truth is merely a blatant manifestation of prejudice. Like the misologists to whom Socrates refers in the *Phaedo*,[31] he has been deceived by certain arguments. Therefore, he distrusts all argument, confusing knowledge with opinion and freedom with anarchy. But, as Socrates remarks, "No worse thing can happen to a man than this."

How then are we to distinguish between knowledge and opinion? What is the criterion? Where is the infallible sign?

Plato's answer is clear. There is no such criterion or sign. There is no sure and easy pathway to the truth. The only pathway lies through the arduous exercise of the individual intellect in a Socratic questioning, examining, and sifting of the relevant evidence. Then, the truth may be seen, or it may not be. But the individual intellect alone is the test.[32] In his dialogues, Plato has recapitulated this questioning, sifting process, and has given us many hints and reminders,[33] which may assist the individual reader in apprehending certain moral truths. Whether they are actually true or not can be decided only by the reader, as the result of dialectical question and argument.

Neither Niebuhr nor Crossman presents us with any argument of this sort. They give us statements and decrees. Niebuhr says that not only Plato, but moral theory itself, is pretentious opinion resulting from intellectual pride, and he then retires to the authority of revelation.[34] Crossman says similar things and ends finally with a ceaseless flux of unstable concepts and opinions, which he calls "the democratic spirit." Nevertheless, he seems to *know* an opinion when he sees one and also its falsity when examined. Genuine truth, however, never emerges.[35]

Who, then, is the more dogmatic and authoritarian, he who

proceeds through Socratic questioning and sifting of the evidence to a theory for which he can give an intelligible account in terms of evident fact, or he who brushes aside all argument with a wave of the hand and relies on formulations which he cannot explain and for which he gives no evidence at all? Who is more dogmatic and irrational, Plato or his antiphilosophical enemies? In Part II we shall attempt to present some of the evidence on which Plato's moral philosophy of natural law is based. But we must now pass on to a second general charge.

Section II. Plato as a Militarist

One of the commonest charges now made against Plato is that he is a militarist, a believer in the use of force and violence for the attainment of his ends. Thus, Warner Fite says that "the nobility that Plato had in mind was a military nobility," and that "character, indeed, receives a military definition—and likewise truth";[36] and Crossman states that he would approve the use of force, violence, and murder as in modern dictatorships if employed for noble ends.[37] According to Popper, the Platonic politician is committed to a policy of bloody revolution and useless force. "He must eradicate the existing institutions and traditions. He must purify, purge, export, deport, and kill."[38] This is his interpretation of *Republic* 501 A, where Plato uses the simile of painting on a clean canvas in explaining the possible establishment of a better community.[39]

Charges of this sort are also made by Arnold Toynbee, though the general attack on Plato which runs through his masterful *Study of History* is opposed in many respects to that of Popper. According to Toynbee, Plato is essentially a contemplative philosopher. His ultimate aim is to achieve inward peace, "a detachment from life,"[40] through the contemplation of the eternal ideas. Hence, the abstract philosopher, having attained this vision of the truth, is reluctant to return to the Cave.[41] He lacks that impassioned love for his fellow men that has been inspired by Western religion at its best.[42] He is a cold and detached philosopher, unable to elicit from others any sacrificial devotion to his futuristic dreams.[43] Hence, in order to realize them, he is far too ready to employ the sword.[44]

Is there any evidence to support these charges which can be derived from what we know of Plato's life or from his writings?

So far as Plato's personal life is concerned, we know of no acts of violence with which he was directly connected. Nor is there any evidence to support the view that he himself favored militarism and violence. Plato's *Gorgias* is written in a tone of passionate conviction and personal feeling. In this dialogue the might-makes-right philosophy of Callicles is bitterly condemned. Similar views of Thrasymachus are similarly, though less vehemently, treated in the *Republic*. At 569 B, the ambitious tyrant who is prepared to use force against the "democratic" city which has nurtured him is called a "parricide." In the Seventh *Epistle* the use of violence against one's paternal city is similarly condemned. "One ought not to apply violence to his fatherland in the form of a political revolution, whenever it is impossible to establish the best kind of polity without banishing and slaughtering citizens, but rather he ought to keep quiet and pray for what is good both for himself and for his state."[45] Though Plato may have fought for a time as a young man at the end of the Peloponnesian War, the major part of his life was certainly devoted to the peaceful occupations of teaching and writing.

If we may rely on the traditional accounts of his Sicilian adventures, they were not marked by any use of force on his part. His idea was to persuade and educate the youthful tyrant to introduce necessary reforms. It is true that Dion was his student and friend, and that many other students of the Academy joined him in his expedition. But Plato himself attempted to reconcile Dion with Dionysius. In view of doubts concerning the letters, all this is highly speculative. There is no reason, however, for attributing militaristic attitudes to Plato as a man.

When we turn to the dialogues themselves, a clear and consistent doctrine is expressed. Plato holds that slavery is worse than death.[46] Hence, the use of force in defending one's self or one's city is justifiable. Plato sometimes carries this principle of the defensive use of force too far, as when he advises the use of the death penalty against those who threaten the welfare of the state by spreading atheistic and nihilistic doctrines, to which he traced the decline of Athens.[47] This is, no doubt, a mistake, though it is to be used only as a last resort after other less drastic measures have failed. But it is surely inaccurate to confuse this with a defense of aggressive militarism and bloody revolution.

Wild animals and other subhuman entities lacking intelligence must be dealt with through the use of force. But according to the *Politicus*,[48] man, possessing reason, the source of human unity, is a tame animal, susceptible to rational persuasion and voluntary guidance. The use of compulsion against such a being is, therefore, tyrannical,[49] rendering to men what is due only to tigers or beasts of prey. This is injustice,[50] and it is not so bad to suffer injustice as to do it. How can this be reconciled with militarism?

According to the *Phaedo*, war is due to unconstrained greed for material possessions, the greatest obstacle in the way of the philosophic life.[51] Social schism, which has its roots in a schism in the soul, and social conflict are the major diseases of the human community. One cannot heal these diseases by intensifying them. They can be healed only by the use of true rhetoric guided by the insights of philosophy. Hence, Plato abandoned a political career and devoted his life to teaching and contemplation. If man fails to guide his life by reason, then he may become a misologist who "no longer makes any use of persuasion by speech but achieves all his ends like a beast by violence and savagery. . . ."[52] Popper's idea that Plato is an apostle of violence[53] is wholly unsupported by any direct evidence from the texts. How, then, can we explain the origin of this charge?

In Popper's case the answer seems clear. Plato is not a rationalist at all, but a "pseudo-rationalist"; and "what I shall call 'pseudo-rationalism' is the intellectual intuitionism of Plato. It is the immodest belief in one's superior intellectual gifts, the claim to be initiated, to know with certainty, and with authority. According to Plato, opinion—even 'true opinion' as we can read in the *Timaeus*—is shared by all men; but reason (or 'intellectual intuition') is shared only by the gods, and by very few men."[54] Popper calls this "authoritarian intellectual-

ism" and holds that it is "diametrically opposed" to true
scientific rationalism,[55] which is philosophically agnostic. If
there is no philosophic insight, then Plato, of course, is an ir-
rationalist working under a deceptive disguise. This makes the
charge of militarism plausible, for, as Plato constantly reminds
us, if reason abdicates then force dictates.

Both Popper and Plato condemn the use of force. There is
no disagreement here. The issue concerns the nature of the
other alternative. What is reason? Is the human mind restricted
to the quantitative perspectives of "science"? Is every attempt
to know other modes of being such as virtue, knowledge, and
freedom unjustifiable? Or can we hope to gain some insight
into existence and the basic structure of things? Is philosophy
really possible, or is it a fantastic delusion? This is the basic
issue between Plato and his modern enemies.

Toynbee's criticism of Plato as an abstract philosopher whose
cold ideas are incapable of arousing the intense devotion of high
religion is made from a Christian point of view. As such, it has
some truth, though the idea that Plato is a philosopher of "detachment" is very dubious. This idea was characteristic of the
nineteenth-century epistemological interpretations of Plato,
which gave an exclusive emphasis to the theory of ideas and
attached little importance to Plato's practical philosophy.
Toynbee's view of the Platonic good as an Epicurean "imperturbability"[56] is even more questionable. The good for man is
the active living of a complete human life in which intellectual
activity is no doubt the highest *part*, but not the whole.[57] *Republic* and *Laws* are a sufficient witness to that primary and
persistent interest in ethics and the actual life of man which is
rightly stressed by such commentators as Taylor[58] and Cornford.[59]

One looks in vain throughout the dialogues for any articulate
and perfect expression of Christian *agapē*. This, of course, must
be granted. But the notion of sacrificial devotion to common
causes is certainly not absent. The seeds of *agapē* are there.
Certainly the portrait of Socrates which Plato has given us is
not wholly lacking in sacrificial benevolence. After all, the
philosopher who has ascended into the sunlight does return to

the Cave to help his fellows, at the cost of his life.[60] And the motive for this sacrificial act is not to be confused with an abstract Kantian duty, having no connection with natural need or interest, as Toynbee suggests.[61] This conception of a radical opposition between duty and basic need is wholly foreign to Plato's thought. Virtue, what we *ought* to do, is not opposed to interest and happiness. It is conceived as the proper functioning of an entity, acting well.[62] It is thus required for happiness and is an essential *part* of it.[63] Plato's aim was not merely to attain inner peace and "imperturbability," but rather the complete realization of all the essential human faculties in a wisely ordered community.

The relation between the fundamental conceptions of Toynbee and those of Plato is an interesting subject. In spite of Toynbee's sustained polemic, the similarities of the two philosophies of history are deep and far-reaching, far more important than the differences. For both philosophers, human nature is one; the problems confronting different civilizations are basically the same.[64] Both reject any form of historical determinism;[65] but both hold that human choices are governed by laws of *moral* necessity.[66] Unless problems are met in sound and rational ways by intelligent choices eliciting common agreement and devoted aspiration, a culture will disintegrate. Both agree that such disintegration, originally psychic and then social, is the chief disease to which human culture is subject.

Both hold that the solutions to human problems must be first conceived and carried out by individual persons. Plato calls these gifted individuals *guardians;* Toynbee calls them a *creative minority*. Both hold that culture is healthy only when such persons are able to formulate sound plans, and to lead their fellow men by common agreement, and that when this does not happen, the culture must fall into disorder and lethargy which require force for the preservation of any social unity. But such enforced unity breeds further opposition and further force in an intensifying vicious circle. Both agree that the last stages of such corruption are militarism and tyranny.

Both also maintain that there are three essential activities which must be carried on at least with some degree of effectiveness in any genuinely human culture—noetic (including science, philosophy, and religion), political, and productive or technological. In Plato's *Republic* these three functions are performed by the guardians, the auxiliaries, and the artisans.[67] Of these functions, the first is the most important, and the last the least important.[68] Thus, civilizations do not decline primarily from external physical causes, or from technological failures, but rather from mental lethargy and sterility, and from moral weakness and vice.[69] They are not so much destroyed from the outside by physical causes; they rather commit suicide and kill themselves by moral failure and self-disintegration.

The chief difference is that Toynbee's approach is primarily religious and theological, whereas Plato's is primarily scientific and philosophical. But, as we have just noted, these two approaches are not necessarily opposed. Plato's philosophy certainly does not exclude high religion,[70] nor does Toynbee's religion necessarily exclude all reason and philosophy,[71] although at certain points Toynbee seems to speak as if it does.[72] Unfortunately, we possess only unfinished fragments of the late works in which Plato might have more fully explained his own philosophy of history. But from what we do possess, we may learn, if we make allowance for Plato's lack of modern information and for Toynbee's lack of respect for human reason and philosophy, that the basic categories of the two philosophers are markedly similar. This can be seen from an examination of a brief passage in the *Laws*, Book III to 697 D, where we find the basic pattern of Toynbee—the challenge to human culture and the response of human choice with God in the background; the transition from primitive patriarchal government to larger empires, their breakdown from intellectual and moral failure, and their disintegration from militarism and tyranny.

Section III. PLATO AS A TOTALITARIAN

We must now turn to a widespread attack upon Plato which has arisen from the persistent modern attempt to interpret him as an "idealistic" philosopher. Such influential idealists as Kant and Hegel tried to absorb certain aspects of Platonism into their idealistic thought, and a host of modern commentators have fol-

lowed their example in working out idealistic interpretations of
Platonic doctrine. For English readers, the most influential
work of this kind is the famous Jowett translation of Plato,
written under the influence of Hegelian ideas. Hence, it is no
wonder that we now often find Plato referred to as an idealist.
Since the totalitarian view of the state as a peculiar sort of
superindividual organism is peculiar to idealistic thought,[73] this
theory is also now commonly attributed to him. Popper, for example, follows many others in attaching this epithet of idealism
to Plato and to Aristotle[74] and accuses them both of holding the
German totalitarian theory of the state.[75] Is there any truth in
these contentions?

Idealistic metaphysics and epistemology have been so predominant in the modern period that the term *idealist* is often
applied by recent authors in a very loose way to anyone having
a serious interest in systematic philosophy as opposed to logic
and scientific method. In this sense, of course, Plato and Aristotle were *idealists*. But when this term is more carefully analyzed, such a usage is seen to be very misleading. Two essential theses distinguish idealism from other types of philosophy.
The first is epistemological. According to it, all the objects of
knowledge are either subjective states of the knowing agent or
indirect inferences from these states. The second is metaphysical. All being is mental, either mind itself or states and
relations conditioned by mind.

Neither of these theses is compatible with the thought of
Plato—even less with that of Aristotle. So far as Plato is concerned, he went out of his way to reject the subjectivist epistemology of Protagoras. Man is not the measure of all things.[76]
The human mind can know things in themselves as they really
are without distorting and twisting them into mental con-
structs. Knowing is a kind of finding or discovery, not a making.
Hence, those who seek knowledge are compared to hunters.[77]
Plato is certainly not an epistemological idealist; nor is he an
ontological mentalist. Being is not exhausted by experience or
mental being. Physical things exist as well as minds.[78] The accurate term for such a philosophy is not idealism, but realism. It
cannot be assumed a priori that a realistic philosopher will have

any special predilection for the idealistic theory of society as an organic mental entity, living a life of its own apart from the individuals included within it. In the case of one like Plato, long antedating the period of Kant and Hegel, this must be proved by clear and unambiguous evidence. Such evidence does not exist.

This does not mean, of course, that Plato was a social pluralist or individualist who believed that the human community has no unifying structure of its own, but is constituted by the mere coincidence of the acts of independent individuals. Modern social philosophy has been dominated by a mutually destructive conflict between these opposed extremes, which has helped to diffuse the widely held opinion that these two views exhaust the alternatives—either anarchic individualism or totalitarianism. As a matter of fact, there is a third possibility which is no mere compromise, but qualitatively distinct from the other two.

According to this view, the community does not result from the proximity of separate physical organisms or from the automatic expression of undeviating instincts like those of the so-called social animals. Human beings have no such automatic social instincts. The human community has a peculiar unity of its own. But this is not the substantial unity of an organism or mind, which lives a life of its own, apart from the individual members. It is a moral unity of shared idea or purpose. The same common good can be conceived by different individuals and sought by co-operative action. Such an ideational structure can be transmitted by education to successive generations. It founds the unity of the human community. This was Plato's view.

Nowhere in the dialogues is there any reference to a group mind or a group will. The community is made up exclusively of the individual members, each with his own thoughts and aspirations, and social structure arises from the characters of the citizens.[79] But so far as they are adequately criticized and rationalized, they may be led into common agreement concerning a common goal and the rationale of its co-operative realization. This is the *politeia*, the constitution or rational order of social life, which is the traditional title of Plato's major work on politics. If the group possessed a unity of its own, apart from the thoughts and aspirations of its members, Plato would not have been so concerned with the unifying power of ideas. He would simply have described the social leviathan and those peculiar modes of superindividual behavior which Hegel called *objectiver Geist* and would have analyzed those laws of social dialectic before which the individual is supposedly as helpless as a single cell within a giant organism. But this is clearly not his attitude. Social life is a manifestation of activities, especially intellectual activities, proceeding within the souls of individual men.[80] The rationale or logos of the human community must be present not in a group soul, but in the souls of intelligent individuals.[81] Agreement with respect to a sound common purpose is the very heart of the *Republic*, as Plato conceives it. Hence, education is the chief preoccupation of the whole community. When this common purpose is no longer clearly understood and disagreement arises, the community begins to sicken and disintegrate.[82]

It is true that Plato is deeply concerned with the social welfare, the good of the community as a whole. But this is not the good of some super-entity, distinct from all the citizens.[83] For Plato, every whole is simply all its parts,[84] and the good of the whole community is simply the good of all the citizens—the common good, as it was later called.[85] It is true that Plato compares the structure of social life with the structure of individual life. He also compares the relation of individual happiness to communal happiness with that of the painted eye to the whole statue.[86] But these are analogies or *relational* similarities, not univocal similarities. As the individual is to his individual purpose, so is the group to its conceived common purpose; or *as* the eye is to the whole statue, so is the relation of the individual to the community. From these relational similarities we cannot deduce that the individual alone is like an eye, or that the community alone is like a statue, any more than we can deduce from the famous analogy of the ship of state[87] that the community is some kind of a ship with sails and a tiller. For Plato, the good of the whole community, though not a mere sum, is not the good of something else apart from the members, but the common good of all—a collective whole, including the good of every one.

Popper is committing a serious historical error in attributing the organic theory of the state to Plato and accusing him of all the fallacies of post-Hegelian and Marxist historicism—the theory that history is controlled by the inexorable laws governing the behavior of superindividual social entities of which human beings and their free choices are merely subordinate manifestations.[88] Plato's view is rather the opposite. According to him, it is social order which is the manifestation of what is going on within the individual soul—the individual soul writ large, the more visible sign from which may be inferred the invisible thoughts and aspirations of the individual minds determining them.

Book VIII of the *Republic* is not an account of concrete history, as Popper interprets it,[89] but rather a description of the different possible forms of social purpose which may be conceived by the human mind, and their ideal order from the best form to tyranny, the worst. It is not a record of how things have happened in the concrete, but of how they would happen if an authentic human community were ever realized, and if it should then continuously degenerate into the worst state.[90] It is true that this reveals the working of a natural law in human affairs. Man is as much a part of nature as the tiger and the snake. But his nature is rational. He can understand his end or misunderstand it; and he can choose alternative ways of realizing it.[91] He is not automatically propelled towards the goal like subrational beings. Hence, the natural law of human action is a moral law and is hypothetical in character.[92] If men neglect the discipline of education and fail to exercise their reason properly, social disagreement and conflict will arise. This must lead to class war, anarchy, and ultimately to tyranny.

Either reason or force must control human affairs. These alternatives are always open.

Individuals here and there may resist corrupting tendencies and achieve authentic human life, even in the midst of a degenerate society.[93] Even a tyranny in the last stages of social decay must not be abandoned as hopeless. Those wielding tyrannical powers are open to rational persuasion. If they can be educated, they may be led to take steps which will reverse the trend towards dissolution. Human history is a mixture of freedom and necessity. But the individual alone is free. It is with him that the ultimate decision rests. Whether the course of social change be up or down, it is the individual who must lead the way. There is no mass ascent from the Cave. The individual must fight his own way and then return by himself to help others to help themselves by the exercise of their rational freedom.[94]

Plato's social philosophy is, no doubt, imperfect in many ways. His passion for reason and human unity led him to exaggerated hopes for the scientific control of human breeding. As Aristotle first pointed out, the idea of turning the human community into one great family by eugenics and the breaking down of natural family ties is ungrounded and even fantastic. But whatever other errors he may have committed, Plato did not fall into the fallacies of totalitarianism and historicism. The conceptions of group soul and totalitarian state are entirely foreign to his thought. He did not believe that recorded history is the record of an inevitable decline from a past Golden Age.[95] In his view, the ideal republic has never actually been realized, and indeed is incapable of being perfectly achieved in the concrete.[96] It is an ideal that may function as a standard and may be more or less approximated.

Plato is often accused of being indifferent to the worth and dignity of the human individual,[97] and even of "hostility towards the individual."[98] But these charges are hard to justify. The human individual, who begins life as a helpless infant, is, of course, deeply influenced by the structure of the society into which he is born. But, according to Plato, he is not a helpless pawn in the hands of irresistible social forces. No matter how debased the conditions are, as soon as he exercises his reason possible alternatives will be revealed. Then, he may choose either to drift with the ever-present forces that lead towards materialism and tyranny or to struggle against these towards a life of reason and humanity. The great battles of history are fought within the invisible regions of the human soul. Social schism results from schism in the mind.[99] Social justice is the manifestation of an order that must first be achieved within.[100] The ultimate choice rests with the single person and, whatever his lot, there is always room for such a choice.[101] No matter how degenerate a culture may become, it is always possible for the individual to rebel, and to initiate a process of reversal.

A primary aim of Plato's life was to preserve the life and spirit of such a rebel and, so far as this was possible, to continue this rebellion. According to Plato, Socrates was born into a community suffering from intellectual confusion and lethargy, and from social disorder and power politics. In his portrait of Socrates he is trying to show how the weak and fragile individual person can use his unique powers of reason and rational aspiration to combat such tendencies in thought and word and deed. Plato's final answer to totalitarianism is the life and work of Socrates.

To anyone who is seriously in doubt about this, the only possible suggestion is: read the dialogues for yourself and see.

Section IV. PLATO AS A RACIALIST

Popper is not the only critic of Plato to make the charge of racialism in the modern sense of the word. Toynbee has also made this accusation.[102] According to Popper, Plato is an anti-equalitarian thinker who has "correlated the natural inequality of Greeks and barbarians to that of masters and slaves."[103] Furthermore, there is in Plato "nothing but hostility toward the humanitarian ideas of a unity of mankind which transcends race and class."[104] Can these charges be substantiated by a careful examination of the texts?

In order to check this interpretation of Popper, we should turn first of all to the myths of creation, where Plato presents his opinion concerning the origin of mankind. None of these myths asserts any natural original distinction between different races. In the myth of the *Phaedrus* it is asserted that some souls follow the divine forms with difficulty; but this is not due to any original handicap, rather to a failure on their own part to exercise their faculty of insight and to control their passions.

The Promethean myth of the *Protagoras* (320–23 A) is expressed in an exalted tone without satire, which makes it reasonable to take it seriously as something to which Plato himself would agree, even though it is stated by Protagoras. It clearly and unmistakably asserts the moral unity of all mankind, for all men were given *aidos*, respect, and *dike*, justice. Nowhere do we find any reference to racial distinctions, but rather a strict philosophical neutrality between Greeks and other races.[105]

At *Politicus* 262 D–263 D, it is suggested that men should be classified into Greeks and barbarians. This is ridiculed and compared to a crane who might similarly try to divide all life into cranes and other creatures. It is clearly implied that there is no original natural basis for such a distinction. Contrary to Popper's charge, there is no statement anywhere in Plato that barbarians are *by nature* slaves.

Popper refers to Plato's interest in eugenics as a proof of "racialism."[106] But the two are not equivalent. It would be absurd to bring the charges of racialism against all those in democratic countries who now favor sterilizing certain criminal types. Racial traits are hereditary. But it does not follow that all hereditary traits are *racial*. If we adopted Popper's mode of argument, we could also deduce that most biologists at the present time are racialists—a conclusion which he himself would hardly wish to draw. This is clearly a *non sequitur*. Plato certainly held that intelligence and quickness of mind could be inherited. Some persons are more readily educated and, thus, disposed to virtue.[107] But virtue itself is not an inherited trait. It is something that must be learned and in some sense taught. This is presupposed by the discussions of the *Meno* (88 ff.) and the *Protagoras*, where Socrates finally suggests that, in spite of many possible objections, virtue is something that can be taught.[108] Indeed, unless this is true, the basic concern for education in the *Republic* would be meaningless. Virtue is certainly not a *racial* trait, nor is it even hereditary. In the *Republic* the native intellectual talents of clever persons who through a lack of *paideia* devote themselves to vicious purposes are said to be a disadvantage rather than an advantage.[109] This is directly opposed to any form of racialism.

The guardians are not a hereditary caste, but are to be selected on the basis of examinations which test their intellectual and moral qualities.[110] These tests are carefully described at the end of Book III of the *Republic*. That they are an essential feature of the educational system is shown by the reference to them in Book IV (429 E 9). Children of guardians who cannot meet these tests are demoted. Children of artisans who *can* meet them are promoted. Nettleship has suggested[111] that these provisions, explicitly stated in Book III, are later rescinded in Book V. But he gives no reasons, and there is no definite evidence in the text to support this view. Popper refers to *Republic* 546 A and 435 C as showing that "the intermixture of classes is forbidden";[112] but the texts, when examined, fail to justify this assertion. He attributes to Plato the view that virtue in its entirety can be inherited and sustained in a "golden soul," irrespective of all environmental influence. This, of course, would make the whole Platonic scheme of education meaningless.

Plato's discussions of virtue, law, the soul, and moral philosophy in general are uniformly permeated with a universal feeling. Thus, taking one of his characteristic doctrines at random, the philosopher-king thesis[113] asserts that until philosophers are kings there will be no end of troubles for *all mankind*. At *Republic* 499 C he states that the ideal republic may at that moment be closely approximated in some distant *barbaric* region. Popper himself noticed this, and he called it an "afterthought" in the first edition of his book since, as he argues, Plato is a racialist with no ethical concept of humanity—which leads one to wonder how such a concept *could* be revealed.[114] In a passage of the *Phaedo* (78 A), Socrates urges his hearers to seek for wisdom to quiet the fear of death, not only among the Greeks but among the *barbarians* as well. Popper takes no notice of this at all.

Republic 469 B–471 has been criticized by many commentators. Plato here maintains that Greeks should not enslave Greeks, but should remember the common danger of enslavement by the barbarians. It is in commenting on this passage that Popper makes the statement that Plato has "correlated the natural inequality of Greeks and barbarians to that of masters and slaves."[115] To understand this passage, we must make a real effort of imagination to try to recapture a sense of that most constant and terrible danger that threatened life in the ancient world, the danger of being sold into slavery after one's city had lost its independence. Plato is saying that all Greece should be the motherland of a Greek, and that no Greek should be sold into the slavery of a fellow Greek, although the long-standing war against the barbarians is accepted as a fact.

It is true that Plato here is regarding the barbarians as historic enemies. Of course, he is not alone in this. He thus shows himself in this respect to be a child of his own time, which limitation probably no philosopher has ever completely transcended. Perhaps he may be criticized for this. He is recognizing the barbarians as in some sense traditional *enemies*. But Popper goes further in his accusations.

He has confused the recognition of traditional *enmity* and long-standing military threat with an assertion of moral inequality and racial superiority. Popper is reading Nazi feeling— the idea of a master race—into Plato, thus showing himself to be a child of *his* own time, and to be reading his own experiences into an ancient author in a wholly irresponsible manner. There were slaves in every ancient society, though there is no official recognition of them in the *Republic* and, as we have said, no statement anywhere in the dialogues that barbarians are *natural* slaves. What would have happened if the Persians had won a war against the Greeks? The citizens of different Greek states would have been intermingled and sold abroad.[116] Plato never defends aggressive war. From his earliest youth he had been trained in the idea, certainly not without foundation, that the war of Greek cities against Persia and other barbarian countries was *defensive*. In his mature years the Greek cities of Ionia were subjected to Persia in a humiliating manner. This dread of slavery cannot be equated, as Popper equates it, with an overbearing racialism.

Popper also criticizes Plato for stating at *Republic* 563 A that foreigners and resident aliens should not be regarded as the political equals of citizens. No nation known to history has ever admitted all foreigners to perfect equality without restriction. Judged by contemporary standards, Athens was liberal in this respect. In the *Laws*, Plato goes into this question in some detail[117] and insists that they are to be protected from all injustice. Such a view may perhaps be legitimately condemned as provincial from the standpoint of a Utopian idealism, but is Popper justified in confusing it with the theory of the master race? If so, this disease is far more widespread than he himself—and certainly most historians—seem to imagine.

Popper attempts to justify his charge of racialism by building an imposing theory of what he calls "the Great Generation" of Athenian democratic and equalitarian liberals who were opposed and finally overcome—until Popper rediscovered them—by the racialist totalitarianism of Plato.[118] Two leading members of this great generation of democrats who opposed Plato on the equalitarian issue were the sophist Antiphon and the philosopher Antisthenes. By an amazing display of constructive logic, Popper erects a vast web of speculation on the slight evidence we possess concerning these two men.

Antiphon did appeal to nature in attacking the distinction between Greek and barbarian. Hence Popper calls him "equalitarian."[119] In some sense of the word this is true. But the exact sense is not clear and depends on one's general view of the fragments. According to Taylor[120] and Field[121] he is a selfish pleasure-seeker; according to Greene[122] a socially minded utilitarian. Winspear attributes democratic principles to him.[123] Popper agrees. He also associates him with what he calls "the Athenian movement against slavery."[124] There is no evidence to support these last affirmations.[125]

Popper reserves his more elaborate techniques for Antisthenes. Wilamowitz in his book on Plato[126] gives a general warning against overly imaginative interpretations of the very limited evidence. But Popper in his text[127] builds up a tremendous case for Antisthenes as "the last of the Great Generation" of Athenian liberals "who developed the fundamental tenets of antislavery and of antinationalism: i.e., the creed of the universal empire of men";[128] who defended "the unity of mankind";[129] a believer in "the brotherhood of Greeks and bar-

barians,"[130] a phrase with a Christian ring; an advocate of
"equalitarianism";[131] and a man of "very liberal and humanitarian outlook."[132] All this is said of a man who considered
Cyrus, the absolute despot of Persia, as the model of a wise
monarch. Popper's interpretation cannot withstand a critical
analysis.[133]

He also states that Antisthenes was a pupil of Socrates—an
"old friend," and "old companion," and even "the only one
worthy successor of Socrates."[134] The only actual evidence for
these assertions is Plato's statement in the *Phaedo* that Antisthenes was present with Socrates during his last day in prison—
together with twelve others. Xenophon in his *Symposium* also
reports the admiration of Antisthenes for Socrates, though Popper does not refer to it. Hence, it might be reasonable to conclude that he may have admired Socrates, but there is no real
evidence for any of Popper's extravagant assertions.

It is characteristic of Popper's method that he should use his
highly imaginative picture of Antisthenes as a weapon to dis-
credit Plato. Antisthenes probably denied the validity of the
current distinction between *phusis* and *nomos*. He believed, as
Wilamowitz remarks, in one God, a commonplace belief for the
intellectually sophisticated of that time. He may have held that
God makes the same moral demands on all men; much of this is
highly speculative. But even if we grant that it is so, it will not
justify Popper's further procedure of imagining a bitter, deep-
seated personal enmity between Plato and Antisthenes, and then
of deducing that, therefore, Plato could not have believed in the
moral unity of man.

In Plato's case we may refer to the texts, and their evidence is
clear. He certainly believed in the moral unity of man. This is
proved by the myths of creation, and by countless passages
which may be quoted from his discussions of the human soul
and of wisdom and virtue, which are the same everywhere for
all men. Plato recognized the distinction between Greek and
barbarian as a matter of profound cultural significance and of
long-lasting historical enmity; but he recognized no distinction
in personal dignity and worth. It is fantastic to think of him as a
racialist, in the modern sense of this word.

Section V. PLATO AS A REACTIONARY DEFENDER
OF THE CLOSED SOCIETY

Plato conceived of the good for man as the realization of human nature in all its phases under the guidance of reason which alone deserves to rule. His ethics is based upon his anthropology. Human nature is composed of many parts, of which reason and rational aspiration are naturally fitted to guide the rest. In the life of Socrates he found a concrete example of an individual life guided by reason, and in most of his dialogues he attempts to convey something of Socrates' love of wisdom, and his impassioned application of it to thought and word and deed. But with respect to social life, he could find no such concrete example. All existing communities, when examined in the cold light of reason, seemed full of diseases and corruptions. No one could emerge unscathed from such a rational test. Indeed, this seemed to be a clear implication of the life of Socrates himself, for he had consistently opposed the policies of his mother city of Athens, certainly the most advanced and cultivated of the Greek communities. He had criticized the politicians of the fifth-century democracy;[135] he had defied the commands of the Thirty Tyrants in the case of Leon of Salamis.[136] The returned democracy had put him to death as a subversive corrupter of the youth. If he could not get on in Athens, the most civilized of the Greek cities, as he himself said, how could he hope to live elsewhere in peace and happiness?[137]

But man is by nature a social being who cannot live a human life alone by himself. Was there anywhere a city in which Socrates could live at peace? The answer seemed clearly negative, for no city, not even Athens, could survive this radical questioning. So in trying to think through the social implications of the life of Socrates, Plato was forced to use his imagination in giving concrete content to these implications. In the *Republic*, Plato attempts to describe a city built on rational principles in accordance with the natural needs of man, in which the Socratic spirit might find itself at home. This is a rational ideal and, like any rational ideal, is expressed in terms of timeless, changeless principles. Furthermore, its essential productive, political, and noetic functions are hierarchically ordered in accordance with the structure of the human soul. It is a hard, cold, fact of nature that science and intelligence alone are capable of guiding human life. This timeless and hierarchical structure of Plato's ideal republic has called forth many bitter attacks from modern thinkers, who assert that it is a reactionary attempt to dam the current of change and progress, and an apology for arbitrary class rule.

Thus, Popper follows Winspear in maintaining that Plato believed in a past Golden Age from which all historic change had been a retrogression.[138] The stable structure of Plato's *Republic* is interpreted as an effort to return to this glorified state of the past, or at least to obstruct social change. The Golden Age idea is sheer fantasy. There is no shred of evidence in the texts to support the view that Plato believed an ideal society to have existed in the past and then to have declined through a retrogressive law of history. The Promethean myth of the *Protagoras* asserts the direct opposite. Owing to a blunder of Epimetheus (After-thought), the human race was brought into the world originally naked and helpless and was saved only by the intervention of Prometheus (Fore-thought), who gave man the subordinate arts. Even then, the unfortunate race would have been extinguished by fratricidal disagreement and bloody strife had it not been for the divine gifts of respect and justice, which were presented in the course of human history.[139]

According to Plato, this history is dominated neither by a continuous, automatic progress, nor by an inevitable law of retrogression.[140] It is rather a cyclic sequence in which periods of advance alternate with periods of decline.[141] There are divine powers which have an interest in human affairs,[142] but their influence always leaves room for the exercise of human decision,[143] and the course of history is largely determined by the moral choices of human agents, particularly those in positions of authority.[144]

But Plato is a rationalist who believes in the capacity of human cognitive powers to apprehend the truth when subjected to Socratic critical discipline. Hence, he holds that moral choices are not purely arbitrary. Certain general principles, at least, must be followed *if* human life is to be lived in a genuinely human way, or as he phrased it, in a *natural* way (cf. chap. 5). In the *Republic* he has attempted to describe the general structure of a genuinely human society. From the standpoint of this ideal, which can never be more than approximated, any change would be a degeneration. The *ideal* pattern of such a degeneration is described in Book VIII of the *Republic*, which Popper has misinterpreted as a Platonic account of the concrete events of history.[145] This has also led him to accuse Plato of attempting to arrest all social change by the establishment of a reactionary "tribal" society in which human life is regimented to the last degree by the suppression of personal freedom.

With respect to the first charge of arresting social change, two points should be mentioned. In the first place, this society is an abstract ideal which, as we have said, has never actually existed, and can never be more than approximated. But such an ideal is implicit in any moral aspiration for a better state. When carefully formulated, it provides us not with a description of any factual situation, but with a standard, no matter how vague and confused it may be. In the *Republic* Plato attempted to formulate such a standard, based on the natural needs of man, with great precision.

There is no general condemnation of change to be found in his works. In verification of this strange assertion, Popper refers to *Laws* 797 D to show how Plato teaches "that change is evil, and that rest is divine."[146] What Plato says, however, is: "We shall find that the change of all things, *save only what is bad*, is most perilous, of seasons, winds, bodily diet, mental disposition, all things, that is, with the single exception, as I just now said, of the bad."[147] In other words, change from an evil state to a better one is good; from a better state to an evil one is bad. This is far from any condemnation of change, as such. In fact, it would seem to express a position to which Popper himself, who holds very strong views on ethical matters, would seem to be committed unless he is prepared to defend the very dubious doctrine that all change, as such, is good. But there is a second and deeper issue involved.

Popper is not merely criticizing Plato's ideal republic; he is also criticizing any attempt to formulate a general conception of the good society as "utopianism."[148] Such an ideal, which penetrates to the root structures of human society, according to Popper, is always dangerous because it tends to radical criticisms of existing social orders and to dangerous and sweeping revolution.[149] As opposed to this, he advocates "piecemeal social engineering," a method of "searching for, and fighting against, the greatest and most urgent evils of society, rather than searching for, and fighting for, its greatest ultimate good."[150] He says that this method is "less risky and for this reason less controversial. . . . It is easier to reach a reasonable agreement about existing evils and the means of combatting them than it is about an ideal good and the means of its realization."[151]

Is evil, then, totally disconnected from good? How can men possibly agree on what is evil without at the same time agreeing on what is good? How can men work gradually for the slow improvement of a diseased condition or institution without at least implicitly committing themselves to some general view of the human good and the good society? One human condition or institution is surely not totally disconnected from others. Is it sound to think of a human institution as a distinct, logical atom which can be altered and "improved" without any reference to other institutions? Is it not clear that even the most gradual and piecemeal social engineering if it is to be clearly and adequately conceived must be guided by a sound insight into the nature of the human good? Plato, who condemned all aggressive use of force and who never advocated bloody revolution, certainly accepted this basic principle. He believed in gradual, piecemeal social engineering guided by a clear and rationally defensible conception of the human good.[152] To follow Popper in defending the former and in rejecting the latter would seem to imply either a hatred of all coherent rational thought or a complacent acceptance of uncriticized popular opinion in basic matters of ethics—or both.

With respect to the second charge of tribal regimentation which Popper, following Winspear,[153] brings against the *Re-*

public, the careful reader of both authors will find himself in some bewilderment. By a closed or tribal society Popper says he means one which is rigidly dominated by uncriticized customs and magical taboos. An open society, on the other hand, is one in which "personal decisions may lead to the alteration of taboos, and even of political laws which are no longer taboos."[154] As he says, "the great difference is the possibility of rational reflection on these matters."[155] At first the reader will be deeply puzzled by Popper's interpretation of the *Republic* as an insidious attempt to arrest political progress by a return to a tribal society of uncriticized custom and taboo. Where in all literature do we find a more evident effort to defend the power of "rational reflection" to deal with moral matters and to reach defensible results?

The discipline and training of the rational faculties, education in the Socratic sense, is certainly the central institution of Plato's ideal community. No phase of individual or common life is to be free from the searching light of Socratic criticism. Plato holds that even if a human individual devoted the whole of his vital energy to rational reflection, this would still be far from adequate for the education of his soul.[156] In the United States of America, which Popper apparently holds to be an advanced example of his ideal, or open, society, more money is now spent every year on alcohol than on education. In the *Republic* Socratic education is the chief concern to which all else is subordinated. How, then, can Popper attack it as a disguised return to an irrational, pre-Socratic, tribal society?

The answer is, of course, to be found in a most decisive issue concerning the nature of "science," "reason," and "Socratic criticism"—a philosophic issue, to be more precise. According to Popper, "science" excludes any attempt to gain clarity about the meaning of such basic terms as "knowledge," "good," "evil," "man," "virtue," etc., or to arrive at any disciplined answer to the Socratic question *ti esti*, what is it? Popper says that the quest for universal definitions (the Socratic quest), which he refers to as "the essentialism of Plato and Aristotle,"[157] "not only encouraged verbalism, but also led to the disillusionment with argument, that is, with reason."[158] As Popper uses the term "reason," or "science," in the modern positivistic sense, "only nominalist definitions occur . . . and we can at once see from this that definitions do not play any very important part in science."[159]

Socrates, on this view, had nothing whatsoever to do with philosophy as it has been conceived for the last two thousand years, for Plato "betrayed Socrates, just as his uncles had done."[160] Plato and his decadent disciple, Aristotle, tell us that Socrates was a moral philosopher with an impassioned interest in defining the virtues and other moral terms. As a matter of fact, he was a nominalist, as is shown by the sensible doctrines of Antisthenes, his only true disciple, who believed that nothing could be defined. In the *Apology*, which, according to Popper, is a reliable picture of Socrates' defense, Socrates says that he is sure of certain truths—that the soul is more than the body, that vice is worse than death, etc. As a matter of fact, he is the father of modern ethical skepticism and conventionalism, holding that all value rests upon personal preference.[161] Plato tells us that Socrates lost interest in physical science and turned to ethics and other connected matters. Popper claims that Socrates was really the father of modern positivism and scientism, completely skeptical of all philosophical truth, trusting only in the variable conclusions of the physical and social sciences, and believing any conception of moral *truth* to be naïve.[162]

In erecting this highly novel picture of Socrates as the first scientific humanist and of Plato as an apostle of "the Inquisition," "Secret Police," and "romanticized gangsterism,"[163] Popper is, of course, disguising the basic issue. It is not that Popper stands for science, reason, and Socratic criticism, whereas Plato stands for the reverse of these things. This is so absurd that it can be corrected even by the most superficial reader of Plato who also believes in science, reason, and Socratic criticism. The issue is a philosophic one, which affects the meaning of every term.

By science Plato means not merely what Popper means, but philosophic science as well—the science of knowledge, ethics, and being. By reason he means not merely the logical and experimental processes by which the different restricted sciences gain control over, and a certain amount of theoretical insight into, the processes of subhuman nature, but philosophical and moral insight as well. Finally, by Socratic doubt and criticism he means not only the search for science and wisdom, but also the achievement of some results, without which the whole life of Socrates would have been silly and futile. What is the use of seeking a wisdom which no one will ever attain in any sense?

Is there or is there not such a thing as philosophy? This is the basic question to which Popper and Plato give divergent answers, the question which divides them on all other basic issues. With the rise of modern positivism, which Plato in his day called sophistry, this has again become a living issue of our time. Is philosophy in the Socratic sense—the search for ethical knowledge and insight into the basic structure of reality—to survive? Or is it to be abandoned for an idolatry of the restricted hypotheses of the separate sciences and for the loose and slipshod theories of popular opinion, which must, then, take its place? With these questions in mind, we may once again turn to the pages of Plato with hope for understanding them.

Popper's second charge against the *Republic* as a regimented society is based upon a purely negativistic view of human freedom, as well as a failure to distinguish what was later called natural law from positive law. To him, all freedom is freedom *from* constraint of some sort.[164] There is no positive freedom *to*. This is, no doubt, excusable in one who has suffered personally from Nazi tyranny and oppression; but freedom cannot be adequately conceived in exclusively negative terms. No one would think of an abandoned child, not subject to any external interference, as being free. Constraint necessarily involves something positive that is being constrained against its natural tendencies. In the case of man, these natural tendencies cannot be expressed without co-operative aid and nurture. Such care and nurture, even if resisted, must be distinguished from the forceful oppression of a person attempting to carry out a deliberate purpose.

Human freedom includes the exercise of choice in certain matters. It also includes the spontaneous realization, with external assistance, of those basic faculties which make deliberation and choice possible. In his *Republic* Plato is trying to delineate a human society in which the noetic, politic, and poietic needs of man are cared for in such a way that these basic rights, as they were later called, may be realized. If this is oppression, then any social pattern must be oppressive, and the whole distinction between oppression and freedom becomes impossible. Plato's view was that man is free in so far as he is enabled by proper nurture and the spontaneous exercise of his higher rational faculties to live a genuinely human life. He is oppressed in so far as he is deprived of the opportunity to live in an ordered community, to satisfy his material needs, and to receive intellectual nurture; or in so far as he fails to make use of these rights and thus enslaves himself. There is nothing opposed to freedom in this conception.

In fact, such a recent document as the Universal Declaration of Human Rights, proclaimed by the United Nations in 1948, is based upon the natural-law philosophy which received one of its earliest formulations in the writings of Plato (cf. chap. 5). That which furthers the realization of the nature of man is liberating; that which thwarts and impedes that nature is tyrannical. Popper, as a nominalist, cannot, of course, focus this conception. Hence, he constantly confuses Plato's use of the term *natural* in this sense, those traits and tendencies which all men share in common, with an imagined early state of man, a pristine Golden Age.[165]

Natural law is always universal. But men exist only in the concrete, and face unique and shifting circumstances. Hence, natural law must always be specified by further determinations of positive law to meet new situations as they arise. Plato clearly states that he is concerned only with the basic structure of society (the principles of law) and is neglecting the need for legislation "about business matters, the deals that men make with one another in the agora—and, if you please, contracts with workmen and actions for foul language and assault, the filing of declarations, the impanelling of juries, the payment and exaction of any dues that may be needful in markets or harbors and in general market, police or harbor regulations and the like."[166] These must be left to the free decision of those who concretely face the varying circumstances. In so far as they decree what is in accordance with the universal law of nature, the enactment will be sound and liberating. In so far as they decree what thwarts or distorts a natural right, it will be unwise and oppressive.

Warner Fite charges Plato with a failure to appreciate the value of personality, and with a disregard for the true dignity of the individual.[167] Popper repeats this accusation in a more violent way, attributing to Plato a "hatred" of the individual person.[168]

Plato certainly held that the welfare of many individuals in a community is even more valuable than the welfare of one;[169] but it is hard to see how this justifies the charge of hatred for the individual or even of an indifference to personal values, especially in view of the fact that, according to Plato, human welfare can be achieved only through the authentic exercise of those rational faculties which the individual alone possesses. The whole conception of a group mind is entirely foreign to Plato's way of thought. The *Republic* asserts that the many are incapable of philosophy, and that the community is bound to fall into chaos and tyranny unless the universal structure or idea of community life is clearly held in the minds of one or more individuals. The Socrates of the dialogues is constantly expressing his disapproval of long speeches and mob oratory.[170] Thus, in the *Gorgias* he tells Polus that his arithmetic is quite peculiar, for he regards it as much more to convince the questioning mind of a single opponent than to convince a vast inert audience by the tricks of oratory.[171]

Popper says that Socrates is one of the great persons, one of the great individualists of all time.[172] Most of those who have delved at all deeply into the dialogues would agree. But it is primarily through Plato that our knowledge of Socrates as a living person has come. Indeed, it is one of the chief purposes of the dialogues to undo the work of the hemlock, and to keep alive the spirit of this man. Is it, then, reasonable to maintain that Plato had little understanding for the peculiar dignity and value of the individual? Where is the actual evidence in support of this charge? It seems to be refuted on almost every page of the dialogues.

CHAPTER TWO

PLATO AS AN ENEMY OF DEMOCRACY

THE most serious charge against Plato from a modern point of view is that he is an enemy of democracy. This term is now used in many ambiguous ways to cover a wide variety of meanings. Hence, the refutation of such a charge is difficult, involving as it must, an analysis of the meaning of the term *democracy* as now employed. Those who accuse Plato of being antidemocratic seldom present such an analysis. They begin by referring to passages in which Plato criticizes certain political phenomena of late fifth- and early fourth-century Athens under the name democracy. They then usually infer that Plato was an enemy of his own home city, the Athenian Democracy, as we call it, and finally conclude that he is a universal enemy of all democracy, including the great democratic ideal of modern times. Let us now examine these charges. Is it reasonable to believe that Plato was an enemy of his own home city? Is his political philosophy opposed to the modern ideal of democracy?

Section I. PLATO AND THE ATHENIAN DEMOCRACY

That Plato was opposed to early Greek democracy, especially as he experienced it at Athens in the last years of the great war, and even as it had manifested itself earlier in the Age of Pericles, must be granted. According to Plato, the ruthless imperialism of Athenian war policy and the cultural decay which followed the war must be traced back to certain sophistic movements which began in the Age of Pericles. He identified this form of democracy with irresponsible anarchy and condemned it both in itself and in being the mother of tyranny. Indeed, in Book VIII of the *Republic*, he places the pure form of democracy under oligarchy and holds that it is exceeded in degeneracy only by tyranny. From this, it has been inferred that Plato must have held that democratic Athens was inferior to timocratic or oligarchic

40

Sparta, and that he must have belonged to that minority of his fellow citizens who secretly supported Sparta.[1]

This inference, however, is very dubious, for in Book VIII of the *Republic* he is not considering concrete history, but pure social forms or abstract structures, which are never exemplified in the concrete without admixture. There is good reason to believe that Plato did not hold Athens to be a pure form of democracy, exemplifying all the corruptions described in Book VIII,[2] though it may have closely approximated this at the end of the war when he himself may have heard drunken rhetoricians clothed in armor stepping up to the rostrum to persuade the popular assembly by impassioned oratory to embark on acts of mad and hopeless aggression. He probably held that during much of its history Athens was a mixture of democracy with oligarchy and timocracy. In his view, Sparta was also not a pure timocracy, but a timocracy probably tinged with oligarchy and even tyranny. No safe conclusions concerning Plato's attitude towards his mother city can be drawn from the formalistic discussions of Book VIII of the *Republic*.

For further light on this question, we must turn to such indirect evidence as is afforded by the dialogues and to the *Epistles*, though their authenticity is dubious. An examination of all this evidence gives us good reason for holding that Plato, in spite of his bitter disapproval of many phases of Athenian policy, especially towards the end of the war, nevertheless held his own city in high filial esteem and never took sides with Sparta or with oligarchic Athenians against his own city, as Winspear and Popper suggest.[3]

First of all, we must attach some weight to the portrait of Socrates as a loyal Athenian citizen who fought throughout the course of the war. In the light of the filial feeling he expresses towards his mother city in the *Apology* and in the *Crito*, it is inconceivable to think of him engaging in anti-Athenian activities or attitudes, though he was, no doubt, severely critical of many Athenian policies. If this is a true account, and if it is also true that Socrates was the determining influence over his whole life, it is not reasonable to believe that Plato was anti-Athenian as well as antidemocratic. If this picture is wholly or partly Plato's own creation, then Popper's supposition is even less likely. In the *Apology* Athens is referred to as "the great and mighty and wise city."[4] It is hard to think of these words as being penned by a militant enemy.

Finally, there is the first part of the Seventh *Epistle* which, if genuine, provides us with the strongest evidence of all. Here plotting for the overthrow of one's own native city is compared to patricide, and the earlier democracy is referred to as a Golden Age in comparison with the rule of the Thirty Tyrants in which Plato's uncles participated.[5] There is not a shred of evidence to support the opposed view of Popper that Plato sympathized with these oligarchic plots.

He certainly held that the skeptical, materialistic views of the sophists and rhetoricians of the Periclean Age, whom Popper calls "the Great Generation," sowed the seeds of Athenian degeneration. He was bitterly opposed to the ruthless imperialism and militarism of later Athenian policy. But this does not show that he was pro-Spartan. From his point of view, all existing states and parties were degenerate. Hence, as he states in the Seventh *Epistle*,[6] after watching the giddy course of events until his head was in a whirl, he finally decided to abandon his proposed political career and to devote his life to the study and teaching of philosophy. How can justice ever be achieved until men spend some time in disciplined thought about it, and about those other basic structures which are presupposed by it?

There is no reason to distrust this assertion, which is closely approximated by many passages from the dialogues. Plato thought of his purpose as quite distinct from the policy of any existing power or party. His aim was to bring about a new cultural revolution by peaceful means—a revolution far more radical than any change which could be achieved by the shedding of blood or the mere interchange of power, a revolution of the whole human soul turning from the confused experience of the senses to an intelligible structure seen only by the eye of the mind, which might eventually culminate in the establishment of a society ruled by reason and philosophy.[7] Such a revolution has not yet been achieved. But through the ages of Western history, the influence of Plato's writings has worked in this direction.

In order to understand more clearly what Plato is criticizing under the term *democracy*, the modern reader should follow Thucydides' account of the last years of the great Peloponnesian War. Some modern interpreters have inferred from this criticism that Plato must have been a Spartan sympathizer and an enemy of his own city. Thus, according to Fite, "Plato deliberately turned his back upon the civilization of Athens—upon what is still today regarded as the highest point in Greek civilization—and embraced the barbarism of Sparta."[8] This view is shared by many other critics, including Winspear and Popper.[9] We have suggested reasons for believing that it is most hazardous.

Section II. PLATO AND THE MODERN DEMOCRATIC IDEAL

Crossman,[10] Popper,[11] and others have inferred that Plato is also an enemy of *modern* democracy, filled with a bitter "hatred" of democracy in general.[12] This, of course, brings up the whole question of what is now meant by "democracy." We shall not try to discuss this very complex question thoroughly. But we shall offer some reasons for holding that this inference is even more hazardous than the first one. Let us first briefly consider the chief characteristics which enter into the modern ideal of democracy and then, second, the major criticisms of Plato's *Republic* urged by certain "defenders" of this ideal.

The word *ideal* is important, for we must remember that the *Republic* is not the description of any concrete situation but the outline of a goal or standard, formulated for the guidance of action. Hence, the question we are raising should not concern the relation between this ideal and current practice, but rather its relation to the current democratic ideal. Many factors—including pre-Cartesian, realistic philosophy, Judaeo-Christian religious tradition, and skeptical elements from modern philosophy—have entered into various formulations of this ideal, which are often marked by differences in emphasis and content. In spite of these differences, it can be suggested, without arguing the historical points involved in detail, that there are at least three essential elements in the democratic ideal, each derived from one of the major movements mentioned above.

First of all, still unfinished modern struggles against feudalism and class tyranny, and the skeptical intellectual movements
associated with these struggles, have contributed a deep distrust
of unchecked political power and dogmatism of any kind. From
this negative factor has been derived the abolition of hereditary
political tenure, the right to remove public officials from office
by free ballot—which is characteristic of all present-day democ-
racies—and the separation of powers in the Constitution of the
United States. This is an essential aspect of the modern democratic ideal. But when exclusively emphasized, as it often is by
such modern apologists as Popper, it becomes one-sidedly negativistic, and omits other positive factors which are also essential
to the democratic ideal.

When thus defended, democracy is represented as a wholly
negative doctrine, its aim being exhausted in the avoidance of
tyranny. All common action and government are viewed as
evil, though perhaps necessary in minimal degrees. From this
point of view, co-operative action of any sort is regarded as
undemocratic, and the function of government is reduced to
that of removing all checks to individual action, no matter how
capricious or even vicious this may be. Presented in this negativistic manner, democracy would seem hard to distinguish from
anarchy; and modern experience, to say nothing of the experience of the ages, has shown that freedom, when thus identified
with license, leads inevitably to the domination of those who are
most greedy and self-assertive, as Plato pointed out. But fortunately there are other positive factors in the democratic tradition.

From the Judaeo-Christian tradition, though not exclusively
from this, it has derived a sense of the dignity and worth of human life (as opposed to oriental pessimism), the fundamental
equality of all under God, and the universal brotherhood of
men. These three elements, when working together, are responsible for that daring faith in the common man and that burning
hope for a positive, co-operative conquest over the problems of
life, which has been responsible for the recurrent dynamism of
Western civilization as contrasted with the relative quietism of
the East. This positive factor of faith in the common man and

in his ability to co-operate in the realization of common dynamic purposes, often seemingly impossible, has made essential contributions to the still unfinished movement to abolish every trace of slavery, to other humanitarian projects, and especially to the principle of majority rule, that faith in the opinion of a majority as the wisest way of settling basic matters of common policy.

When exclusively emphasized, as it has been by certain apologists, as the very essence of democracy,[13] it is subject to certain unanswerable criticisms which have often seriously weakened the case for so-called democracy. What if the majority betrays this trust? What if, as has often happened in recent times, the majority loses all interest in freedom and democracy, and develops an urge for the easier way of tyranny? If democracy is defined exclusively in terms of majority assent, no matter what is assented to, then mass tyranny, the most awful kind, must be regarded as essentially democratic. But this is an impossible conclusion.

So fatal is this objection that Christian influences, as in the time of Luther, making use of the religious doctrine of original sin, have often gone to the other extreme—undiluted mistrust of the common man—and have thrown their support to reactionary forms of rule. But these have been special perversions of the central stream of Christian doctrine. If man is totally depraved, the Incarnation, the central dogma of Christianity, would be absurd and impossible. Man's nature has been thwarted and damaged by sin, but it is still a genuinely human nature, made in the image of God, and retaining its immaterial faculties of reason and free choice. Hence, the appeal to reason can be made, and with divine assistance an authentic human life can still be lived in the world.

In spite of many corrupt manifestations, the Western religious influence has been felt throughout our history as predominantly hopeful and dynamic, an ever-present pressure towards the theological virtues of faith in the powers of man, a burning hope for human causes—though often seemingly hopeless—and an openness for sacrificial love. These religious factors have an essential place in the modern democratic ideal. But to be purified of dangerous fantasy and delusion, they need to be reinforced by a third influence.

This is derived from the tradition of realistic philosophy which originated in ancient Greece, and has since been cultivated and refined and developed down to the present day. It was this tradition that first worked out a clear and articulate theory of natural law, natural rights, and natural duties which has played a decisive, positive role in the evolution of democratic concepts and practices. In the Middle Ages it was merged with Christian faith, often in such a way as to be almost overwhelmed by it. Hence, many modern writers have failed to focus it as a distinct doctrine having an integrity of its own, and have viewed it as a mere appendage to religious dogma. As a matter of fact, however, as we shall see, it was independently developed by Plato and Aristotle, apart from any Christian influence.

This tradition has contributed to the democratic tradition a definition of human goodness as the realization of a nature shared by all men. It has also defined certain universal rights and duties prescribed by such realization, which are binding on all men and on all communities. Such principles are permanent and inalienable by any form of tyranny. They are prescribed not by any ruler, class, or arbitrary constitution, but by nature itself and the cosmic powers which produce man. They remain in force no matter what a human majority may decide, and must be clearly recognized by any rationally ordered society in which authentic human life is to be possible. Hence, modern democratic communities offer protection to the weak and evanescent human individual, who alone possesses the precious faculty of reason, against ruling opinion. No matter what a majority may decide, these principles remain in force; the ruling opinion may be in error. Free discussion and criticism must proceed. Hence, in all genuinely democratic countries the rights of access to information, of assembly, and of free expression of opinion are recognized and protected.

The United Nations Declaration of Human Rights specifies *other* rights presupposed by these, such as the right to sufficient nurture and medical care and the right to education. In Great Britain and the United States education is not yet recognized as a *right*, but there is a general understanding that adequate training of the cognitive powers is required for the intelligent exercise of democratic functions, which has already led to the establishment of public schools and universities. This recognition of the importance of reason as the only power naturally fitted for the guidance of human life, and of those individual rights which are required for its exercise, is the peculiar contribution of realistic philosophy to the modern ideal of democracy.

When exclusively emphasized, as in ancient times by Plato and Aristotle, this natural-law tradition has produced political ideals which stress the rule of reason—the realization of basic human needs, especially the need for rational nurture and education. Compared with the least inadequate statements of the modern democratic ideal, such as the United Nations Declaration of Human Rights, the more extreme formulations of the natural-law ideal, like Plato's *Republic*, suffer from a lack of certain elements provided by the other two sources we have noted. We miss some of the effective checks against dogmatism and tyranny which have been discovered in modern times, and a robust faith in the capacities of the common man for practical insight and sacrificial endeavor. But in the *Republic* at least we find that these are not wholly lacking.

Plato also was acutely aware of the dangers of tyranny. As a protection against it, he suggested a concentration of community energy on the primary task of education, and a system of rigorous civil service examinations for public office. That other protections are advisable may be granted. But that this must always be the most basic protection is, at least, an arguable point. Plato may have had an exaggerated conception of hereditary differences in intellectual endowment. But he certainly recognized the *basic* unity of all men as possessing a common human nature and the need for giving equal opportunity to all. His *Republic* is not a hereditary caste society. The theory of natural law, which lies at the heart of his whole conception, is still an essential ingredient in our modern democratic ideal.

In view of these facts, it is reasonable to hold that Plato's *Republic*, when compared with the modern ideal of democracy, is deficient in certain respects, but not totally opposed to this ideal or essentially undemocratic, as is often supposed. This ideal, one-sided as it may be, is not so deficient as those antirational interpretations of democracy which identify it with philosophical skepticism and anarchy or with unrestrained majority rule. We shall now attempt to confirm these tentative conclusions by a brief consideration of the major objections which are urged against Plato by modern "democratic" apologists.

Section III. CLASS RULE

Many commentators repeat the charge that Plato in the *Republic* is defending an aristocracy in the sense of a small privileged class or caste, ruling for its own interests. Thus, according to Fite,[14] the whole community is an "aristocratic Republic" to be controlled by "a ruling-class,"[15] a privileged minority. He claims that this is the Spartan ideal of a regimented state.[16] These charges are repeated by Crossman[17] and Winspear.[18] The most extreme version of this criticism is to be found in Popper's claim that Plato's guardians—whom he calls "leaders,"[19] "elite,"[20] a "ruling class,"[21] a "master race,"[22] and "herders of human cattle,"[23] are a hereditary caste selected on racial grounds.[24] Beginning with this last of Popper's charges, it is quite clear that Plato's guardians (φύλακες) are in no sense arbitrary rulers, but guardians of a law of nature, which they have in no sense decreed or determined but have discovered by rational dialectic. Popper's slanted translations, for which he offers no justification, are perhaps to be explained as a result of his legal positivism, which regards any law whatsoever as the expression of an arbitrary and tyrannical preference. It is only from such a standpoint that these translations become understandable.

But it is hard to see how, then, rational government can be distinguished from tyranny. If there are no basic practical principles which can be recognized by reason, then all government is the expression of arbitrary preference and, therefore, equally tyrannical.[25] Yet Popper himself certainly opposes "the open society" to what he calls dictatorship and tyranny. What, then, is this open society? Either it is a community with no government or the very minimum of co-operative action, in which case he is defending a diluted anarchism; or it is merely a form of unjustifiable, arbitrary rule to which everyone agrees, in which case he is defending mass tyranny. With respect to these alternatives, we may certainly ask the moral relativist for evidence to show either that anarchy is possible for man or that mass tyranny, in the light of recent political experience, is not the most dangerous form of oppression.

Moral relativism, of course, is not Plato's point of view. He believed that all men possess a partly rational nature in common, and that this nature includes basic tendencies which must be co-operatively realized if human life is to be lived.[26] To understand these essential tendencies is to grasp the moral law. Plato's guardians are not arbitrary rulers at all, but guardians of the law, who try first to understand it, then to apply it for the benefit of the whole community, including themselves, and finally to preserve it through the flux of varying circumstance. They are not a hereditary caste. At *Republic* 415 C 3 and at 423 C 8 he clearly states that all citizens are eligible to become guardians, including the children of artisans, whom Popper calls "drudges," and female children. Plato has a rather extreme view of the importance of heredity in these matters; so he believes that guardians will tend to produce guardians. But he specifically provides for exceptions. No child of a guardian will be chosen for office simply on the grounds of birth. He must show his special qualifications by meeting very stringent tests and examinations which are given to all. This is not a caste society.

Nor is it correctly described as "class rule" in the usual sense of this word—government by a privileged group for the attainment of special interests denied to others. Plato's guardians and auxiliaries are not a *class* in this sense. They are civil servants selected by rigorous examinations for the performance of certain functions necessary to the attainment of the common good. The development of a sense of *class* distinctions and *class* interests is the sign of social decline. In the *Republic* all are friends and mutual supporters of one another.[27] Popper speaks constantly of the "privileges" of the guardians. But in Plato's view the sound exercise of the governing function for the common good is no privilege, but a burdensome responsibility. If the guardians do anything for their own special interests, they are obstructing the common good and thus betraying their function. They are provided with no material goods beyond their necessary needs, and live an arduous life, intensively devoted to a common good in which, of course, they justly share. Even though we may disagree with such a view, it is not correct to refer to it as the rule of a privileged class in the modern sense of this word.

Plato is often attacked as a defender of slavery. According to Popper, all the inhabitants of the *Republic* except the guardians are in a state of slavery.[28] If by *slave* we mean a human being whose natural rights are disregarded and violated, this charge is certainly erroneous. The artisans perform productive functions for which they are naturally fitted. As rational beings, they are given the same education primarily in music and gymnastics that is given to all, until they reach the age of twenty.[29] If Plato had been able to conceive of modern machine production, he might have extended this age and modified his whole scheme. But unfortunately this lay beyond the range of his imagination. Necessary material artifacts must be produced by the labor of the artisans. But they are allowed to have adequate property to satisfy their material needs, though an upper limit is set.[30] Their material standard of living is higher than that of the guardians; their fundamental rights are recognized; they participate in all the fruits of communal endeavor. They are not slaves, unless an unusual meaning is given to this word.

The question as to whether Plato takes slaves for granted in the *Republic*, but never refers to them, is a controversial one. I believe that the answer is definitely *no* in view of his explicit remarks at *Republic* 547 C ff. where the introduction of slavery is attributed to the class feeling and violence which attends the establishment of a timocratic state. The timocratic "aristocrats" "enslave their own people who formerly (in the ideal *Republic*) lived as free men under their guardianship . . . and holding them as slaves and drudges, devote themselves to war (as in Sparta) and to keeping these subjects in bondage." To this we may also add the further argument that slaves in the *Republic* would be superfluous, since all the necessary productive functions are performed by artisans whose natural rights, including the right to an education, are definitely recognized. If this is true, Plato's imagination was politically far ahead of his own time, as it certainly was in the case of the rights of women.

Section IV. LYING PROPAGANDA

As a result of our intellectual heritage, of which Plato and Platonism are important parts, we have attained a respect for reason and truth, and a deep sense of the need for an educated and informed electorate, if democracy is to be maintained. Hence, the idea of rulers who deceive the people rightly offends us as undemocratic. Plato's defense of the "noble lie" at *Republic* 414 B strikes us as peculiarly obnoxious and even reminds us of unscrupulous totalitarian propaganda. This objection has been singled out for special emphasis by political thinkers like Crossman and Popper. Thus, Crossman interprets the passage as an approval of noble lies for "cajoling the civilian masses into obedience."[31]

Popper's accusations are even more violent. He compares this procedure to the activities of the nefarious Nazi Propaganda Bureau, and attacks the noble lie of Plato as an attempt to infuse racialist doctrines of blood and soil and the master race into the innocent inhabitants of the republic.[32] I am not prepared to defend Plato's concept of the noble lie in all respects; but I believe that these charges rest on serious misunderstandings.

First of all, Plato has a somewhat elaborate and complex doctrine concerning the lie,[33] which may be summarized as follows: the worst kind of lie, according to him, is "the lie in the soul," the belief by one's self of what is not so, whether or not the truth is suspected. Such lying to one's self is involuntary, for no one really wishes to be deceived. Hence, it is utterly indefensible, unmitigatedly evil without exception. Socratic education—radical questioning of self—is required to root it out. What *we* commonly refer to as *a lie* is something quite distinct. This consists in telling someone else what the teller himself knows to be false, because he knows what is really true. In Plato's view, this is secondary and derivative, for at least someone knows the truth.

Hence, he calls this merely a lie in words. Such a liar is not deceiving himself, unless he is using the lie for a mistaken or immoral purpose. If so, it involves a lie in his soul, which is a disastrous evil. Sometimes, however, the lie in words is justifiable. This is when those to whom we are communicating are not in a position to understand or gain any benefit from the truth which we understand.

Thus, at the beginning of the *Republic*[34] Socrates brings up the case of someone who has lent us a deadly weapon and suddenly returns to demand it from us in a fit of homicidal mania. In such a case, it would seem reasonable for us to say that we had left it somewhere else or misplaced it. Another less extreme case is that of children who may ask us questions, the abstract answers to which they are not as yet able to understand. When they ask, we usually give them some concrete story or picture, which may convey something of the truth to them, but certainly not the clear, abstract truth as we understand it. We do not refer to such practices as lying. Plato, whose standards in this respect are very high, calls this "a lie in words." He says that the guardians of the ideal republic are in a similar situation. They possess a coherent body of abstract knowledge concerning human nature and the obscure noetic powers of man— the source of human unity—which they cannot explain in full detail to the artisans and auxiliaries, who see radically different functions being performed by different members of the community.

No society can live in a healthy state unless there is an underlying sense of unity and a feeling of devotion to the common purpose. The full nature of this purpose and the complex doctrine on which it is based cannot be fully explained. So the guardians simplify it and clothe it in the concrete imagery of a patriotic myth of common origin and of different natural endowment fitting men for different functions in the co-operative living of human life. This is the "noble lie"—a simplified version of the truth concerning diversified endowments and common origin, like simplified heroic versions of past history, and other symbols capable of eliciting group loyalty and common aspiration.

Wild's defense of Plato's "Noble lie"

I believe that Plato overemphasized the need for such patriotic mythologies, but it is at least true that all human communities so far have developed them. In any case, this is the noble lie. The guardians know that it is not exactly true. Nevertheless, in a simplified version it does convey the gist of the truth. Men are brothers, though the earth is not their common mother. Souls are not gold or silver; this is mythological language. But that some are endowed with superior intelligence is true. The purpose of the myth is to elicit feelings of brotherhood and loyalty to the whole community as members of one family. This purpose is morally sound, though not exactly and abstractly stated. So this is a lie in words, a noble lie.

Popper claims that this myth is an expression of racialism.[35] "These metals are hereditary, they are racial characteristics."[36] This is a *non sequitur*. We may grant that the metals refer to what Plato held to be hereditary tendencies toward greater or less intelligence. But from this it does not follow that these differences are racial. Racial traits are hereditary, but all hereditary traits are not racial.

According to Popper, the purpose of the myth is to emphasize these differences, and to strengthen "the rule of the master race."[37] As a matter of fact, Plato makes it quite clear that the purpose is rather that of emphasizing a unity of race, so far as race means common ancestry, and thus of eliciting a loyalty to the whole community which transcends differences of intelligence and social function.[38]

If, as Popper supposes, the guardians were using this myth as political propaganda to support their own unjust rule, they would be guilty, on Plato's view, of ignorance and self-deception concerning the most important matters—the lie in the soul.

Section V. THOUGHT CONTROL

Philosophical skeptics, like Crossman and Popper, for whom the very concept of philosophical truth is synonymous with dogmatism, accuse Plato of advocating a tyrannical form of thought control, which strikes at the very heart of democracy. Thus, Crossman says that the greatest flaw in the reasoning of the *Republic* is that "human reason is capable of infallibility and that the scientific spirit should be prepared to force others to accept it as infallible."[39] Popper asserts that the *Republic* rests on "an educational monopoly of the ruling class with the strictest censorship, even of oral debates," and opposes this to the intellectualism of Socrates which "was fundamentally equalitarian and individualistic."[40] This criticism raises a certain question of fact, as well as the basic issue of philosophic truth which underlies the whole debate.

That Plato was intensely critical of the dominant art of his own time, including that of Homer, on philosophical grounds, and that he defended a policy of censorship with respect to art which might exercise a demoralizing influence on the young, must be granted. I believe that he went too far in this direction, and that censorship beyond the period of youth should be left to the educated individual to exercise for himself. But is it true that the citizens of the *Republic* are to be passively molded and indoctrinated with one theory alone—"oral debates" being eliminated—so that they are to be totally unfamiliar with any opposed point of view? This would, indeed, be a vicious blow at intellectual freedom, the very heart of true democracy. Both Crossman and Popper assert that this is the case. But in the *Republic* itself there is no evidence to support this view.

The work is a dialogue in which Thrasymachus, Glaucon, and Adeimantus are given ample opportunity to express opposed views. Surely, we may take this as an indication of what Plato would regard as a normal mode of argument in his ideal community. For him, Socrates remained the ideal teacher, and the dialectical method of question and answer, in which the mind is free to take any position whatsoever and to follow the argument wherever it may lead, remained the ideal form of intellectual procedure. Even the soul, when thinking within herself, follows this dialectical pattern.[41] There is no statement in the *Republic* which provides any legitimate basis for the thesis that the expression of certain opinions is to be suppressed. Of course, many opinions are not to be accepted. But this is because they are constantly shown to be unable to meet the Socratic test of maintaining themselves in searching questioning and debate.

There is no suggestion that the nonguardians of the republic, when they reach maturity, are to be kept in a state of artificial ignorance concerning such false doctrines. In fact, there is definite evidence pointing clearly in the opposite direction.

At every stage of education after the elementary level, the students are to be given examinations to test their advance. Some of these tests are to be moral, but others are intellectual.[42] The students are to be presented with false doctrines of every kind, defended with the greatest possible skill in order to test their capacity to see through fallacies and to avoid becoming confused by clever argument.[43] Any opinion can be expressed by anyone. There is no restraint on freedom of thought. Without such freedom the whole concept of Platonic argument and education would be absurd. But not every opinion can be accepted as true.

The *Republic* is an imagined ideal community which in Plato's conception demands the discovery of actual truths, especially concerning the most important and basic matters of a moral and philosophic nature. Crossman and Popper claim that there are no such truths.[44] Therefore, they cannot distinguish between the claim to possess such truth and undiluted dogmatism and tyranny. As we have already suggested, this is the basic philosophical issue between Plato and his most bitter critics. This is why they attempt to defend a violent contrast between Socrates, "the agnostic," who believed in no "final truth" at all and Plato, the totalitarian dogmatist, who betrayed his master by openly defending an articulate and full-fledged philosophy.[45]

We have already called attention to the dubious nature of the thesis that Socrates himself was a pure agnostic in the light of the *Apology*, which Popper accepts as genuinely Socratic.[46] At this point, we shall add only a brief comment on the *Gorgias*, which he also holds to be a true picture of Socrates.[47] In this dialogue Socrates presents a long and elaborate defense of the distinction between true and false art, and the relation of the arts to one another,[48] argues at length in defense of his positive belief that doing injustice is worse than suffering it,[49] analyzes the virtues as they are analyzed in Book IV of the *Republic*,[50] clearly defends the distinction between human goodness and pleasure,[51] and expresses a definite belief in immortality and a detailed, mythical picture of the fate of the soul in the after-life.[52] Is this agnosticism?

Socrates was certainly an enemy of uncriticized opinion and prejudice. He believed that all ideas must be subjected to the test of free argument and debate, as Plato also believed. But where in any dialogue, in Xenophon, or anywhere else, is there any evidence to support the view that Socrates held all truth to be unobtainable? If this negativistic doctrine is true, how can we, then, avoid the conclusion that Socrates' passionate quest for philosophic truth, to which he devoted his life, was a stupid mistake? What is the use of going on seeking for something that cannot in any sense be found? Of course, even the theory that there is no philosophic truth, if true, is a philosophic truth, requiring justification and support. Even this is a philosophy. Was it the philosophy of Socrates? If it was, we cannot trust the *Apology*, the *Gorgias*, or any dialogue of Plato or Xenophon—or indeed any evidence available to us. What, then, shall we trust?

Plato, who knew the man, did not accept this negativistic theory. He certainly held that Socrates' quest was not futile—that he had found certain truths, at least those suggested in the *Apology*, that there is something higher than man, that man is more than a mass of flesh and bones, that the cultivation of the soul is more important than the cultivation of the body, that vice is worse than death, etc. In his own life he attempted to elaborate the implications of these Socratic convictions. In doing this, he did not merely repeat what Socrates himself had said; he went further. Was this a betrayal? If so, the whole history of Western thought in its major currents has been a betrayal of Socrates. Can the modern ideal of democracy be defended and justified against other alternatives on the basis of a complete philosophical skepticism? Can freedom of thought be adequately maintained without some true insight into the nature of freedom, the nature of thought, and the complex nature of man? If so, democracy will be preserved by accident or historic destiny rather than by responsible human choice and effort.

Section VI. THE ATTACK ON PLATO: CONCLUSION

We have now studied the major criticisms urged against Plato by his modern enemies: first, that he is a dogmatist; second, a Spartan militarist and advocate of ruthless force and violence; third, a totalitarian defender of historicism; fourth, a racialist; fifth, an enemy of individual freedom, working for the return of a tribal, closed society; and finally, sixth, a militant opponent not only of ancient democracy but of modern democracy as well. Having examined these charges in the light of evidence provided by the dialogues, our conclusions may be summarized as follows:

1. Plato is a dogmatist only in the sense in which anyone defending basic philosophical convictions is a dogmatist. In this sense, Socrates was also a dogmatist, for even if the *Apology* alone is accepted as an authentic picture of him, he held many basic philosophical convictions. Uncriticized opinion and prejudice are inimical to freedom. But unless freedom is identified with anarchy, it has nothing to fear either from critical knowledge, which is able to defend itself by reference to evidence available to all, or from the untrammeled search for such knowledge in every field of human experience.

2. Plato's impatience with social corruption and his zeal for reform may have led him at times to make statements which seem to imply an approval of militant means to achieve what he conceived to be worthy ends. Such statements cannot be defended when separated from their contexts. The facts known about Plato's life, however, and what can be reasonably inferred from his writings in general give no ground for attributing to him any sympathy for militaristic and dictatorial practices or attitudes. So far as his definite doctrines are concerned, they are antimilitaristic and uncompromisingly attack all aggressive use of force. In this respect, Plato's social philosophy is very close to that of Toynbee, in spite of Toynbee's anti-Platonic polemic.

3. Plato is not an idealist, and the organic theory of society, as well as political totalitarianism, are altogether foreign to his thought. The human community, as he conceives it, is neither a mere juxtaposition of atomic individuals nor a superorganism

living its own life apart from the individual members. It is
rather a group of individuals unified by a shared purpose
capable of eliciting co-operative acts—not a physical or substantial unity, but a moral unity of purpose and aspiration.
Neglect of reason and rational nurture thus lead to social disintegration and attack the community at its very roots.

4. The charge of racialism seems to have no justification, for
the distinction between Greek and barbarian has no implication
of racial inferiority in the modern sense. A traditional cultural
enemy is not necessarily a racial inferior, and was not so conceived by Plato. An interest in eugenics does not imply the theory of a master race. Plato's myths of creation are all unitarian.
The whole human race is one flock under one divine shepherd.
Human cultures may vary widely in their excellence, but human
nature is everywhere the same.

5. The *Republic* is a universal ideal to be approximated in the
concrete realm of flux, not the description of any past Golden
Age. Plato was opposed to degeneration—change from a better
to a worse state—but not to change in general, which he recognized as an essential trait of physical existence. The *Republic* is
no more a closed society than any other rationally articulated social ideal. Even the most piecemeal social engineering must be
guided by some such articulated conception of the ultimate end
to be striven for. If by *tribal* is meant a society ruled by uncriticized prejudice and arbitrary decree, the *Republic* is certainly
not a tribal society.

6. Plato was opposed to the hysterical mob rule which he
knew by the name "democracy" and which he had experienced
at first hand during the end of the great war. He was also opposed to the philosophical skepticism and relativism which it
presupposes. But there is a grave question as to whether the
inference that Plato must, therefore, be opposed to modern
democracy is justifiable, since this is a complex idea to which
many historical movements have contributed. Three movements especially have made essential contributions to this modern ideal of democracy: first, skeptical ways of thought associated with the modern rebellions against feudalism and class oppression; second, an appreciation of the dignity and worth of

human existence and a trust in the common man, derived primarily from Christianity; and finally, the concept of natural law as equally binding upon all men everywhere, and a respect for reason and rational education, contributed by Greek philosophy and its later developments.

Plato's ideal is, of course, most closely related to the last. But it is not totally deficient in the other two respects. He also hated tyranny and suggested ways of guarding against it, especially Socratic education. Nor was he devoid of all sense of the worth of individual life and the natural equality of men as possessing a common human nature. Plato's ideal may reasonably be described as deficient from a democratic point of view, but not as antidemocratic, unless the democratic ideal is uncritically identified with anarchism.

Section VII. REASONS FOR THE ATTACK: MISUNDERSTANDING OF PLATO'S MORAL PHILOSOPHY

If these conclusions are not entirely mistaken, we must regard the widespread opinion that Platonic thought is somehow deeply opposed to all modern progressive ideals as a tragic misunderstanding, and we must raise the question as to why it is that able thinkers have been seemingly so predisposed to embrace it. Why is it that these dialogues, which in the past have aroused so many minds to Socratic questioning and the impassioned quest for philosophic truth, why is it that they have recently been studied by so many English and American thinkers with so little sympathy and understanding?

One basic reason we have had occasion to comment on. This is the subjectivist trend of modern thought and the skeptical distrust of philosophic reason which have now come to exert such a dominant influence not only on academic thought but on common-sense philosophy as well. Such skepticism places a yawning chasm between the present-day reader and the unhesitant realism of Plato and Aristotle, who accepted the fact of human knowledge, and dared to apply their cognitive faculties to the most obscure and basic questions. It is so easy for us to confuse this trust in reason with naïve dogmatism, and to ignore or misconstrue the actual evidence offered in its defense.

There are no doubt other reasons connected with Plato's style. But whatever the causes may be, there is a surprising vagueness and diversity of opinion among Plato's modern critics, and even among his more careful commentators, concerning the nature of his moral doctrine.

In Germany the word *eudaemonism* is widely used in this connection. Thus, in Ueberweg's monumental *Grundriss der Philosophie* we are told that "Plato's Ethics is eudaemonistic."[53] This term of course is derived from a term often used by Plato. But its present-day connotations are not the same. Having been widely used by idealistic thinkers, like Paulsen, it now suggests to the modern reader a theory of self-realization according to which the human good is regarded as a maximal satisfaction of any interests that happen to prevail in a given institution or society. Without any stable criterion for distinguishing what is essential from what is incidental and ephemeral, such a view is closely allied to utilitarianism and other forms of moral relativism.

Hence it is not surprising that in Anglo-Saxon countries where utilitarianism is very influential, Socratic and Platonic ethics are often referred to as utilitarian. Professor Fite is not niggardly in attributing diverse views to Plato, but utilitarianism is one which plays an important role in his campaign of vilification and attack. According to him, Platonic ethics lack any warmth of personal feeling. "His attitude towards truth, moral or other truth, is everywhere impersonal and objective."[54] Socrates also is a Spencerian moral mechanist attempting to settle moral issues by a quantitative calculus. Thus in commenting on the *Gorgias* he writes: "Socrates is still as ever a utilitarian, only now (from the Spencerian point of view) a more scientific utilitarian. In both dialogues the ethics is an ethics of calculation."[55]

As we have already noted, the opposite view of Plato as a philosopher of rigid repression haunted by scenes of debauchery is also expressed by Fite and by others. Thus, Niebuhr conceives of Plato as a "dualistic" thinker for whom everything connected with the body is evil.[56] Winspear, for whom Plato is "an idealistic, authoritarian reactionary,"[57] shares his view. According to him, "the logical (and historical) outcome of Platonic theory was asceticism, and an asceticism which became increasingly stern and harsh"[58] (*The Genesis of Plato's Thought*, p. 214). Crossman also repudiates any eudaemonistic interpretation of Plato whose "bias in favor of aristocracy led him to identify the 'gentleman' with the good man. . . ."[59] But Plato was not concerned about the human welfare of even this favored class, since he demanded of them "a virtue far beyond their reach," while to the "lower orders" he denied "any possibility of self-realization."[60]

None of these commentators pays any attention to Plato's constant use of the term *nature* in a normative sense. Popper, however, does notice this, and rightly sees that the concept of *nature* plays a determining role in the whole structure of Platonic ethics.[61] He refers to this doctrine as "Spiritual naturalism." But he can see nothing determinate in the term nature. Hence "spiritual naturalism can be used to defend anything, and especially any 'positive,' i.e., existing norms."[62] He thinks that the *nature* of a thing, according to Plato, is its "origin."[63] The more ancient something is, the more natural it is. Hence this view reduces to a reactionary moral conservatism. As we have indicated, it is possible to show that this is certainly not Plato's meaning. But then what did he mean? What is the Platonic moral philosophy?

It is only by attaining a satisfactory answer to this question that we may hope to explain the misunderstandings we have been considering, and the variety of conflicting views attributed to him by his modern critics. Surely all of these attributions cannot be correct. I believe it will be possible to show that none of them is. Plato's realistic ethics of natural law represents a mode of thought diverging fundamentally from the dominant subjectivist trend of modern philosophy. During the nineteenth century this tradition was completely submerged. Hence it is no wonder that modern interpreters of Plato have difficulty in focusing it.

As we have seen, almost every influential modern ethical position has been imputed to Plato. The Germans have confused him with Kant, the English with utilitarianism. Many other views have also been attributed to him. But with a few exceptions no one has recently thought of him in connection with the realistic tradition of natural law, of which he was actually a founder. These exceptions, however, deserve to be mentioned.

One is Professor Solmsen who in his recent book *Plato's Theology* has dared to question the accepted opinion that natural-law philosophy began with the Stoics.[64] The other is Mr. H. Cairns in his book on *Legal Philosophy from Plato to Hegel*, who suggests that "by insisting upon a rigid distinction between the idea of law and the positive enactments of the state, Plato prepared the way for natural-law speculation and the perception of an ideal element in law making."[65] These assertions are made incidentally and are left undeveloped by their authors. But they constitute noteworthy exceptions. For the most part, Plato's moral realism, like the concept of natural law itself, has been unnoticed and confused with essentially alien tendencies more familiar to the modern mind.

Thus in spite of their diversity, the views which the modern critics of Plato attribute to him all have one thing in common, that norms are man-made constructions, legislated into existence by arbitrary human interest or decree. It is quite clear, as we shall see, that Plato held no such conception. As a matter of fact, he identified this sort of moral subjectivism with his enemies, the sophists, and bitterly attacked it in his dialogues. What an irony that in a time when subjectivism has become almost a philosophical truism, a peculiarly obnoxious variety of it should be imputed to Plato himself! In fact, as we shall attempt to show, Plato was a moral realist. As such, he must be classified with the tradition which later came to be known as that of *natural law*. Unless we succeed in clearly focusing Plato's moral realism, we shall never understand the confusions we have been discussing, nor the resulting issues between him and his modern critics.

But before we can hope to understand Plato's realism and his position in the tradition of natural-law philosophy, we must first briefly examine this theory and attempt to distinguish it from those alien views with which it is so prevailingly confused. What is meant by the term *natural law?* How and why is it so generally misunderstood? It is to these questions that we shall turn in the following chapter.

CHAPTER THREE

BASIC MISCONCEPTIONS OF NATURAL LAW

THE theory of natural law is not merely of historical interest in connection with the thought of Plato and Aristotle. Since its first formulation in ancient Greece, it has played a crucially important role in the great crises of our cultural history, and is now being revived once more after a century and a half of neglect. It is a concept of great significance, even for moral philosophers who cannot accept it, and is now a vital ideational factor in international politics and the movement for world unity. For all these reasons, we shall now turn to a provisional consideration of this theory: first, its general nature and the radical differences which distinguish it from influential types of modern moral theory; and second, certain prevalent misconceptions of the theory.

Section I. NATURAL LAW AS A DISTINCTIVE TYPE OF ETHICAL THEORY

By natural law, or moral law, I mean: *a universal pattern of action, applicable to all men everywhere, required by human nature itself for its completion.*

This concept, like any basic ethical category, is founded on certain ontological and epistemological principles. Even though modern moral philosophers have been notoriously lax in this respect, it is of the first importance to make such basic presuppositions clear. Otherwise, the fundamental concepts of an ethical argument will remain confused and indeterminate, and the whole theory will be plunged in a fog of obscurity. Let us, then, first consider the ontological presuppositions of the theory of natural law and then its epistemological presuppositions.

The most basic thesis involved in this theory is that value and existence are closely intertwined with one another. If the completion of existence is good, then existence itself must be valuable. Goodness is some kind or mode of existence, evil some mode of nonexistence, or privation. But this thesis would seem to lead us to the assertion that existence as such is good—that what is, is right—an equally embarrassing conclusion which rules out the possibility of existent evil. Indubitable empirical evidence shows us that evil in some sense really exists, as well as what is good. Hence, we must reject the conclusion that existence as such is good. We must qualify it by recognizing that existence in a certain mode is bad. It is only a certain mode or sense of existence that is good. What sense? What mode?

The answer of the theory of natural law is indicated by the word *completion* in our formula. If existence is deprived of what it requires for its completion, evil arises. Furthermore, this is a positive existent evil, for such deprived existences actually are. The privation, abstractly considered in itself, is nonexistent. But privations never exist in this way. They are always attached to a concrete existent entity. Such an entity, taken together with its privation, is a positively existent being in a thwarted or evil condition. It is only existence which fulfils itself and attains existential completion that is good. Such *completion of being* is the general ontological sense of terms such as *goodness* and *value*. This notion of completion involves further ontological implications of great significance.

It implies that being has an active or tendential character. Such acts or tendencies are at first imperfect or incomplete. They may be either frustrated with a resulting evil, or completed with a resulting good. Such a dynamic view of existence is incompatible with any form of logical atomism which would regard existence as made up exclusively of units which are fully determinate and actual. At the present time, such ontological views are widely assumed, though only rarely consciously defended. In opposition to them and in accord with great ranges of evidence which strongly indicate that the world of nature is in flux towards what is not yet fully possessed, the theory of natural law holds that natural entities are in a state of incompletion or potency, and that they are ever tending further towards something they now lack. What determines the nature of these existential tendencies? The answer to this question is suggested by the word *nature* in our formula.

This term signifies a certain determinate structure, or form, which is possessed in common by all individuals of a certain kind or species. Thus, all individual human beings share in a common human nature. As in the case of other finite entities, this determinate structure or nature, when given existence, produces certain determinate tendencies towards fulfilment. Such a tendency lies at the root of the human feeling of obligation (cf. chap. 7, B). This view is inconsistent with any conception of nature as consisting exclusively of inert passive stuff, incapable of action.

The theory of natural law also presupposes certain realistic epistemological principles. It implies that human nature is an ordered set of traits possessed in common by every human individual and essential to his being. This is inconsistent with nominalism. It also implies the capacity of human reason to apprehend this essential common structure and the perfective tendencies characteristic of the human species. When so understood and expressed in universal propositions, these tendencies are norms or moral laws. This realistic doctrine is inconsistent with any view which would regard norms as separated from existent fact or as arbitrary constructions made by man.[1]

Such a separation of fact from value has dominated the whole course of modern ethical theory. Being has been thought of as the realm of fully actual atomic fact with *value* as an extraneous realm of norms. The *is* is not what *ought to be*, the *ought* is not the *is*, and there is no natural bridge between the two. As a result of this separation, the whole idea of a normative law based on natural dynamism and tendency has been rejected as an equivocation. As is usually said, this confuses a purely descriptive law of nature, which merely records a succession of disconnected finished facts, with an imperative prescription or command with no natural basis in fact at all—an arbitrary dictate or decree. Critical discussion, however, has revealed many serious difficulties in this view.

In the first place, when the notion of being is focused, it is clear that values and disvalues are facts *of some kind*. Existent entities are certainly judged, sometimes truly judged, to be in a sound or an unsound condition. So far as such judgments are true, they must refer to *some kind* of existent fact.

Furthermore, the values which men strive for are not indifferent to existence. It is true that the value as conceived, which elicits aspiration, is only an intentional object, a possibility. But this is not what we strive to achieve. We strive for its realization. It is literally impossible to seek for a merely possible object. Of what real good are the sublimest values if they remain unrealized? This shows that the values really moving us are not separated from existence.

Another serious difficulty, which is now in the forefront of ethical discussion, concerns the obligation which binds or moves us to certain values. This is clearly a factual urge, or tendency, which existentially links us or propels us towards certain values. If there is no connection between the two realms, how is this factual link to be explained? Why should certain objects move us positively, others negatively?

Finally, what is the nature of moral reasoning and deliberation if value is totally divorced from fact? Either it must be identified with theoretical truth concerning existence, in which case it will be irrelevant to what we ought to do; or else it will concern arbitrary preferences which cannot be rationally justified.[2] Moral reasoning will be reduced either to abstract theorizing, having no moving power except by accident, or to the rationalization of irrational bias. Neither of these alternatives seems to accord with the actual evidence of moral experience where we recognize certain ways of justifying ends and means as both rational and binding.

The theory of natural law has an answer to these difficulties, which seems to square with the factual evidence. This answer rests on a basic denial of that false metaphysical atomism which rejects the idea of tendency, and thus leads to an unbridgeable chasm between so-called finished fact and nonexistent value. Finite existence is always unfinished. As such, it is essentially characterized by tendencies towards fulfilment and completion. Some tendencies are peculiar to the individual entity. But other essential tendencies are shared in common by those possessing a similar nature. Such tendencies, when they are rationally understood, constitute what is commonly referred to as the moral law. The realization of these tendencies is always good;

their frustration is always evil. Hence, the chasm between fact and value is bridged. In the physical world of time and change, there are no fully finished atomic facts. All such existence is tending to further fulfilment. The world is dynamic and moving towards completion. There are natural norms embedded in the structure of all material existence.

Man is no exception. Hence, the nature of obligation becomes clear. It is based on those existential tendencies which all human beings share, and which move them to their natural end. When this end is grasped by rational insight, together with those modes of action which are required to realize it, we are physically moved or bound by the urge of obligation or oughtness. This is neither a pure theoretical judgment, having no basis in natural desire, nor a mere appetitive bias, having no connection with cognizable fact. It is rather a union of the two—a natural urge, together with the rational justification of this urge or, as Aristotle put it, *a desiderative reason, a reasoning desire.*[3]

This makes it possible to avoid the dilemma concerning the nature of practical reason.[4] A question about the justification of some envisaged end can be rationally answered by showing that it is in agreement with the natural end of man. A question about the justification of means can be rationally answered by showing that it coincides, or is not incompatible, with the moral law, the universal pattern of action required to achieve this universal end. Such practical reasoning is not purely abstract and theoretical, since it is united with actually felt urges of natural desire. But neither is it the rationalization of an incidental appetite, since it is guided by a natural end that can be theoretically understood as the completion of an intelligible common nature. Thus, practical reason can be understood as *both* cognitive and desiderative, and the dilemma is avoided (cf. chap. 7, C). In thus defending the principle of natural norms grounded in factual tendencies, the philosophy of natural law differs from all the major types of ethical theory which have been developed in the modern period. It also differs from each of these in further definite respects.

Kantian ethics is grounded on a radical separation of the *noumenal* realm of value (the "intelligible world") and the *phenomenal* realm of fact.[5] The categorical imperative is laid down by the human mind without being grounded in any observable reality. Hence, it is empty of all empirical content, and seems to reduce to an abstract principle of formal consistency. When the question is raised as to *why* we should be moral, the answer is simply—*you should!* Any attempt to discover a rationally defensible ground for the moral imperative is condemned by Kant as heteronomy.[6] The theory of natural law differs sharply from each of these principles. Value is tendentially rooted in fact. The justifiable moral imperatives are not arbitrarily laid down by the human mind, but rather discovered in the tendential structure of human nature. They do not reduce to an empty principle of abstract consistency, but are filled with the essential content of human nature, on which they are factually grounded.

Utilitarian ethics makes no clear distinction between raw appetite or interest, and that deliberate or voluntary desire which is fused with practical reason. Value, or pleasure, or satisfaction is the object of any interest, no matter how incidental or distorted it may be.[7] Qualitative distinctions are simply ignored, and the good is conceived in a purely quantitative manner as the maximum of pleasure or satisfaction.[8] Reason has nothing to do with the eliciting of sound appetite. One desire is no more legitimate than another. Reason is the slave of passion. Its whole function is exhausted in working out schemes for the maximizing of such interests as happen to arise through chance or other irrational causes. This is fundamentally a moral relativism.

As against this, the theory of natural law maintains that there is a sharp distinction between raw appetites and deliberate desires elicited with the co-operation of practical reason. The good cannot be adequately conceived in a purely quantitative manner. Random interests which obstruct the full realization of essential common tendencies are condemned as antinatural. The maximizing of such appetites is evil, not good. When reason becomes the slave of passion, human freedom is lost and human nature thwarted. Moral relativism cannot explain the fact that all men are subject to certain universal principles of justice which they at least dimly understand.

The idealistic ethics of self-realization, or eudaemonism, as it is often called, is easily confused with the ethics of natural law. As a matter of fact, they are sharply opposed. From the standpoint of natural law, this kind of eudaemonism is closely allied to utilitarianism. No attempt is made to distinguish what is essential to the self from what is ephemeral and incidental, all desires and tendencies being reduced to the same qualitative level. Hence, the good is conceived quantitatively as a maximizing of purposive realization. For the idealist, however, this is conceived in mentalistic terms as the larger self, or the self of the great community. The larger the self or group soul, the better it is. Thus, when the individual finds himself in conflict with society, he is sure to be wrong. There is no universal standard to which an appeal can be made from the judgments of a corrupt community. This position is effectively summarized by Bradley in the aphorism *my station and its duties*.[9] This is a social relativism.

As opposed to this view, the ethics of natural law sharply separates essential needs and rights from incidental interests. The good is not adequately understood as a mere maximizing of qualitatively indifferent purposes, but a maximizing of those tendencies which qualitatively conform to the nature of man and which arise through rational deliberation and free choice. That which exists always contains germinal tendencies towards the right, but these tendencies may become twisted or distorted by chance, by tyrannical manipulation, and by mistaken deliberation. Hence, we cannot infer that what is, is right. Natural rights may remain unsatisfied and natural duties unperformed. There is a stable universal standard, resting on something firmer than the shifting sands of appetite, to which an appeal can be made even from the maximal agreements of a corrupt society. This standard is the law of nature which persists as long as man persists—which is, therefore, incorruptible and inalienable, and which justifies the right to revolution against a corrupt and tyrannical social order.

As against all the modern abortive attempts to build some
sort of a moral bridge over the unbridgeable chasm of a metaphysical dualism between fact and value, the recent emotive
theory of ethics has simply pointed to the futility of all such
attempts and has returned to an undiluted statement of this
dualism without questioning its necessity. According to this
theory, the radical separation of value from fact must simply be
accepted without qualification. Hence, rational ethics is impossible. The theoretical cognition of existent facts has nothing to
do with what ought to be, even though it includes the description of actual preferences *ex post facto*. The fact that someone
has desired something, or that I have desired something, or that
I now desire something, does not justify the inference that I or
anyone else ought to desire it. Reasoning which does not end in
action is irrelevant to ethics and futile from an ethical point of
view.[10] Such evaluational terms as ought, right, and good are
not cognitive terms at all; they are merely the expression of
biases and preferences. Practical reason is merely the rationalization of such preferences. Rational ethics does not exist. Moral
justification is impossible. In fact, moral meaning is noncognitive. Like poetry, moral judgments use language in a nonrational, emotive way and lack all cognitive reference. Modern
ethics has thus ended in the destruction of ethics.

If moral theory is to be saved from this fate, its basic ontological presuppositions must be once again thoroughly re-
examined and clearly focused. In this process, the ancient tradition of natural law may be able to offer enlightenment and
guidance. It is founded on a realistic metaphysics quite distinct
from the dualistic ontology which has given rise to the modern
ethical impasse. As we have just observed, it is distinct from all
the major types of modern moral theory. Perhaps it may help us
to dissipate the confusion into which ethics has fallen. But before it can do this, it must be sympathetically studied and
understood. So foreign has this whole point of view become that
it is hard for us to approach it fairly, or even to come to grips
with it at all.

Section II. Five Current Misconceptions
of the Theory of Natural Law

Having tried briefly to explain the theory of natural law and to distinguish it from four current types of ethical theory, we shall now turn to certain misconceptions of this theory which can be found in the critics of Plato whom we have been studying and which, we believe, are widely prevalent in the recent literature of moral philosophy. Our aim will be to clarify the theory and to defend it against a certain kind of objection.

It is often difficult to distinguish a misconception from an objection. But the distinction we have in mind is this: sometimes we find objections raised against a theory by one who understands the nature of the position he is criticizing. Such objections are, in one sense, the most important, and they need to be carefully considered by anyone defending the theory in question. But sometimes we find objections raised by certain critics in such a way that those defending the theory cannot recognize it as theirs. Misconceptions or objections of this sort are primary in the sense that they must be answered and clarified *before* the theory in question can be intelligently discussed—that is, before it can be either intelligently criticized or defended at all. It is misconceptions or objections of this sort with which we shall now be concerned.

In our opinion, such intelligent discussion is a vital matter, for the issues it raises are basic and of great contemporary relevance. If there is no universal moral law which may be reasonably defended as holding good for all men, then the very existence of ethics as a rational discipline would seem to be subject to serious question. Also, the dream for any world community based upon rational foundations would seem to become pure fantasy. Hence, it is no wonder that there is a widespread reawakening of interest in natural law at the present time. This makes it all the more important that it should be clearly understood by moral philosophers, so that it may be subjected to the grueling test of unprejudiced examination and criticism. However, at present certain misconceptions stand in the way of such a test.

We shall now examine five of these. They can be found in the critics of Plato whom we have been studying, and are closely associated with the prevalent types of ethical theory from which we have attempted to distinguish the theory of natural law. An analysis of these misunderstandings may not only lead to a clearer grasp of the theory; it may also serve to clarify certain aspects of the philosophy of Plato, who, as we shall see (chap. 5), was actually the founder of this theory, so far as Western philosophy is concerned.

A. NATURAL LAW AS BASED UPON A DUBIOUS INFERENTIAL TELEOLOGY

The theory of natural law was developed by a realistic tradition of philosophy, radically empirical in its methodology, and claiming to derive all of its basic concepts from the observation of experienced facts. From a disciplined examination of concrete instances, where there is common agreement that goodness, health, or soundness is present, it has attempted to defend the view that what is meant is always the realization of natural capacities and potencies. For any entity whatsoever, to realize its essential tendencies and capacities for action is to be in a sound or healthy state.

One of the commonest reactions to such a theory is to observe that it rests upon a naïve attribution of purpose or teleology to the universe at large. The critic here takes it for granted that reality, as it is immediately observed, consists of finished atomic facts which simply are what they are. They have no capacities for further development; they are not in flux or transition; they are fully determinate and finished. From this point of view, any attribution of tendency towards what is not actually present is a naïve projection of subjective purpose into nature. Thus, the conception of any universal moral law holding good for all mankind is merely a peculiarly blatant form of dogmatism by which some naïve individual has mesmerized himself into believing that his own particular aims and purposes are somehow ingrained in the nature of man and the universe. As a matter of fact, however, as modern science has shown, while the human individual may possibly be capable of acting teleologically, there is no evidence for the view that other things—and the universe in general—cannot be perfectly well explained without reference to any immanent teleology or "mystical" factors of any kind.

Thus, we find Winspear commenting on a passage at the end of the first book of the *Republic*, where Plato refers to the fact that each thing has a function and that its virtue or goodness consists in performing this function well. "Here," he says, "we have a supreme example of the use or misuse of teleology."[11] That a thing has performed its function well is a mere fact having nothing to do with any purpose. But a moral virtue is something altogether different. It implies a conscious agent who conceives of a purpose, and then relates some act to the attainment of this subjective aim. So "excellence of functioning is not really the same as moral virtue."[12] The whole argument rests on a confusion of fact with moral purpose.

Fite makes a similar comment on the Platonic doctrine that the nature of an entity fits that entity for the performance of certain functions, or that action always follows being. He says that this whole conception of a dynamic or tendential nature is merely a projection of Plato's own subjective point of view into a static universe—a naïve subjectivism.[13]

The assumption underlying all such criticisms is that the basic ontological facts about the universe are obvious. It is obviously fixed and determinate—just what it is. The only alternatives are either to be content with these given facts or to project something analogous to human purpose into the world in a dubious attempt to explain them in an anthropomorphic way. This criticism rests on several serious misconceptions.

In the first place, the issue concerns not merely the interpretation of certain evident facts admitted by all, but two very divergent views of what the facts really are. Plato and others who defended the theory of moral law held that the sensory facts immediately presented to us are not perfectly determinate, fixed and complete, but rather that they are indeterminate, dynamic, and tendential.[14] They are never simply what they are, but also on the way to something that they now are not. The world is dynamic and in flux. This issue cannot be settled by any appeal to logic or to a priori argument of any kind. It can only be settled by careful attention to experience. If change is really a primary datum, then tendency must be recognized as a basic ontological fact, having nothing to do with the projection of subjective purpose or teleology, in the ordinary sense of this word.

Furthermore, to hold that natural entities have similar tendencies determined by similar formal structures is not to imply that such entities act with conscious purposes and know that to which they are tending, as Nicolai Hartmann supposes in his criticism of the realistic category of form.[15] The tide may now be rising and tending to come inshore. This fact may be recognized without committing one's self to the view that the tide is purposively striving for a mentally conceived end. Men have minds which often enable them to act purposively. But as we now know, human individuals may tend towards certain goals without having the least conception of that towards which they are tending. The phenomenon of tendency must be distinguished from that of conscious tendency.

The basic issue is a question of empirical fact. Do I find things actually changing in my experience, or am I always confronted with one fully determinate thing which is then succeeded by another? If I find that things are really changing, that they are not always determinate, but often on the way to determinate goals which they may or may not realize,[16] then the basic ontological categories of natural-law philosophy will be recognized not as inferences but rather as descriptions of facts. The notion of essential tendencies, common to different species of entity, will also be recognized as a necessary consequence, for how can a tendency fail to be determined by the nature of that which is tending?[17] When these ontological facts are clearly recognized, the notion of goodness as the realization of tendency and that of evil as the obstruction of tendency will no longer seem strange or dubious. They will rather be recognized as descriptive categories true of the most basic facts of our experience, so ubiquitous in fact and so often taken for granted as to be opaque and hard to focus without the closest attention to the data of direct experience.

A natural widespread criticism of natural-law philosophy is that the appeal to nature as a norm is bound to be indecisive unless warped by subjective bias. This is because of the all-inclusiveness of factual existence. Everything may be found in existence—the irrational as well as the rational, the bad as well as the good. Hence, as history shows all too clearly, any sort of a normative principle may be justified by this appeal to being. The range of facts referred to by such philosophical terms is far too vast, and the terms too vague, to admit of any precision. Hence, what always happens is the selection of certain facts which happen to agree with an a priori, normative bias of the naturalistic thinker. Both slavery and antislavery have been justified by such appeals to factual existence. What they represent is merely an attempt to evade responsibility and to seek a rationalization for preferences already made on other grounds.

This objection is intensively exploited by Popper in his criticism of Plato.[18] According to him, "this form of naturalism is so wide and so vague that it may be used to defend anything. There is nothing that has ever occurred to man which could not be claimed to be 'natural'; for if it were not in his nature, how could it have occurred to him?"[19] A little farther on, he tells us again that "spiritual naturalism [his name for natural-law ethics] is much too vague to be applied to any practical problem. It cannot do much beyond providing some general arguments in favor of conservatism. In practice, everything is left to the wisdom of the great lawgiver (a godlike philosopher, whose picture, especially in the *Laws*, is undoubtedly a self-portrait)."[20]

This objection rests on several misconceptions. In the first place, the appeal is not made to being but to nature. One cannot make a normative appeal to existence, which is all-inclusive. But natural existence can be distinguished from existence. Many things happen to a man, either from external influences or from his own free choice, which are not in accordance with his nature and his natural tendencies. If this were not true, we could not distinguish between the healthy or sound state and that which is unhealthy and unsound.

What is meant by a natural tendency? This is marked by two distinguishing features: first, it is shared in common by all members of the species; second, its realization, at least to some degree, is required for the living of human life. Thus, the need for food is a natural tendency; the desire to torture other men is not. The first is common to the species, and some degree of realization is required for human life. Hence, it is essential. The second lacks these marks. It is not common to the species. Human life can be achieved without it, and closer examination will reveal that it is an impediment to co-operative modes of action which are essential to human life. Hence, it is unessential or accidental, and also obstructive or evil.

The pattern of action which is universally required for the living of human life is essential. This is the standard of natural law. All other acts are incidental. If they conflict with essential natural needs, they are evil. If they further the realization of such natural needs in the concrete, they are good. If they do neither, they are indifferent. This is the theory. It evidently rests on the possibility of distinguishing between what is essential to an entity and what is incidental, a distinction which Popper categorically rejects.[21]

We have no time here for an exhaustive discussion of the epistemological and ontological issues. But since they are necessarily involved in any attempt to clarify the basic concepts of ethics, we shall briefly comment on the chief arguments which Popper brings up against what he calls "the essentialism of Plato and Aristotle."[22]

He regards the distinction between essence and accident as a peculiar invention of these philosophers, which has unfortunately dominated Western thought ever since, until the rise of modern science.[23] But at the same time, he admits that any attempt to define or clarify the meaning of a term presupposes this distinction. This is because the concrete individual entity can never be defined as such. It is far too rich, and includes far too many irrelevant traits and accidents. We can, of course, simply point at such a concrete blur, or ostensively define it in terms of some arbitrarily selected sensory trait. This is often sufficient for the predictive purposes of what we now call *science*. But if we are ever to gain a clear insight into the thing, whatever it is, and precisely separate it from others, we must, by a more painstaking examination of its behavior, distinguish what is basic and essential in it from what is derived and incidental.

The *essence*, as it has been called, and its tendencies for realization, as well as all acts agreeing with it, are natural; those not agreeing, unnatural. If we are to understand the meaning of any term whatsoever—whether it signifies a substance, a property, or a relation—we must be able to regard it abstractly, separating out those traits which are necessarily involved in the existence of the thing or relation from those which are merely extrinsic and accidental. Popper himself, like any writer who makes himself intelligible, defines or characterizes the things he is talking about in this way. Thus, he briefly describes what he means by a norm, and sharply distinguishes norms from facts.[24] On page 169 he briefly summarizes what he means by an open society and those essential marks which separate it from a closed or tribal one. The words "essence" or "nature," of course, are of no importance. But without some such defining, describing procedure of this sort nothing intelligible could be said at all. This is what Plato and Aristotle meant by the essence or nature of a thing. What are Popper's reasons for attempting to reject it? Basically, they can be reduced to three.

The first is that science makes no use of essentialist definitions which place a term to be defined on the left, and then proceed to a longer defining formula on the right, as when we say "a puppy is a young dog." Popper maintains that science uses only nominal definitions: "it starts with the defining formula and asks for a short label to it." Having arrived at the concept of *young dog*, science then merely asks, "What shall we call this?" seeking for a shorthand label "in order to cut a long story short."[25]

We need not dwell on this argument, for there is nothing

non-Aristotelian about it. Nominal definitions have long been recognized in the tradition of realistic philosophy and, of course, play a certain pragmatic role in al precise disciplines. But, as Popper's own argument shows, such definitions presuppose real definitions or "defining formulae," which descriptively express the real nature or essence of something, telling us what this thing is. The formula when read from right to left is nominal. But since it is a formula or equivalence, it can also be read from left to right. Then, it is a real definition. Any nominal definition presupposes a real definition of some kind. A young dog may be called a puppy in English and something else in French or German. These are nominal definitions of the same thing and are all equivalent. But the reason for the equivalence is that their real definition, the real thing they signify (a young dog), is precisely the same. Popper also admits that defining formulae, tables, and clear-cut distinctions between different kinds of entities occur in science.[26] So there is no argument here. He has said nothing new.

Popper's second argument[27] does raise a significant issue. Here, under the name of "intellectual intuition," he attacks the Platonic and Aristotelian doctrine that the human intellect, in cooperation with the senses (for Aristotle),[28] can actually apprehend some structure as it is, and can express this apprehension in a defining formula. Popper says that "such intuitions cannot even serve as an argument . . . for somebody else may have just as strong an intuition that the same theory is false."[29] So Popper rejects the notion of self-evidence and with it, as he thinks, the whole theory of real definitions. But this is a misconception.

No competent realist has ever maintained that every insight supposedly possessed by anyone is necessarily true. This is a caricature. But a "theory" is not the same as a "defining formula." Before we may either agree or disagree with any theory, we must understand the terms of the theory, what it is about. Such understanding of a real structure, as soon as it becomes clear, may be expressed in a defining formula and checked by other observers. There is no need for claiming infallibility at any stage of this process. But unless certain things were evident to a scientist, as that a needle on an instrument is now passing a

certain hair line, there would be no empirical method. If nothing
were immediately and directly evident under conditions favorable to observation, science itself would be impossible, for no
theories could ever be verified or checked.

The third and last argument is of more importance.[30] Terms
can be defined on the realistic view only by means of more basic
and more general terms, ultimately the basic terms of philosophy which signify the omnipresent existential structure of all
things. But according to Popper, "these, for many reasons, are
likely to be just as vague and confusing as the terms we started
with; and in any case we would have to go on to define them in
turn; which leads to new terms, which too must be defined. And
so on to infinity."[31] Hence, the attempt to define terms "can
only make matters worse,"[32] actually increasing "the vagueness
and confusion."[33] There are several misunderstandings here.

Of course, the infinite regress must be rejected. Popper admits that no theories could be proved if there were no first
principles[34] which, like the law of contradiction, require no
demonstration because they are evident.[35] In the same way,
complex derivative terms must be defined by means of ultimate
structures which are evident by themselves. Hence, the regress
is avoided by reference to the ultimate structures of philosophy,
whose relations and distinctions may be made evident to
reason. Such notions as existence, unity, and difference, are
involved in all other concepts whatsoever. It is only by clarifying the meaning of such fundamental terms that ultimate
clarity may be achieved in the more restricted defining formulae
of the special disciplines. Such clarity, however, is difficult to
attain, requiring disciplined observation and analysis of a basic
level of fact too apt to be taken for granted and thus ignored.

Popper's attempt to reject the notion of definition rests upon
his enmity towards philosophy. For him its basic concepts are
vague and obscure. Hence, the philosophical clarification of concepts, the only way in which they can be ultimately clarified,
seems to him merely confusion piled on confusion. We may
grant to him that philosophy is still in a most imperfect state;
but the answer to a difficult challenge is not to evade it. The
answer is further discipline and effort.

The theory of natural law is the result of such a disciplined effort to clarify the meaning of ethical concepts in terms of the ultimate ontological structures which they exemplify—essence, existence, essential tendency, and fulfilment. In the light of such an analysis, universal moral principles may be rationally justified as founded on real facts which can be understood by all. If no such ontological justification can be given, as Popper maintains, it is hard to see in what sense ethics may be defended as a rational discipline entitled to any respect. He holds that norms are completely divorced from facts and that normative judgments rest entirely on individual preferences.

He tries to save this from the necessary implication of arbitrariness,[36] but his attempt does not succeed. "It must be admitted," he says, "that the view that norms are conventional or artificial indicates that there will be a certain element of arbitrariness involved. . . ."[37] This gives the case away. How can any discipline capable of eliciting universal agreement be based upon conventions which are admittedly "arbitrary"? How can disagreements be resolved if there is no stable evidence to which we may refer? In spite of this, Popper argues that one arbitrary preference may be better than another, though he fails to give any reasons supporting this strange conclusion.[38] No such reason can be given. If moral judgments rest exclusively on preferences having no foundation in any realm of observable fact, there can be no discipline of ethics. Moral nihilism is the only consistent conclusion.

C. NATURAL LAW AS A CONFUSION OF DESCRIPTIVE
WITH PRESCRIPTIVE LAW

Perhaps the most common charge which is made against the theory of natural law is that it rests upon a naïve confusion of two distinct meanings of the term "law." On the one hand, "law" refers to the descriptive generalizations of science, the realm of fact; on the other hand, to normative principles and commands, the realm of values or norms.[39] From the standpoint of those making this charge, the facts are clear and evident. The two realms are sharply separated. Facts are always perfectly determinate and finished. They are simply there, fixed and unalterable. Norms, on the contrary, are simply not there. They belong to an altogether separate realm. For Kant these were the two worlds of the phenomenal versus the noumenal, governed by two opposed sets of laws and principles. Though this Kantian terminology is no longer fashionable, the basic dualism of fact versus value still remains as an uncriticized ontological presupposition of most contemporary ethical discussion.

From this point of view, natural law is regarded not only as a naïve confusion of two things entirely separate, but also, as by Popper, as a naïve confusion resulting from anthropomorphic theological assumptions.[40] If there is a supreme lawgiver, then the laws of nature may be regarded as resulting from normative commands. But without such an inferential assumption, there is no basis in the empirical evidence for any such confusion. And even if this assumption is granted, there is a sharp separation between descriptive laws not subject to human choice, and moral commands which are made by man.[41] Such critics often accuse natural-law philosophy of reducing man to subhuman nature (Kantian *heteronomy*), of leaving no place for human freedom to do as one likes,[42] and of projecting their own moral whims into an imaginary universe. All of these charges are made by Popper in attacking Plato.[43]

He calls his own position *critical dualism* or *critical conventionalism* and asserts it to be "characteristic of the open society."[44] Other views, such as the vague "spiritual naturalism" of Plato, are expressions of earlier, pre-scientific tribal societies.[45] According to him, a natural law is "a strict unvarying regularity,"[46] "which is unalterable."[47] "There are no exceptions to it."[48] A normative law, on the other hand, is alterable and enforceable by men. "It can be broken."[49] The confusion of these two separate kinds of law is inexcusably naïve in failing to recognize "the impossibility of reducing decisions or norms to facts."[50]

It was originally associated with a "naïve conventionalism," which said that "both natural and normative regularities are experienced as expressions of, and as dependent upon, the decisions of manlike gods or demons."[51] It is often reinforced by "our fear of admitting to ourselves that the responsibility for our ethical decisions is entirely ours and cannot be shifted to anybody else; neither to God, nor to nature, nor to society, nor to history."[52] It is also associated with an extreme type of casuistry which hopes for the construction of "a code of norms upon a scientific basis so that we need only look up the index of the code if we are faced with a difficult moral decision."[53] These charges involve several misconceptions.

In the first place, the view that competent defenders of the philosophy of natural law have "reduced" norms to facts in a "monistic" manner, and have failed to make any distinction between theoretical and normative science, is entirely false. Thus, Plato in the *Politicus*[54] clearly distinguishes the purely noetic or descriptive modes of knowing, which seek knowledge alone, from the practical arts which govern effective action. But he does not separate them, as do most post-Kantian moralists. The practical arts involve action, but they also possess insight as part of their inherent structure.[55]

Similarly, Aristotle sharply distinguishes theoretical science which seeks truth alone from practical science which also involves action. But the latter is not wholly deprived of all knowledge. It is reason working hand-in-hand with action, a reasoning desire, or a desiderative reason.[56] This practical reason is distinct from theoretical reason in three ways: first, it works together with appetite, which is irrelevant to pure theory;[57] second, it is concerned with the individual as well as the universal, for we cannot act in general;[58] and third, it deals with what is indeterminate and contingent.[59]

Practical reason attempts to determine the proper norms for conduct—not merely what is, but also what ought to be. Hence, it is distinct from theoretical science which attempts to determine what is. But norms are founded on facts. The good for any entity depends upon the nature of that entity. What is good for a man is not good for a fish. Hence, the natural end of any process or tendency can be adequately determined only by a comprehensive knowledge of the nature to be realized and completed. Norms are not purely arbitrary and preferential. They are grounded on nature. Hence, ethics or practical thought is distinct, but not separate, from descriptive knowledge.

In the second place, the metaphysical view of logical atomism, which holds that all facts are finished and determinate, cannot be granted as a self-evident axiom without critical consideration. There is a great range of empirical evidence, as we have already suggested, which indicates on the contrary that most of the objects of experience are unfinished or changing, and that many entities are filled with tendencies. This issue cannot be decided by an a priori fiat. It can be conclusively settled only by careful and patient phenomenological analysis, very little of which is found in modern ethical treatises.

As a matter of fact, the literature of natural-law philosophy, beginning with that of Plato and Aristotle, is full of such attempts to describe and to analyze the given data. The theory of natural law was first formulated and defended on the grounds of such evidence, not on the basis of theological assumptions. From the standpoint of this tradition, the potential and tendential structure of the natural world was not based on the supposed existence of a supreme lawgiver, but rather the existence of such a supreme being was grounded on the observation of divergent tendential structures, requiring one another for their origin and completion.

The Kantian notion that any attempt to ground moral principles on observable facts must involve heteronomy, as he called it, or loss of human freedom, requires radical qualification. It is true that, if the moral law is grounded on the structure of human nature, we cannot suppose that man is free with no limitation—that he can choose to live the life of a butterfly, for instance. But there seems to be no evidence whatsoever that man has ever possessed or ever will possess such unlimited freedom. The pure Kantian freedom of absolute spontaneity, to do anything at all, is a delusion. The general nature of man's end is determinate. But this leaves many alternatives for free choice. The end may be misunderstood and freedom lost. If the universal end is *rightly* understood, it leaves an infinite variety of different ways by which it may be realized in divergent circumstances. This is the only freedom which man, or any other finite creature, can be reasonably supposed to possess.

In reply to this charge, it may be pointed out that Kantian

norms, having no ground in nature at all, seem singularly vulnerable to the question of possible alternatives. They have no possible defense or justification. If we ask why we ought to pursue the categorical imperative, we are simply told—*because you ought*. Similar difficulties would seem to attach to any theory which follows Kant's guidance in introducing an unbridgeable chasm between what is and what ought to be.

The charge of intensive casuistry has no foundation. The moral law is universal in its structure. It tells us in general what all must do if they are to reach the universal end of man in general. It does not tell anyone precisely what in detail he should do in every concrete situation confronting him. This of course, is impossible and fantastic. But the universal principles of the moral law may give him an unalterable standard which may guide him in his endeavors.

Since man is rational and free, he may through his own choices break the moral law. As we now know, even the descriptive laws of subhuman entities are only statistical averages which admit of many exceptions. They can be explained only as tendencies, fulfilled for the most part, if externally unimpeded.[60] But man's capacity for the free determination of his own acts enables him to violate the laws of his nature by himself. Why, then, should a law that can be broken in this way be called a law? Because even when broken, the moral law remains in force, imposing natural sanctions. A stupid act is punished by the formation of a stronger tendency to perform stupid acts. A community which ignores the natural rights of its citizens is punished by discontent and revolution.

D. NATURAL LAW AS AN EXAMPLE OF
THE NATURALISTIC FALLACY

We shall now turn to a logical criticism of the theory of natural law which is closely connected with the ontological separation of values from facts, and which is widely accepted at the present time, though it has its ancient antecedents.[61] This criticism is directed against any definition of goodness and, therefore, applies to our definition of it as the realization of natural tendencies.[62]

According to G. E. Moore, who initiated this line of attack in modern times, especially in dealing with ethical hedonism,[63] we can still ask if the realization of such tendencies is good. This shows that the defining formula is not really equivalent to the term supposedly defined. In his opinion, any such definition attempts to reduce something which is simple, unique, and ineffable to something else—the complex expressed by the defining formula. This is to commit the fallacy of reduction or, as Moore names it in the case of the good, "the naturalistic fallacy." As a matter of fact, the good is a simple unanalyzable property, which must either be understood by itself alone or not at all. To define the good as the realization of essential tendencies is, therefore, to commit the naturalistic fallacy—to reduce a simple unanalyzable property to a complex really quite different, and thus to jeopardize the autonomy of ethics as an independent discipline.

This kind of an argument is often used at the present time to reject any definition of the peculiar experience of oughtness. Thus, there are certain ethicists who are willing to grant that goodness may be defined or characterized in some intelligible way, but deny that oughtness can be so characterized. Therefore, I may grant the theoretical truth of the judgment x is good without feeling any subjective urge or sense of obligation in connection with x. This feeling of urgency and propulsion to action is held to be the peculiar mark of ethical experience. Moral reflection concerns not what is but what I ought to do. Any definition or characterization of the ought must take the form: *oughtness is so and so.* But this is to relapse into a detached theoretical attitude and to leave the realm of the ethical. Hence, oughtness is regarded as a simple unanalyzable property. Any attempt to define it is an instance of the reductionist fallacy. The theory of natural law which holds that oughtness is a felt propulsive tendency together with an understanding of this tendency as in accordance with human nature, therefore, cannot be accepted. It commits the naturalistic fallacy.

An argument of this sort is presented by Popper. "Given an analysis of 'the good,'" he says, "in the form of a sentence like: 'the good is such and such' (or 'such and such is good'), we would always have to ask: What about it? Why should this concern me? Only if the word 'good' is used in an ethical sense, i.e., only if it is used to mean 'that which I ought to do' could I derive from the information '*x* is good' the conclusion that I ought to do *x*. In other words, if the word good is to have any ethical significance at all, it must be defined as 'that which I (or we) ought to do (or to promote). . . .' All the discussions about the definition of the good, or about the possibility of defining it, are, therefore, quite useless. They only show how far 'scientific' ethics is removed from the urgent problems of moral life. And they thus indicate that 'scientific' ethics are a form of escape, an escape from the realities of moral life, i.e., from our moral responsibilities."[64]

The implications of this passage are quite clear. Ethics as a responsible discipline ("scientific ethics," as Popper calls it) must attempt to define or to characterize its basic terms, to place the realities it is studying in reality as a whole. But oughtness, the peculiar object of ethical study, is a simple unanalyzable entity, which cannot be reduced to anything else. It is simply that which ought to be. Either we understand the meaning of this or we do not. No further analysis can be given. To attempt to do so, as a matter of fact, is to shift to some other theoretical discipline, and thus to abandon what is peculiarly ethical in our ethical responsibilities. This kind of criticism, which attacks moral theory at its very roots, must be answered if ethics is to survive as a rational discipline. A thoroughgoing answer would require more space than we have at our disposal; but certain misconceptions may perhaps be corrected, and the outlines of an answer suggested.

First of all, the atomistic presuppositions of the criticism need to be made explicit. These are three in number. First, the critic is assuming an atomistic pluralism which implies that reality is composed of a number of distinct properties or essences and their combinations. The ultimate kinds have nothing in common; they are simply different. A complex entity may be defined in terms of its component units. But these simple units cannot be further reduced. They must be either directly understood in themselves or not at all. Oughtness and goodness are such simple, irreducible essences. There is nothing more fundamental which such distinct kinds can share.

Second, the critic is assuming that the ultimate components of reality must be simple units of a nonrelational character. For example, one might hold that while goodness is a phase of reality not further reducible to more ultimate units, it is nevertheless a relational structure, analyzable into distinct relational phases no one of which can exist without the other. In this case, goodness could be given a definitive relational formula without reducing it to other atomic entities distinct from itself.

Third, the critic is assuming that the theoretical attitude and the practical attitude are atomically distinct from each other in the sense that they cannot unite with anything else or overlap. For example, one might hold that the act of theoretical cognition involves a union of a certain sort with that which is known. In this case, one might hold that the nature of oughtness can be theoretically known as it is without reduction or distortion. Furthermore, one might hold that while the practical attitude includes an element of urgent appetition, foreign to pure theory, it also includes a cognitive element of theoretical apprehension. In this case, the two attitudes would be distinct, but one (the practical) would overlap the other, and the two would not be exclusively or atomically opposed. But such mediating positions are ruled out a priori by the metaphysical presuppositions of the critic.

All of these atomistic presuppositions are denied by the nonessentialist nonatomistic ontology of classical realism on which the theory of natural law is based. We shall now briefly indicate the realistic doctrines of ontology which correspond to the three assumptions of atomism we have just considered.

Realistic ontology is also pluralistic. The universe is made up of a number of different things and properties, each marked off by its own essence from other kinds of things and from other individual examples of the same kind. But these distinct entities all share in a common existence which links them together in various ways. Existence is distinct from essence.[65] Thus, the very same essence may exist only as a possibility, or it may be brought into actual existence. But even here, there are existential differences. The very same individual may exist in an undeveloped potential condition, or in a developed state. Furthermore, this development may be thwarted by externally and internally imposed obstacles which deprive it of what it needs, or it may proceed to full realization without such obstruction. The terms good and evil refer to these existential modes—good to the latter, evil to the former. They are not distinct essences which may be clearly and univocally defined. They rather refer to those divergent categories of active existence which essences may attain in the concrete. They are not properties, like justice or the color yellow; they refer rather to modes of that omnipresent existence in which all properties, relations, and entities of whatever kind must share.

If good were a simple property, it could not be found anywhere else. But goodness is not so restricted to a single category. There is nothing whatsoever that cannot be found in a privative frustrated mode of existence (evil in the broad transethical sense) or also in an active unimpeded mode of existence (good).[66] But each entity has its own mode of existence. Hence, what is good for a fish is not good for a man. How, then, can this term in such a broad sense have a single meaning? It does not have a single meaning.

However, this does not imply that it is purely equivocal. There is a proportional similarity, or analogy, between different goods, which enables us to embrace them under a single concept. The good of the fish is to the fish as the good of a man is to a man. Goodness in general means that activity which a given finite nature requires for its completion. This definition does not reduce a simple property to something else, for goodness is not a simple property or essence. It is an existential category, the completion of existence.

On the basis of this sort of ontological analysis, we may agree that goodness is something ultimate that cannot be resolved into a complex of distinct atomic properties or essences. But this need not mean that it cannot be given a relational analysis. As a matter of fact, this is precisely what the defining formula does do. Realization is not a simple essence which can exist by itself. There can be no realization that is not the realization of something. Neither is capacity, or tendency, an atomic unit which can exist alone. We cannot even understand a tendency without thinking of that to which it is tending. Each of these factors exists only by virtue of the other. Goodness is not a single atomic unit which cannot be characterized or analyzed. Neither is it a complex of such units. It is rather a relational structure of existence which can be relationally analyzed.

The realistic philosophy, on which the theory of natural law is based, also rejects on empirical grounds that sharp separation of the theoretical from the practical attitude which is presupposed by the metaphysical dualism of fact versus norm. Neither of these is a simple atomic unit incapable of further analysis. Each is very complex. By a fact is meant some reality which is the object of true understanding. This understanding is a relational union of a most peculiar sort. In a certain sense we are the things we understand. Of course, the physicist who understands a certain liquid does not physically become liquefied; but he must nonphysically, or intentionally, become that which he understands.

So the moral dualist is quite justified in pointing out that we do not physically become identified with oughtness when we understand what it is. We do not become physically identified with anything we understand. The astronomer who understands the nature of a stellar explosion does not have to explode. But if this is regarded as a fatal defect in our knowledge and taken to imply that we should, therefore, stop trying to know or to analyze anything, the absurdity would be evident. Fortunately for us, we can become noetically identified with the whatness of things, without becoming physically merged with these things. The same is true of the ought. The task of ethical theory is to perform such an analysis, to grasp what obligation and oughtness are. The fact that such a theorist may not properly apply such knowledge to his own individual existence, which is notoriously possible, does not prove the irrelevance or certainly the futility of seeking such knowledge.

But is it not the aim of moral theory to refine the sense of obligation and to elicit sound moral action? If action is something different from theory, then theory is irrelevant. Here again atomism is at work.

Two structures may be different and yet have something in common. One may include the other, together with something different. Moral action arises from a tendency to pursue some cognized goal. It therefore includes a noetic phase, knowledge of the goal, and an active, appetitive phase, tendency towards the goal. Hence, the urgent propulsion of oughtness, subjectively inherent in the individual, may be enlightened and purified by sound ethical theory, on the condition that it has already developed a proper respect for reason and a readiness to be enlightened. Voluntary appetite is not an isolated globule of pure conation, entirely distinct from cognition. It is rather a relational compound of reason together with desire, an active tendency to a goal that is cognitively apprehended.

Such a tendency may be further illumined and guided by moral insight and theory.

Those who press the objection of the naturalistic fallacy pose the following dilemma: either the good is the privately felt feeling of oughtness, a subjective urge to concrete action, in which case it is unanalyzable, wholly divorced from theory, and unjustifiable; or else it is a universal theoretical concept carrying with it no actual obligation to concrete action, in which case it has nothing to do with ethics—in short, either a subjective urge with no rational basis or justification, or a theoretical justification with nothing actual to be justified.

To this dilemma presented by logical atomism, the theory of natural law offers the following escape between the horns for all those interested in the survival of ethics as a rational discipline. Man is subject to indeliberate raw appetite, elicited merely by a sensed or an imagined object. He is also capable of pure theoretical cognition divorced from any interest, save the urge to assimilate the truth. If this were all, there would be no escape from the dilemma. Appetite would be totally divorced from reason as in the other animals, and theoretical insight would be irrelevant to action.

But man is a creature of many powers and capacities. In addition to blind impulse and raw appetite, he also possesses the capacity for a deliberate rationalized mode of appetition. In addition to a purely detached theoretical insight, he has a faculty not for reasoning in slavery to, nor in tyranny over, but for reasoning with his needs and appetites—a desiderative reason (νοῦς ὀρεκτικός). It is in the realization and development of this unique capacity that human freedom lies.

The voluntary action to which it gives rise is neither blind passion using reason as an instrument nor reason dictating to desire; it is rather a co-operative union of the two. As we say, it knows what it is doing; it is aware of its end, and of its need for this end. It is both active urge and reason all in one—appetite providing the efficient power, reason the guiding end. Such activity can be elicited, aided, and refined by ethical theory and analysis. When assisted in this way, it may become neither a blind, subjective urge with no justification nor a detached theory with no obligation attached, but something in between— a deliberately chosen purpose, theoretically justifiable through a recognition of its natural foundation. This is a way between the horns.

Any definition, of course—even a sound one—may be questioned by those who do not understand its structure, or who do so only vaguely. There is always some difference between the *definiens* and the *definiendum*, a difference in the clarity of apprehension. By the *definiendum* we understand something complex as a whole in a confused way. By the *definiens* we understand the same thing with all of its parts clearly distinguished and analyzed. The latter grasps explicitly what the former grasps only potentially and implicitly. What is apprehended is the same. The mode of apprehension is different, the difference between vagueness and clarity.[67]

The good, of course, may be erroneously defined—for example, as pleasure by the hedonist. The *definiendum* and the *definiens* are strictly different—in no sense the same. One cannot be substituted for the other. In this case, we are guilty of reductionism, the naturalistic fallacy.

The definition of good as the realization of natural tendency can withstand such a criticism. The term *good* is widely applied throughout all the categories or kinds of being. So is this existential formula, for existence is found everywhere except in nothing. This ontological structure is so pervasive that it is difficult for us to focus it. But as soon as we become aware of it, we find that the *definiendum* and the *definiens* are interchangeable. Wherever we find goodness, we find some capacity or tendency in the act of realization. To live a human life in accordance with nature is the good for man, and holds good univocally for every human individual. By terms like *good* and *value* we recognize this complex relational structure in a vague and implicit way. By the *definiens* it may be apprehended more clearly and exactly. What is referred to in each case is one and the same thing. But the mode of apprehension is different. In the one case, we apprehend it confusedly and implicitly; in the other, clearly and explicitly.

If the attainment of such analytic clarity in the *definiens* is to commit the naturalistic fallacy, then all sound definitions commit it, and the passage from vagueness to clarity, an essential phase of the whole noetic enterprise, is impossible. It is hard to believe that this is true. If not, then the theory of natural law is not an instance of the naturalistic or reductive fallacy.

E. NATURAL LAW AS A REACTIONARY INFLUENCE IN HISTORY

Another charge now widely urged against the theory of natural law is that it is fundamentally a conservative or reactionary conception basically opposed to all progressive change. One reason for the prevalence of this idea is the association of natural law in the popular mind with the medieval Church, and with certain policies of the Roman Catholic Church in recent times. This, of course, is a historic accident. Certain progressively minded thinkers, and others who have been influenced by Marxism, make the same criticism for different reasons.

Among the former group we find Popper, arguing in his impassioned defense of "the open society," that the theory of natural law, which he calls "spiritual naturalism," is generally conservative and opposed to social change.[68] This, he says, is because it is so vague that it is readily identified with any status quo and thus easily adapted to the purpose of resisting movements of reform. But as we have seen (pp. 76–77), this rests on the misconception that nature is to be equated with existence as such. When this mistake is avoided and human nature is properly analyzed in the light of what is essential to it, this concept is not vague at all, but filled with a very rich, though specifiable, content, which has inspired many rational ideals and revolutionary declarations of natural rights, the last and least inadequate of which is the recent Universal Declaration of Human Rights proclaimed by the General Assembly of the United Nations on December 10, 1948.

Winspear, however, who has been strongly influenced by Marxist thought, justifies this same charge for very different reasons which require further examination. According to him, the sixth and fifth centuries B.C. in Greece were marked by an intense social struggle of oppressed classes against the rigid hierarchical structure of a "tribal" society towards greater freedom and democracy. In this struggle, the materialistic philosophers and the so-called "sophists" sided with the oppressed classes,[69] while the Pythagoreans and Eleatics took a conservative position.[70] Socrates and Plato, whom he constantly refers to as "idealists," presumably because they believed that human nature includes the faculties of cognition and choice which purely physical entities lack, sided with the wealthy and, therefore, conservative, oligarchic classes.[71] Within this highly imaginative but somewhat questionable framework, he then interprets their defense of natural law.[72] "Whereas the conservatives wanted to make of justice and statute law something inherent in the very nature of things and worthy, therefore, of unquestioning acceptance and obedience, the sophists wished to make justice a matter of convention, of arbitrary external pressure; so that when custom comes into conflict with 'natural laws' and 'human nature' [taken in a purely physicalist sense without reference to freedom] then custom must give way. Such doctrines were clearly skeptical, subversive, and revolutionary. And it is no wonder that they stirred up the hatred, suspicion, fury, and contempt of the conservative and oligarchical class."[73]

Sophistic skepticism and conventionalism is a "progressive"

force. The Socratic and Platonic opposition to the unstable opinions of the many, and their constant emphasis on a stable knowledge of immutable principles, accessible only to the few, is aristocratic and conservative. To believe in unchanging principles of moral law is reactionary. To distrust all such principles and to lapse into a moral relativism is progressive and even revolutionary. What are we to think of this mode of argument? It raises two important issues.

The first is the question as to whether moral skepticism and relativism provide a favorable basis for the intelligent criticism of social institutions and for needed social reform. If we abstract from particular accidents of history, which often present us with peculiar and even inconsistent patterns of attitude and doctrine, and confine ourselves to the logical implications of the position itself, the answer is clear. If one moral view is no more justifiable than another, what rational motive can there be for social reform? If the prevailing situation, while indefensible on rational grounds, is no more indefensible than any other, why change it? Such views tend to elicit a cynical indifference to moral issues, which in the long run leads to social rigidity and reaction. I believe that Popper's judgment on this question is far closer to the truth than Winspear's. "As a matter of historical fact," he says, "ethical (or moral, or juridical) positivism has usually been conservative, or even authoritarian. . . ."[74]

The second issue concerns the moral effect of materialistic doctrines, which either deny or seriously qualify the autonomy of individual reflection and choice. Winspear argues that such doctrines are socially and morally progressive.[75] But apart from historical accident, I believe that such a view is very dubious. If moral attitudes are dependent on physical laws, or on laws of historical development and class differentiation, as in Marxism, this must rather lead to historical relativism in the field of ethics, and to a weakening of moral aspiration. Popper's remarks on this phase of Marxism[76] are very much to the point, though he fails to explain how his own view, which holds that moral attitudes result from partially arbitrary individual preferences with no foundation in fact, escapes from relativism.[77]

The theory of natural law is not relativistic. It does not agree with positivistic legal theory in holding that the term *law* must be restricted to the factual decrees actually made by some sovereign power and enforced by its established sanctions.[78] One of the main reasons for the present revival of interest in natural law is a revulsion against the positivistic view which, if consistent, must accept the fantastic decrees of such recent tyrannies as the Hitler regime as valid laws, no less legitimate than any other positive enactments. Natural law provides us with a standard, founded on human nature and its essential tendencies, by which such decrees may be judged as sound or unsound. Without such a standard we are lost in a chaos of relativism and are finally committed to the view that might makes right.

Natural law is founded on tendential facts of human nature. On the other hand, it is not a mere description of observed and predicted units of behavior—a now widely accepted sense of the phrase. Both physical laws in this sense and moral laws are natural, since they describe tendencies rooted in the structure of changing entities. Both types of law admit of exception and are hypothetical in character. A physical law describes what will happen if unusual external interference is not encountered. Subrational beings are subject to such statistical laws. A moral law describes what should be done by the immanent choice of a rational agent, if his essential tendencies are to be realized. Rational beings, capable of choice, are subject to such moral laws. Like physical laws, they are based on active tendencies physically present in the agent. But unlike them, they are also based on a rational understanding of these tendencies, and a voluntary choice to fulfil them, which is peculiar to rational agents.

Man as a rational being is by nature free, or capable of acting immanently, by his own choice, either to realize or to frustrate his nature. The moral law states what he must do if his natural end is to be achieved. Hence, there is no reduction of moral law to the level of physical law which applies to agents incapable of deliberation and choice. Moral laws are prescriptive as well as descriptive. They describe certain modes of action which are in accordance with the nature of man. They prescribe such acts as ought to be voluntarily performed by free human agents. The materialist tends to confuse these two types of law and reduces the voluntary to the automatic, the human to the subhuman.

Since this moral law is binding on all men everywhere, it is timeless and universal, and must not be confused with any concrete imaginative picture of an ideal society including much that is incidental and ephemeral. Individuals and groups exist only in the concrete. Hence, in addition to realizing the essential tendencies common to all men everywhere, they must also attempt to realize many incidental aims peculiar to themselves and the unique circumstances they face. But the universal pattern of natural law provides us with a standard for judging such changing aims and enactments. If they are consistent with this universal pattern, they should be approved as valid for anyone in such circumstances. If they are inconsistent, they should be condemned as inhuman and, therefore, unfit for any human agent, no matter what his circumstances may be.

When compared with other opposed types of moral theory, it may be seen to be free of many of the weaknesses which modern criticism has revealed in them. While it recognizes the material nature of man and his essential physical needs, it does not follow the materialist in attempting to reduce, or to qualify, his moral freedom and rationality and the distinctively human needs arising from these sources. It does not follow the consistent utilitarian in attempting to reduce all the manifold forms of aspiration and obligation to raw appetite or pleasure and in thinking of reason as a mere slave of appetite. Unlike Kant and the emotive ethical theorists, it refuses to separate the ought from the is by an unbridgeable chasm. The ought is a basic fact of human nature—the actual urge inherent in this nature towards realization, together with a cognitive understanding of this urge. As against positivism and cultural relativism, it maintains that this nature, shared in common by all men, founds certain tendencies, which may be formulated in the universal principles of the moral law. Regarded abstractly, it is hard to see how such a view can be incompatible with a deep respect for human freedom, a hatred for injustice, and an intense aspiration for the betterment of man both individually and socially.

Granted that this principle has often been misused, I believe that an unbiased study of Western history will show that, far from having elicited social indifference and moral lethargy, the theory of natural law has been closely connected with the most important progressive movements which have influenced the Western way of life. It was essentially involved in the moral and social ideals of Plato and Aristotle.[79] In the Middle Ages, it was united with the analogous Judaeo-Christian conception of moral law, and played an important role in the formulation of Christian ideals and in the spreading of this influence. In modern times, it has provided a philosophical basis for the declarations of natural laws and rights which were vital factors in the struggle to escape from feudalism and tyranny. Its most recent expression is the Universal Declaration of Human Rights, which embodies the hope of living men and the purpose of the United Nations—to establish a world community in which the social, material, political, and rational needs of every man may be recognized. This theory is not accurately described as basically authoritarian and reactionary.

Section III. Conclusion

We have now considered five basic objections which are raised against the concept of natural law in the current literature of moral philosophy. We have found that these objections involve certain misunderstandings which we have attempted to clarify.

1. Natural law may be an erroneous theory, but if it is erroneous, this is certainly not because it is based on a dubious anthropomorphic inference of universal teleology. If it is in error, this will be because it can be shown that there is no direct empirical evidence for change and tendency in the world of concrete experience.

2. Those who have been moved by the great declarations of natural laws and natural rights which have marked our Western history may have been deceived. But if so, it was not because natural law was a vague and equivocal notion actually synonymous with being from which anything can be deduced. Nature, when properly understood, is not equivalent to being, and in so far as we can ever clearly understand what anything is, bears a specific and determinate content.

3. The defenders of natural law may have confused many things in many ways, but they did not confuse two evidently separate realms of existence and value—in the first place, because it is by no means obvious and evident that value is totally divorced from fact. If values do not exist in some way, ethical reflection is much ado about nothing. In the second place, those who have responsibly defended this theory have never asserted that value and existence were the same. What has been asserted is that they are distinct, but inseparable.

4. The philosophers of natural law may have committed many fallacies. But they have not committed the so-called "naturalistic fallacy," unless all true definitions and characterizing formulae commit it. They have believed that the basic concepts of ethics, like the basic concepts of other disciplines, can be clarified only by relating them to the basic structure of existence which is common to all entities. Perhaps they have defended wrong ontological formulae, but these are not wrong because they are ontological.

5. Finally, though this conception has been misused by individual thinkers and institutions for illicit purposes, often to justify some decrepit and corrupt status quo, it is not true that the conception itself, when properly understood, is reactionary in its systematic implications. As a matter of fact, it has played an important role in the great progressive movements of Western history.

By attempting to clarify these misunderstandings, we are not so naïve as to believe that we have demonstrated the truth of the theory. We do hope that we may have helped to pave the way for an intelligent criticism of a distinctive moral position which is unfamiliar to the modern mind. In view of the impasse into which recent ethics has fallen and the desperate need for clarity on basic moral issues, we feel that the time has come when this theory should be sharply focused and intelligently discussed.

But before we can do this in any responsible way, we need to learn more about the systematic structure of natural-law philosophy and of its history in the West. It is to these matters that we shall now turn our attention in Part II.

PART II

THE THEORY OF NATURAL LAW

CHAPTER FOUR

THE THEORY OF NATURAL LAW AND ITS HISTORY IN THE WEST

So far we have studied certain criticisms of Plato recently urged by his modern enemies and have seen some reason to believe that these criticisms rest upon misunderstandings arising from the subjectivist trends of recent philosophy and its unfamiliarity with realistic modes of thought. In the last chapter we provisionally identified Plato's ethics with moral realism of the natural-law tradition and analyzed certain prevalent misconceptions of it. But negative definitions are notoriously ambiguous. To know what a thing is not, is not to know what it is. We must now attempt a more exact analysis. What precisely is meant by the doctrine of natural law, and who are its authentic representatives in the history of Western philosophy? At the present time great confusion reigns in this area. No authoritative answers are available. Hence, we shall try to work out an unambiguous answer of our own. It is only in so far as this can be done that we may then be in a position to raise the question, in chapter 5, as to who first originated this tradition of moral realism in the West with any hope of an unequivocal answer.

Section I. Natural Law as Moral Realism

The realistic presuppositions of natural-law ethics are so foreign to the subjectivistic trend of modern moral philosophy that it is hardly ever clearly focused as a distinctive type of moral theory. For the most part, standard treatises and textbooks do not even mention it except in vague and undeveloped historical contexts. The modern student needs to know about the Kantian school, which holds that the human mind autonomously lays down its own moral law, and the utilitarian school, which asserts that values are determined by arbitrary impulse and appetite. Many variations of these dominant

103

themes need to be distinguished. The rest is antiquarian history. The ethics of natural law belongs in this latter category. It is sometimes mentioned as a doctrine which played an important historical role during certain past periods like the eighteenth century, with the understanding that it is now definitely passé. So far as it is analyzed at all, it is usually identified with a "metaphysical" or "theological" theory of natural order as having been imposed by the command of God. This is even true of standard reference books like the *Hastings Encyclopedia of Religion and Ethics*. It gives no careful analysis of natural-law ethics but merely associates it with "metaphysical and theological interpretations of the reign of law."[1]

It is true that most of the ablest defenders of moral realism have ultimately been forced in their metaphysics to recognize those causal arguments which point to some transcendent source of being. But this is peripheral to their ethical doctrine, and even peripheral to the primary ontological presuppositions of this doctrine. To identify natural law with the commands (presumably arbitrary) of a transcendent Deity is certainly to convey an erroneous impression to the modern mind. It is universally agreed, for example, that the Stoics held a theory of natural law. But if they were theists at all, they were pantheists. For them natural law was an order governing the active tendencies of cosmic matter. Certainly there was nothing arbitrary about this, for without it the universe would dissolve into chaos. Of course there have been theistic moral realists who believed that natural law and moral order have their first source in the free decrees of a first cosmic agent. But such thinkers as Augustine and Aquinas never thought of these decrees as arbitrary. They were necessary conditions for the activity, and even for the existence, of finite entities. Without them, there could be no universe at all.

The basic issue between the defenders of natural law and its opponents has never been that of theism versus nontheism. This is a peripheral metaphysical issue. The basic issue concerns the nature of moral norms. Are they grounded in something which exists independently of human interest and opinion, or are they man-made? The philosophers of natural law are moral realists.

They hold that certain moral norms are grounded on nature, not merely on human decree. It is this thesis that binds together the various strands into a single tradition and which radically separates all of them from the subjectivist schools of modern thought.

I believe, therefore, that the best approach to an understanding of the other distinctive doctrines of this way of thought is from a realistic point of view. Let us try to imagine for the sake of the argument that we have broken with modern subjectivist assumptions. Let us suppose that we believe in a moral law that is discovered rather than invented by men. What doctrines will be entailed by such a belief, and what others will be more loosely connected? If we study these questions with some care, we shall soon be led to the most distinctive theses of natural-law philosophy.

Norms that are not man-made must actually exist in some sense. They must be embedded in the ontological structure of things. They are not human constructions but ontological categories. If ethics is a responsible discipline, as the realistic moralist believes, it must be founded on ontology. How can this be? How are norms related to actual being? Let us first explore this question of moral *ontology*, and then consider those distinctively *ethical* doctrines to which a moral realist must be led from these foundational principles.

Section II. EXISTENCE AND VALUE

That which exists, as a complex essence, may be good and evil, in different respects. The same act may be good so far as realized, evil so far as deprived. But unless it is wholly equivocal, the act of existing, *as such*, cannot be both good, evil, and neutral. Hence there are three possible positions concerning the relation of existence to value: (1) the act of existing is evil, and goodness lies in nonexistence; (2) it is neutral to value, neither good nor evil; and (3) existing is good.

The first alternative if held consistently must lead to a radical nihilism incompatible with the assertion of life itself and, indeed, of any ethics. If goodness is nonexistent, there is no object for moral study. This is the end of ethics. But it conflicts with a vast range of evidence which indicates that various kinds and modes of value do exist. Hence, this alternative is rejected both by realist and by subjectivist schools of thought.

The second alternative implies a separation of value from existence which is accepted by most subjectivist moral theory: Existence and nonexistence have no valuational significance. If something is valuable it retains its value-quality whether given existence or not. The way is then open to interpret value as resting on arbitrary human interest or enactment. Sometimes an effort is made to preserve the "objectivity" of values by allotting them a special realm of *subsistence*, divorced from actual existence in space and time. No realist can accept this alternative for the following reasons.

There is no evidence for any realm of subsistent entities which are neither real entities in nature nor objects of human thought, dependent on mental operations. If they do not really exist in nature, then only the last subjective alternative remains. Values and norms are human constructions. But this conflicts with the concrete evidence of such experiences as obligation, justification, and guilt, which clearly indicate that values and norms have a real foundation independent of fluctuating human interest and decree. Obligation often conflicts with haphazard wants. Men know that an act is right not merely because they desire to perform it. Something more universal and lasting than variable enactments of men is required to elicit the genuine experience of moral guilt. Furthermore it is simply false that value is indifferent to existence. Nonexistent values are no good at all. What we strive for is not to attain a nonexistent value, but rather to bring some value into existence. Hence, any separation of value from being must be rejected by a realistic thinker. Only the third alternative remains.

Existence itself must be good. As a matter of fact, this thesis has been accepted by all the representatives of natural-law philosophy. How, then, is evil to be explained? As we have pointed out (chap. 3, A), the answer is to be found in the dynamic nature of finite entities. Empirical evidence shows us conclusively that such entities are always in an unfinished or imperfect state, tending towards further existence. When essential tendencies are being fulfilled, they are in a sound condition; when they are distorted or frustrated, they still exist, but in an unsound or evil condition. Good and evil are modes of existence, existential categories. The essential structure of the entity, determining its tendencies to proceed in a certain direction, is a natural norm, not constructed by man but embedded in the very being of a changing thing and discovered by ontological analysis.

Furthermore, these finite entities are limited, weak, and fragile. They cannot exist and act by themselves alone. They require the sustaining support and influence of other entities. An influence that enables something to act is good for that entity. One that frustrates it is bad. Unless the diverse tendencies of different entities were adjusted to one another so as to sustain each other at least for the most part, no action would be possible. But action does proceed. We must, therefore, recognize the existence of a universal natural law or order which, on the whole, governs the manifold tendencies of finite things and adjusts them to one another. This notion of a cosmic order is also characteristic of realistic ethics. The moral law to which man is subject as a part of nature is a special phase of this universal cosmic order.

Section III. FIVE RELATED MEANINGS OF THE TERM NATURE

The basic conception is the realistic thesis that there are norms grounded on the inescapable pattern of existence itself. This pattern is an order in which many diverse factors are brought together into a relational unity. From the time of its first origin in ancient Greece, realistic philosophy has employed the term nature (φύσις), meaning growth or change, to refer to this normative order which is manifested in the acts of changing things. This order has many distinguishable aspects adapted to one another by the peculiar normative relation of fitness. The good is always ontologically proper or fitting, what is owed to a thing in virtue of its tendential structure.

In order to express this, it was necessary to find a unifying word (and concept) which could be used to signify not only the general relation but also the more important relata. The word *nature* was chosen to exercise this unifying function, holding together in a single concept several distinct but related meanings. Different writers vary with respect to the number of meanings distinguished and the clarity of these distinctions. But taking the tradition as a whole, five meanings of the term nature have proved to be especially important.

1. The word is used to express the general relation of fitness, and the dynamic entities ordered into a world or cosmos by this normative relation. This usage is universal. The other senses are sometimes only vaguely distinguished, and sometimes not at all. But in the more careful and systematic writers they are made explicit.

2. The word signifies the form or definite structure of a finite entity which determines its basic tendencies, and the kind of activity which will fittingly complete these tendencies.

3. The word nature is often used in a richer sense to indicate not only the form (2) but also the tendencies determined by this form.

4. It commonly signifies the fitting direction of these tendencies in such a way as to lead them towards fulfilment. Such "fitting" activity in its incipient stages is said to be natural, or in accordance with nature.

Finally 5, the word is often used to describe the good or fitting condition of existential fulfilment. A close approximation to this condition is also said to be natural. Sometimes it is said to be the real nature of the thing, for it is only in this state that the whole nature becomes manifest, without privation and distortion. Whether or not these distinctions are clearly defined, they are implicit in any realistic moral philosophy which recognizes the empirical fact of change.

When these fundamental ontological conceptions are applied to the specific case of man as a part of nature, they entail three moral doctrines which are characteristic of realistic ethics.

1. The moral law, which is the abstract pattern of such activation, is in no sense an arbitrary construction based on human wish or decree. It is founded on the specific nature of man and the essential tendencies determined by this nature. Hence

it is not merely a moral law in the usual sense of this word, but a law of nature, applying equally to all men everywhere.

2. Human nature is incomplete or tendential. In order to fulfil these tendencies, human acts must be governed by certain general rules applying to all men alike. In subhuman animals this direction proceeds automatically and for the most part without cognitive activity. But in man it requires the exercise of rational reflection and choice, free from automatic determination and physical constraint. Violations of natural law are punished by natural sanctions of distortion and privation. Acts which are in accordance with natural law are commonly referred to as *virtues*. Such acts are not means to a final value from which they are separate. They are themselves included in this final activation and are, therefore, ends in themselves.

Finally 3, the human good is the existential fulfilment of the human individual. Since each individual shares certain traits with other members of the species, this fulfilment will include two distinguishable aspects: (*a*) acts elicited by his peculiar characteristics and circumstances; and (*b*) acts required for the completion of common tendencies he shares with other members of the species.

This conceptual pattern must be approximated to some degree by any realistic moral philosophy which does not deny the fact of change and tendency in the world of nature. Let us now turn to a brief examination of certain thinkers and schools of thought which are commonly held to belong to the tradition of natural law. With this pattern in mind, we may be able to abstract from what is only incidental and variable in their formulations, and to concentrate on what is essential. In this way, we may hope to emerge with a clearer conception of what natural-law ethics actually has been and is. Then with such a conception in mind, we may turn to Plato and Aristotle and raise the basic question we are constantly holding in mind—did they actually hold, and did they perhaps originate the realistic theory of natural law?

There is no time, of course, to examine every thinker who is commonly regarded as belonging to this vaguely defined tradition. In making a necessarily arbitrary selection of schools and authors, we have had two criteria in mind. In the first place, we have chosen thinkers widely separated from one another in time and place, in order to test the theory we have just outlined as to the essential realistic content of this pattern of thought. If we find these doctrines expressed in authors of widely varying background, we may have greater confidence that we have penetrated through the special formulations of a certain school to the basic core of the doctrine. In the second place, we have tried to avoid controversial figures and have chosen those concerning whom there is authoritative and widespread agreement that they are in some sense defenders of natural law. Guided by these criteria, we shall now briefly consider the moral theories of the early Stoics (400–200 B.C.), Marcus Aurelius (A.D. 121–80), Aquinas (1225–74), Hooker (1553–1600), Grotius (1583–1645), and Thomas Paine (1737–1809).

Section IV. THE CENTRAL TRADITION OF NATURAL-LAW PHILOSOPHY

A. THE EARLY STOICS

The old Stoics of the fourth and third centuries B.C. taught that the universe is single, limited, and round in form.[2] Everything happens in accordance with an indwelling law or fate (εἱμαρμένη).[3] The word nature (φύσις) is used to refer to this cosmic order as well as to the structures of its component parts.[4] This order is maintained by two universal material principles. One is passive (τὸ πάσχον) and made up of grosser particles, the other active (τὸ ποιοῦν) and made up of finer particles.[5] This active force was identified with fire. It is responsible for the growth of plants, and the active tendencies of animals.

The word nature was also employed in a more restricted sense to signify this active power in a single living being.[6] Man is no exception. Each individual tends to maintain himself and to develop into proper perfections.

This cannot be achieved without guidance from an overarching theoretical insight into cosmic structure. The old Stoic school differed sharply from the Cynics in this high regard for theoretical knowledge as the only sound basis for practice. According to Zeno, moral insight (φρόνησις) is the foundational virtue, capable of guiding every tendency by right reason. The correct control of distributive tendencies is justice; of positive urges, temperance; of suffering, courage.[7] The individual tends by nature to maintain himself and to attain what is fit. But as he gains a deeper knowledge of himself and of his social union with others, he comes to identify himself with an ever-widening circle—his family, his friends and associates, and finally the whole of humanity. The wise man, recognizing these ties of nature, will think of himself as a citizen of the world and will strive for the welfare of all men as peculiar and proper to himself (οἰκείωσις).[8] To act virtuously in this way is to live in agreement with nature.[9]

This is also to attain happiness, for "to live happily and in accordance with nature are one and the same."[10]

Early Stoicism was a materialistic adaptation of Platonic and Aristotelian philosophy. This resulted in a strong trend towards determinism which was hard to reconcile with moral freedom. But apart from these difficulties we find in the early Stoic fragments five characteristic doctrines of natural-law philosophy: (1) the world is an order of interdependent tendencies which are the ground of objective moral norms; (2) the human individual possesses a rational nature which he shares with all other rational beings; (3) this nature determines certain tendencies requiring completion, if human life is to be lived; (4) virtue is the rational direction of these tendencies in accordance with nature, towards their proper goal; and (5) such fulfilment is the happy or blessed life. The word nature is used in all these distinct but related senses. It is commonly agreed that this realistic ethics is properly referred to as the theory of natural law. Do we find this theory in the later Stoics? In order to answer this question, let us turn to the *Meditations* of the Emperor Marcus Aurelius (A.D. 121–80).

B. MARCUS AURELIUS

Does he believe in an ordered cosmos in which objective norms are grounded on constant tendencies, sustained by other beings? This question must be answered with an emphatic affirmative. He constantly uses a phrase, ἡ κοινὴ φύσις, which Farquharson translates as "universal nature." By this he means an order of entities which mutually sustain and support one another. "Reflect on the bonds which hold together all things in the cosmos, and their relations to one another. For in a certain way all things are woven together and friendly to one another."[11] As we shall see, this is a normative order, for value is the realization of essential needs in any given nature.

Is this really so? Does Marcus hold that each individual entity possesses a nature of its own with needs requiring satisfaction, if privation and distortion are to be avoided? Let us examine the following text:[12] "See what your nature (σου ἡ φύσις) needs, so far as you possess a purely material nature; then do this and accept it if only your animal nature (ἡ ὡς ζῴου φύσις) is not thereby made worse. Next observe what your animal nature needs and take all of this if only your rational nature (ἡ ὡς λογικοῦ φύσις) is not thereby made worse."

Does he conceive of being in an active or tendential manner? Let us look at the following passage:[13] "Remember that what controls the springs is something hidden within you: this is activity (ἐνέργεια); this is life (ζωή); this one may say is the man." Are these existential tendencies wholly creative and chaotic, or are they determined by the natures underlying them to act in similar ways? Take the following:[14] ". . . universal nature loves nothing so much as to transform things and to make them into something new but similar to what was before. For all being is the seed of what will emerge from it."

How are these tendencies to be directed? Does Marcus hold that a knowledge of natural structure, and of those acts which will realize this nature, is a safe guide to virtuous action? His answer is given in many passages. We shall select the following:[15] "bearing all these things in mind, imagine nothing to be great but this: to act as your nature (ἡ σὴ φύσις) guides. . . ." Does he believe that we can gain a normative knowledge from the observation of such tendential facts? Does he hold that such knowledge is really objective and not merely the result of personal or social bias? His answer is given in these sentences:[16] "Judge that you are worthy (ἄξιον) of every saying and of every

deed that is according to nature (κατὰ φύσιν) and do not let the
blame or speech of anyone else deflect you; but if it is right
(καλόν) to be done or said, do not think you are undeserving of
it. . . . Do not look around at them but pursue the straight
path, following your own and the common nature (τῇ φύσει τῇ
ἰδίᾳ καὶ τῇ κοινῇ), for these are one way."

Is it Marcus' view that value consists in the fulfilment of
tendency? Take the following quotation:[17] ". . . the end of any
entity lies in that towards which it tends (πρὸς ὃ φέρεται); and
where the end (τέλος) is, there also is the advantage and good
of any nature (τὸ συμφέρον καὶ τὸ ἀγαθὸν ἑκάστου)." Does he hold
the view that the true and authentic nature of anything becomes manifest only in the full realization of that nature? His
answer to this question is found in a passage from the Tenth
Book:[18] "Short is the time left for you. Live as on a high pin-
nacle, for whether you are here or there matters little if everywhere one lives in the whole universe as in his city. Let men
see, let them behold a true man living in accordance with nature
(ἄνθρωπον ἀληθινὸν κατὰ φύσιν ζῶντα)."

It is commonly agreed that the Stoic ethics is a specific example of the generic ethics of natural law. We have seen that
this ethics, from the time of its origin in the fourth century
B.C. until its end in the second century A.D., includes five basic,
interconnected principles: (1) norms are not man-made, they
are based upon a natural order of interdependent tendencies;
(2) each individual entity possesses a nature which it shares
with other members of the same species; (3) this structure determines expansive tendencies towards further development; (4)
human virtue consists in the rational direction of these tendencies towards their natural end; (5) this end is the authentic
realization or fulfilment of the nature.

It is fitting that such a realistic doctrine should be called an
ethics of natural law. Norms are not legislated into existence by
man. They are grounded on the nature of things which remain
just what they are, independent of all human opinion and
desire. Though it may vary in many incidental ways, any
authentic human life must realize certain essential tendencies
of human nature. This general pattern of action required for the

living of any human life is *the law of nature*. Let us consider other more recent formulations of this realistic ethics. Do they also exemplify these same basic principles? We shall turn first of all to the ethics of Aquinas (1225–74), which is generally recognized as an ethics of natural law.

C. THOMISTIC ETHICS AND NATURAL LAW

Aquinas' philosophy differs from Stoicism in certain important respects. The universe was created *ex nihilo* by the free act of a transcendent Deity. Owing to the influence of Plato, and especially of Aristotle, the reductive simplifications of materialism are avoided. Even in the case of subhuman entities, form is clearly distinguished from matter. The human soul is a subsistent form, the highest intellectual and voluntary parts of which are immaterial and capable of existing apart from the body. Thus, physical determinism is avoided. Men can gain a rational understanding of their nature and of its end. They can also devise alternative ways of achieving this end in the concrete and freely choose between them. But in spite of these differences, Aquinas is consciously and openly defending an ethics of natural law[19] with marked affinities to that of the Stoics. Does he accept the five basic principles we have discovered in them? Let us take them up one by one.

1. The universe is an order of entities dependent upon one another and upon God. "This world is said to be one by a unity of order according to which certain things are ordered to others. All the entities created by God have an order to one another as well as to God."[20] There is a factor of indeterminacy in nature which makes exceptional coincidences (chance) always possible. But on the whole, natural beings sustain and influence each other in regular ways. This order is constantly referred to in the Thomistic texts by such phrases as "according to nature" (*secundum naturam*) and "law of nature" (*lex naturae*). This order is established and supported by causes utterly independent of man. As we shall see, it is the ground of real objective norms.

2. Aquinas also regularly uses the term *nature* in referring to the essence (form and common matter) of an individual thing[21]

which determines it, marks it off from other entities, and grounds its peculiar operations.

3. This nature is not only a determinate structure or form. It is also an internal source of motion. "Every nature tends towards its perfection."[22] The original nature is incomplete and lacks certain acts which it requires for realization.

4. Unless they are properly guided, these tendencies are liable to be dominated by chance and irresponsible external powers, in which case they fall into conflict and distortion. Reason alone can guide them to ordered or virtuous activity. "Since the rational soul is the proper form of man, there is a natural inclination in any man towards rational action, or action according to virtue."[23] Moral norms are not founded on reason conceived as a constructive power legislating its own values. But rather "reason naturally apprehends those acts to which man naturally tends as values, and consequently as goods that ought to be actively pursued, and their contraries as evils that ought to be avoided. The precepts of the natural law follow the order of natural inclinations."[24] These precepts are valid for the acts of all men everywhere. To act virtuously as we ought to act, is to direct our tendencies in accordance with the order indicated by nature—those naturally fitted to rule governing those not so fitted.

5. An entity is good in so far as it acts or exists in its own proper mode. ". . . every existent entity, so far as it actually exists is good. For every entity so far as it is, is in act, and in a way perfect, because every act is a certain perfection."[25] Evil is privation and frustration. ". . . No being is said to be evil so far as it really is, but only in so far as it lacks a certain existence, as a man is said to be evil in so far as he lacks virtuous action, and an eye is said to be evil in so far as it lacks visual acuteness."[26] What is good for any entity is to activate itself, to be authentically what it really is. Thus the good for man is to live a genuine human life, realizing human powers to the highest degree.

Here we find the same basic principles of moral realism which we have already noted in a less precise form in the Stoic texts. The world of nature is a great dynamic order in which a vast array of divergent tendencies of divergent beings sustain and influence one another. Each entity is characterized by a certain structure which determines it to act in a certain way. So far as its tendencies are directed towards their natural fulfilment, it is in a sound condition. So far as they are distorted or frustrated, it is unhealthy and evil. For every entity, including man, to exist and to act in accordance with nature is good. Certain basic needs are common to man. The principles which must be followed if such tendencies are to be satisfied constitute the law of nature. They are the same for all men everywhere.

Aquinas is presenting this body of doctrine as a conscious representative of natural-law philosophy, and his right to speak for this tradition is nowhere seriously questioned. Hence, we must regard his precise statement of our five principles as an important confirmation of our thesis that they must be regarded as the essential core of authentic natural-law philosophy. Let us now turn to certain later thinkers who are also commonly classified as representatives of this tradition. Can we find the same doctrines in them?

D. THE MORAL PHILOSOPHY OF RICHARD HOOKER

The Anglican theologian Richard Hooker (1553–1600) devotes a number of pages in his great work *The Laws of Ecclesiastical Polity* to a consideration of natural law, the basic concept of his moral philosophy. He is commonly regarded as an eminent representative of this tradition. Let us now address our five questions to him.

1 and 2. Does he believe that each substantial entity possesses a determinate nature, and that the realization of this nature not only preserves the entity in question but also contributes something to the interdependent order which binds all things into a single universe? A concise answer to these questions is stated in a single sentence.[27] "For we see the whole world and each part thereof so compacted that as long as each thing performeth only that work which is natural unto it, it thereby preserveth both other things and also itself."

3. Does he accept the category of potency or incomplete being? Does he believe that finite entities are always marked by

such imperfection and by active tendencies to realize their capacities? His assertion in the passage we have just examined that each entity has a natural work to perform would seem to imply this. Is this tendential view of finite being confirmed by other clearer texts? Take the following statement:[28] "All other things besides [God] are somewhat in possibility which as yet they are not in act. And for this cause there is in all things an appetite or desire whereby they incline to something which they may be. . . ." It is clear that this question must be given an affirmative answer. All things are inclining or tending towards further perfections they have not yet achieved in act. The essential human values consist in the realization of essential tendencies or needs. Thus, human society with its values of co-operative activity arises from basic human "need."[29]

4. Does he really think of nature in a normative sense? Does he hold that by directing incipient tendencies in accordance with the nature determining them, good will be achieved? Take the following brief sentence:[30] "Good doth follow unto all things by observing the course of their nature, and on the contrary side evil by not observing it. . . ." The formal structure or nature of any entity determines the course of action which will fulfil this nature. Such action is good for the entity, and normatively prescribed as the law of its nature.

All individual creatures, including individual men and human groups, have incidental tendencies that are fitted to their circumstances and should therefore be realized. But the term *law of nature* is reserved for those universal tendencies that are shared by every member of a given species. ". . . We do not therefore so far extend the Law of Reason as to contain in it all manner laws whereunto reasonable creatures are bound, but (as hath been showed) we restrain it to those only duties which all men by force of natural wit either do or might understand to be such duties as concern all men."[31]

5. Granted that Hooker believes in nature as a standard determining certain duties by which we are bound, does he also believe that goodness and duty are united? Is duty directed towards goodness conceived as the fulfilment of natural tendency? Let us return to the passage already quoted in the

answer to Question 3. As we have already noted, he says:[32] "there is in all things an appetite or desire whereby they incline to something which they may be." Let us now note how he continues: "and when they are in it, they shall be perfecter than now they are. All which perfections are contained under the general name of goodness." Duty and value cannot be opposed. This is an essential doctrine of all authentic natural-law philosophy. Goodness in general means the perfection or realization of natural tendency. Hence, it includes those incipient acts which are the first completions of tendency and which lead on to further completion. Goodness is how we ought to be, and to do what we ought to do is certainly good.

Hooker, therefore, meets our five criteria of authentic natural-law philosophy. He holds a tendential theory of finite existence. These existential tendencies are mutually sustaining or fit for one another. Subrational creatures are automatically determined by their formal natures to act in certain appropriate ways. Man is also initially determined in this way towards human realization. But this realization cannot be fittingly achieved without the direction of his rational capacities which alone can understand all the various tendencies of his complex nature and spontaneously guide them toward a fitting goal. Hooker is a realistic philosopher of the natural-law tradition. Let us now turn to Hugo Grotius (1583–1645), a near contemporary, living on the continent of Europe, who is also widely believed to belong to this tradition.

E. HUGO GROTIUS

1. According to Grotius (1583–1645) individual animals, including men, are marked by tendencies which lead not only to their own preservation but also to the welfare of others.[33] In man this social urge is spontaneously clarified and strengthened by his intrinsic power of rational insight. In nonrational entities it must be ultimately derived "from a certain extrinsic, intelligent source."[34] The world is regarded as an order of interdependent tendencies. This conception underlies the whole work.

2. These tendencies are necessarily determined by the essential nature and the existence of each entity. "For as the exist-

ence of things after they are brought into being, and the essential nature by which they are, do not depend on anything else, so it is with the properties and tendencies which necessarily follow this existence."[35] What is good and what is bad for an existent entity are inexorably determined by its nature. "This natural law is so immutable that it cannot be changed by God Himself. . . . Thus God cannot make twice two not to be four; and in like manner He cannot make what is intrinsically evil not to be evil."[36] This is an uncompromising moral realism. Norms are not due to fluctuating opinion and desire. They cannot be enacted or retracted by human decree. They are immutably founded on the nature of things, and the cosmic order into which they must fit to some degree if they are to exist at all.

3. Grotius refers to those tendencies which are determined by the specific nature of an entity as "first principles of nature" (*prima naturae*), quoting this phrase from Cicero.[37] Thus "as soon as an animal is born, it tends to care for itself and to seek the means of preserving its sound condition, as well as to shun destruction and all things which seem to bring destruction."[38] Man is characterized by many natural appetites of this kind, for food, for children, for knowledge, etc. Of peculiar importance for Grotius, following the Stoics here, is the appetite for society and social order. "Among those activities which are proper to man there is the appetite for the society of his fellow men which the Stoics called οἰκείωσις, not any sort of society but peaceful society ordered in a rational way."[39] These invariable needs of human nature are the objective foundation for the human law of nature as Grotius conceives it.[40]

4. These basic needs are rights, and the modes of action required to satisfy them are prescribed by the law of nature. Acts which frustrate such tendencies are wrong and unjust. "Natural law is a judgment of right reason concerning the moral necessity or turpitude of any act based on its agreement or disagreement with the rational and social nature of man."[41] There are two ways of demonstrating that something is a law of nature. This may be proved a posteriori with a high degree of probability if it is found that all races and nations, or at least all that are civilized, believe it to be morally binding. It may be strictly and

exactly proved only in the light of a clear and adequate conception of human nature and its essential tendencies. A mode of action which is necessarily required for the realization of such tendencies is a law of nature.[42] Such principles lie at the root of individual and social ethics.

5. Co-operative activity which fulfils the nature of man is good. That which frustrates or obstructs such activity is unjust and evil. Thus, "to take from another for the sake of one's own convenience is against nature . . . because if this were ordinarily done the common life of men would be impossible."[43] To exist in a thwarted condition is evil; to exist in a state of active fulfilment is good.

Grotius writes consciously as a moral realist believing in norms founded on tendential facts of nature. We have found that he measures up to the test of our fivefold criterion. So we must conclude that his claim is justified, and that he is an authentic representative of the tradition of natural law. His special contribution was to emphasize in a period of growing nationalism the existence of a law with natural sanctions which holds good irrespective of the waxing claims of national states to absolute sovereignty. Let us now turn to one last example taken from the eighteenth century.

F. THOMAS PAINE

It is of course well known that many of the revolutionary writers of the eighteenth century made a constant appeal to principles of natural law. But natural law may be defined in very different ways. So the mere use of the term proves little or nothing. Did they hold the realistic conceptions we have found in the earlier authors so far studied? If so, our thesis that these conceptions are essential to any authentic natural-law philosophy will be confirmed and strengthened. We shall select Thomas Paine (1737–1809) as a typical representative of this revolutionary mode of thought and address our five questions to him.

1. Does he believe that the universe is an ordered whole which exists independent of human language, desire, and legislation? Take the following passage from *The Age of Reason*, where

Paine is speaking of the Creator:[44] "The Creation speaks a universal language, independent of human speech or human language, multiplied and various as these be. It is an ever-existing original which every man can read. . . . Do we want to contemplate His power? We see it in the immensity of the creation. Do we want to contemplate His wisdom? We see it in the unchangeable order by which the incomprehensible whole is governed." Man is in no way responsible for this natural order. He did not bring himself into being. Nor can he alter the laws of nature.

2 and 3. Does Paine hold that finite being is tendential and that there are uniform tendencies of man, for example, founded on a common nature essential to the very existence of a member of the species? He certainly conceives of nature as a dynamic order. "As to that which is called nature, it is no other than the laws by which motion and action of every kind, with respect to unintelligible matter, are regulated."[45] Man belongs to this order. Those constant tendencies which must be realized to some degree if human life is to be lived are called *natural rights*. "Natural rights are those which appertain to man in right of his existence. Of this kind are all the intellectual rights or rights of the mind."[46]

Not being founded on arbitrary desire or decree, but rather on nature, they have a natural right to be fulfilled. Man is rational by nature. Hence, by his very existence he possesses a natural right to education and the free exercise of his mind. He is necessarily a material being with physical needs. Hence he possesses a natural right to "property" and "security."[47] He possesses a faculty of choice for the voluntary direction of his life. Hence, he possesses also a natural right to "liberty" and "resistance of oppression." Such a nature is shared by all men. In this sense they are created equal, and should be granted equal opportunities for its realization.[48]

4. Paine agrees emphatically with a central thesis of authentic natural-law philosophy that man is a social being not by contract but by nature, and originally endowed with tendencies that fit him for social life. "As nature created him for social life, she fitted him for the station she intended."[49] But social co-

operation is not founded merely on certain special tendencies. It is required by every dynamic phase of his being. No human want can be adequately realized without the support of others. "In all cases she [nature] made his natural wants greater than his individual powers. No one man is capable without the aid of society of supplying his own wants; and those wants acting upon every individual impel the whole of them into society, as naturally as gravitation acts to a center."[50]

This is a radical departure from Hobbes and all those who would oppose civil law to natural law. Paine sharply criticizes the view of Locke, who follows Hobbes in this respect, that certain natural rights are surrendered with the establishment of civil government. "Man enters society not to have *fewer* rights but to have original rights better secured."[51] Civil law, when soundly conceived, must be founded on natural law. "Every civil right grows out of a natural right."[52]

The common needs of man lie at the root of human obligation and duty. When the individual reason understands such a natural need, it also understands the co-operative action required for the satisfaction of the need, and possible acts of this type which he also might perform. Such insight, united with the urge towards realization subjectively felt by the agent, is the so-called sense of obligation. Rights therefore imply duties. "A Declaration of rights is, by reciprocity, a Declaration of duties also. Whatever is my right as a man, is also the right of another; and it becomes my duty to guarantee as well as to possess."[53] Human virtue, the acts that we ought to perform, is achieved by insight into the natural ends of man, and the rational direction of incipient tendencies towards such ends. What are these ends?

5. The ultimate end of all individual and social morality is to attain the common good—that ordered co-operative action in which basic needs and legitimate individual wants are realized. "Whatever the form or constitution of government may be, it ought to have no other object than the general happiness."[54] The word "happiness" here is employed not in a hedonistic sense, but in the classical sense of activity crowned with satisfaction. "Every man wishes to pursue his occupation, and enjoy the fruits of his labors. . . ."[55]

There is no necessary opposition between the collective or

common good, and the individual good when these are properly conceived. When conflict arises this is a sign that one or the other has been misunderstood. "Government is nothing more than a national association; and the object of this association is the good of all, as well individually as collectively."[56] In working for what is really the common good, I am also working for my good; and in working for what is really my good, I am also working for the common good.

Paine is a political pamphleteer embroiled in the revolutionary conflicts of his time. Hence, the major aim of his polemic tracts is not so much to demonstrate and to clarify the basic propositions of his realistic philosophy as to reveal their implications for the burning problems of the day. He performed this practical function with great effectiveness and originality, often making explicit and clear what had previously remained implicit and vague. His cogent defense of the radical social needs of men, natural equality of human rights, and the natural harmony between natural and civil law must be mentioned in this connection.

But while he had no time to dwell on the realistic conceptions which underlie these applications, one cannot read his writings carefully without realizing that they are there. The universe is a dynamic order of dependent tendencies supporting each other in regular ways. That which is necessary and essential in each individual entity can be distinguished from what is accidental. The human person possesses a set of such essential traits which he shares with all other members of the species. These traits determine common needs and tendencies. When these are clearly understood, they constitute the objective ground of an authentic and realistic ethics. We must, therefore, regard Paine as a genuine representative of the central tradition of natural-law philosophy. We may see this more clearly if we now briefly contrast this position with that of two deviating versions with which it is now often confused.

Section V. Two Modern Deviations

A. THOMAS HOBBES

Thomas Hobbes (1588–1679) makes a constant use of the phrase *law of nature*, and his peculiar conception of it plays an important role in his moral philosophy. His works, especially the *Leviathan*, have been widely read, so that many thinkers and writers of the Anglo-Saxon tradition have formed their ideas of natural law under his influence, believing this view to be normal and representative of the tradition. As a matter of fact, this is not true. Hobbes' view is so eccentric that, unless we are to be misled by purely terminological considerations, we cannot judge him to belong to this tradition at all. His position is definitely opposed to the central theses of authentic natural-law philosophy, as we shall now show by comparing it to the fivefold standard we have found to be confirmed by our examination of representative authors.

1. Hobbes says very little about natural order. He seems to recognize the contingency of finite beings, and the existence of an infinite Creator.[57] But even this Deity is conceived as an unlimited power, completely beyond all rational understanding and lacking both will and intellect.[58] The bodies which make up the world obey the laws of motion. Each tends to preserve itself, but is constantly threatened with destruction by alien bodies. Nature is conceived as a chaos of opposed rather than mutually supporting tendencies. Thus, individual human organisms in their natural state are in a war "of every man against every man."[59] There is no natural ground for moral norms. "To this war of every man against every man this also is consequent; that nothing can be unjust. The notions of right and wrong, justice and injustice have there no place."[60] In this state of nature, as Hobbes describes it, there are "no arts; no letters; no society; and which is worst of all continual fear and danger of violent death; and the life of man solitary, poor, nasty, brutish and short."[61]

To be sure, Hobbes has to qualify this description. He has to admit "a possibility to come out of it" consisting partly in the fear of death, and partly in man's rational capacity to devise means for peace.[62] If this were not so, society would never be formed. But this is a clear-cut inconsistency. If Hobbes had consistently followed this line of thought, if man were rational and desirous of peace by nature, then social life would be natural to man, and there would be no opposition between natural and civil law. But this is precisely the most "original" feature of Hobbes' thought, where he breaks completely with the realistic tradition of natural-law philosophy. Nature is a state of anarchy and strife. The usual view of naturalism is that nature is neutral to value. Hobbes goes much further. Not only does nature offer no positive ground for moral norms. It is opposed to them.

2 and 3. Does Hobbes believe that each individual is marked by an essential nature determining necessary tendencies which he shares with other members of the same species? The answer to this question is definitely and clearly negative. Hobbes as a consistent materialist is also a nominalist. A universal concept is not grounded on anything actual in nature. ". . . This word *universal* is never the name of anything existent in nature, nor of any idea or phantasm formed in the mind, but always the name of some word or name . . . that is common to many things."[63] There is no real reason in things which can explain our calling them by the same name. This is due only to subjective association.

The distinction between essence and accident is also arbitrary and subjective. An individual entity is a cluster of innumerable traits. That one which we single out with some purpose in view is called *the essence*. In nature all are equally important. "Now that accident for which we give a certain name to any body, or the accident which denominates its subject, is commonly called the essence thereof. . . ."[64] "Essence and all other abstract names are words artificial belonging to the art of logic, and signify only the manner how we consider the substance itself."[65]

Each individual exists alone by itself as an isolated atom, sharing nothing in common with others. Hence, it is no wonder that Hobbes denies the whole idea of formal causation. Blind efficient force is the only cause he recognizes. The idea that an active tendency might be determined by formal structure is dismissed as a scholastic superstition. "For as for those that say anything may be moved or produced by itself, by species . . . by substantial forms . . . occult quality and other empty words of schoolmen, their saying is to no purpose."[66]

4. Realistic ethics maintains, as we have seen, that moral

laws are grounded on universal tendencies common to all members of the human species. These prescriptions are enforced by natural sanctions independent of all arbitrary decree. Thus, if men fail to recognize the natural right to education, they are punished by ignorance. If they fail to recognize the natural need for rational social unity, they are punished by the natural sanction of war. This whole conception of natural laws with natural sanctions is foreign to Hobbes' subjectivist way of thought.

The only law he can recognize is an arbitrary human decree—the only sanction a punishment inflicted by the power of a sovereign ruler. Thus, since war is not consciously decreed by a human king, he cannot recognize it as the sanction of a natural law, but confuses it with the natural state of man. The laws of nature do not rule or reign. "For he only is properly said to rule or reign that governs his subjects by his word, and by promise of rewards to those that obey it, and by threatening them with punishment that obey it not."[67]

There is no real justice and injustice. "Before there was any government *just* and *unjust* had no being, their nature only being relative to some command: and every action in its own nature is indifferent; that it becomes *just* or *unjust* proceeds from the right of the magistrate."[68] Whatever the magistrate rules so long as it keeps the peace will be just. But in this sense justice loses all content and becomes equivocal. In the *Leviathan*, Hobbes defines law of nature as "a precept or general rule." But this universality is deceptive and really ambiguous. For it merely commands a man to avoid anything not destructive of life in general, but "destructive of *his* life."[69] Thus, the cold-blooded murderer taking shrewd precautions against discovery is obeying this law as exactly as the innocent victim. Like the so-called universal principles of utilitarian ethics (seek always the greatest amount of subjective pleasure), this law is universal in logical form alone. Its object is individual, particular, and indefinitely variable.

The moral realist thinks of law as guiding incipient tendencies to full realization. Hence, he does not oppose law to freedom. How can a man be free if he cannot fulfil his basic needs? Hobbes, however, thinks of freedom as unlimited power to achieve any desire, no matter how unnatural it may be. Hence, for him "law is a fetter, right is freedom."[70]

Having thus identified right with any arbitrary *desire* rather than with natural *need*, Hobbes is forced to the conclusion that in joining a society, men must give up their natural rights and yield them to a tyrannical sovereign.[71] As we have seen in Paine, this peculiar doctrine runs counter to the very essence of natural-law philosophy. No authentic representative of this tradition has ever maintained that social life was a fetter.

5. The basic issue is that between moral realism and subjectivism. Natural-law philosophy holds that goodness lies in the realization of essential tendencies, and of other tendencies as well, so far as these are not unnatural. Such goodness is really good, and retains its value irrespective of whether anyone wishes it or takes pleasure in it. Hobbes, being a materialist, cannot accept any such realistic conception, for materialism always leads to subjectivism. So, like other utilitarian philosophers, he holds a completely subjectivist theory of value. Nothing is really valuable apart from individual interest and pleasure. "Every man for his own part calleth that which pleaseth and is delightful to himself *good* and that *evil* which displeaseth him: insomuch that while every man differeth from another in constitution, they differ also from one another concerning the common distinction of good and evil. Nor is there any such thing as absolute goodness. . . ."[72] Norms are not founded on the independent nature of existence, but rather on shifting desire and subjectively felt pleasure. This is a radical break with the principles of realistic ethics.

On the basis of every one of our five criteria, Hobbes fails to qualify as a genuine representative of moral realism. We must, therefore, conclude that in spite of his deceptive use of natural-law terminology, he cannot be regarded as an authentic representative of natural-law philosophy. This conclusion, I think, can hardly be seriously questioned. We must now turn to another thinker whose position is more ambiguous.

B. JOHN LOCKE

Locke (1633–1704) is another author who, in his writings, makes constant use of the phrase law of nature. Hence, it has been widely supposed that he understands this phrase in its traditional sense and is speaking as an authentic representative of natural-law philosophy. Let us now test this assumption by an application of our criteria.

1–3. What are Locke's ontological views? Does he hold that the world is a tendential order? Is each individual entity marked by a stable essential structure distinct from the incidental traits which may be gained or lost? Does this essential structure determine basic *needs* which are distinct from shifting *desires?* We may consider these questions together since Locke's ontology is never made thoroughly explicit, and his answers are vague and ambiguous.

It is clear that he recognizes the contingency of himself and other finite existents. Hence he accepts a causal argument for the existence of a creative Deity.[73] He also accepts the idea of efficient causal efficacy. Natural entities act on and suffer from one another.[74] But his subjectivist theory of knowledge makes him very skeptical of our capacity to know the real nature and inner constitution of natural entities. Hence, he refers only rarely to a natural order, and it is dubious whether this conception ever played any vital role in his thought. He rejects the Hobbesian conception of the natural state as one of unlimited war and anarchy,[75] and holds that each individual ought not only to preserve himself but ought "as much as he can to preserve the rest of mankind." Nevertheless, he defends the peculiar Hobbesian opposition between the natural state and that of civil society, and asserts that life in the former is "uneasy and unsafe."[76] We must regard his answer to the first question, therefore, as uncertain.

His answer to the second is only slightly less ambiguous. The upshot of his discussion of nominal versus real essences in the Third Book of the *Essay* seems to be that we can never know the real structure of any natural substance but only its sensible effects on us.[77] This leads him to an apparently categorical denial of the distinction between essence and accident, for what we call the essence is always only a nominal essence, some sensible property which we arbitrarily select as important for some purpose. "All such patterns and standards being quite laid aside, particular beings, considered barely in themselves, will be found to have all their qualities equally essential; and everything in each individual will be essential to it, or, which is more, nothing at all."[78] Nevertheless, Locke does continue to speak of the real essence, the internal constitution of natural things from which all their properties flow, though it is clear that we can never know them as they are, and quite unclear from the nature of his epistemology how we can even suspect that there is any such thing at all. Do natural entities have a determinate essence? Locke's answer seems to be: yes, they probably do, but this essence is entirely unknowable by us.

Does the essence determine constant existential tendencies towards realization? The answer to this question seems definitely negative. Efficient power seems to be the only type of causation he recognizes.[79] The question as to what determines an active or passive agency to act as it does is simply never raised. Since this ontological conception of stable needs or tendencies underlies all realistic ethics, it is not surprising to find that Locke's moral theory is marked by a thoroughgoing subjectivism.

4. Are there universal normative principles grounded on the nature of man which may guide our confused, incipient tendencies towards sound and humane realization? This is what has been meant by natural law. Does Locke use the phrase in this sense? The answer is definitely *no!* The realistic view is that there is a stable human nature, always determining basic needs. Hence, man can never escape from this natural condition. Locke, however, does not believe in any such inescapable tendential nature. For him, the "natural state" is something which men may leave by common agreement in setting up a commonwealth. "And this puts men out of a state of nature into that of a commonwealth by setting up a judge on earth with authority to determine all controversies and redress the injuries that may happen. . . ."[80]

Locke quotes Hooker, apparently thinking of him as an authority for this conception.[81] But the very words he quotes unmistakably refer to a radically different view. The laws of nature can never be superseded, no matter what men do. According to Hooker, they "bind men absolutely, even as they are men." We do not engage in social intercourse by a constructive act beyond nature but rather "we are naturally induced to seek communion and fellowship with others."[82] Immediately after quoting these unambiguous words, Locke proceeds to express his own contrasting doctrine "that all men are naturally in that state and remain so till, by their own consent, they make themselves members of some politic society. . . ." No authentic representative of natural-law philosophy could speak in this way. For such a point of view, the supposed escape of a natural entity from its natural state would be regarded as a sheer contradiction.

In accepting this Hobbesian conception of social order as "a new state"[83] in some sense opposed to nature, he also accepts another dubious doctrine of Hobbes. By entering into society, men must "give up" certain natural powers and "part with" much of their natural liberty.[84] As Paine saw very clearly, this is basically opposed to the theory of natural law. Unless it is corrupt, social life requires no abandonment of any natural right or power.

In Locke's view, natural law in the classic sense of norms founded on basic needs of man is not law at all, for it works of itself. He reserves the term *law* for the arbitrary decree of a ruling power supported by arbitrary sanctions. Thus, according to the *Essay*:[85] "It would be in vain for one intelligent being to set a rule to the actions of another, if he had it not in his power to reward the compliance with, and punish deviation from, his rule by some good and evil that is not the natural product and consequence of the action itself. For that, being a natural convenience or inconvenience, would operate of itself without a law."

What Locke here calls "a natural convenience or inconvenience" is precisely what has been called the natural sanction of a natural law. For Locke, it is not a law at all. To act spontaneously in this way is to act in liberty, and law is conceived by him always in the mode of Hobbes as a hindrance or restraint. "Moral laws are sent as a curb and restraint to these exorbitant desires. . . ."[86] Law and liberty are opposed. According to the theory of natural law, this is to confuse liberty with license. Law may restrain accidental interests and pleasures. But unless it is vicious and mistaken, it cannot oppose the essential needs and spontaneity of man.

As a result of this analysis, I think we must conclude that Locke is using the phrase *natural law* in a peculiar sense quite opposed to that of the classical and medieval thinkers who developed this terminology. The concept of natural law as they conceived it is entirely lacking in his system of thought. Thus, he proposes a general classification of all types of law in which he recognizes three divergent types: (1) the divine law; (2) the civil law; and (3) the law of opinion or reputation.[87] It is (1) divine law, to which Locke ordinarily refers when he speaks of natural law. But this is not a coherent rational order of supporting tendencies—the law of nature in the classical and Christian sense. It consists rather in a set of arbitrary decrees laid down by the Deity concerning the attainment of pleasure, enforced "by rewards and punishments of infinite weight and duration in another life."[88] This may be a distorted version of what is often referred to as *Divine positive law*. It is certainly not natural law in either a classical or a Christian sense. This concept is simply lacking in the thought of Locke.

5. What does he hold concerning the fundamental category of goodness? Does he conceive of it realistically as the fulfilment of existence? Here again the answer is a clear-cut negative! "Good and evil, as hath been shown, are nothing but pleasure or pain, or that which procures pleasure or pain to us."[89] Nothing can be said to be good unless it gives pleasure to someone, nor evil unless someone feels pain. Value thus becomes something purely private, subjective, and incorrigible. If someone is feeling pleased, no more can be said. We cannot maintain that a mode of action is intrinsically good in itself, whether anyone likes it or dislikes it, is pleased or displeased. Value is wholly at the mercy of accident and idiosyncrasy. Furthermore, the term becomes equivocal, for there is nothing of any sort whatsoever that may not become pleasing to someone under certain conditions.

This is indeed the end of moral realism, and indeed of ethics itself as a responsible rational discipline. No generalizations with an intelligible, univocal content are possible. How about the principle that pleasure should be maximized? But how can the maximizing of that which is equivocal be anything but equivocal? What are we to maximize? That which procures pleasure? What is this? Anything at all! No meaningful norms can be elicited from this type of subjectivism. Each individual is simply referred to his own desires, whatever they may be. We are thus led to a moral relativism which is the antithesis of natural law.

Section VI. Conclusion

We have now examined the thought of different philosophers living at different times who are generally regarded as representing the tradition of natural-law philosophy. We have discovered in them a basic core of central doctrine on which they all agree— the realistic theory of natural law. We have tried to clarify our understanding of this theory by contrasting it with the views of other writers who, in spite of their deceptive use of the phrase *natural law*, do not actually belong in this realistic tradition.

The theory of natural law is incompatible with any supposed opposition between an imagined chaotic state of nature and the order of social life. It cannot be reconciled with a nominalistic denial of the distinction between essence and accident, or of that between basic needs and ephemeral desires and interests. It does not hold that normative principles are made by man, nor can it be made consistent with any utilitarian theory which identifies value with subjective pleasure or interest.

In opposition to these views, the theory of natural law is a radically realistic point of view which has been defended by able thinkers from the time of the Stoics to the eighteenth century and after. Five basic doctrines are found to be always characteristic of it.

1. The world is an order of divergent tendencies which on the whole support one another.

2. Each individual entity is marked by an essential structure which it shares in common with other members of the species.

3. This structure determines certain basic existential tendencies that are also common to the species.

4. If these tendencies are to be realized without distortion

and frustration, they must follow a general dynamic pattern. This pattern is what is meant by natural law. It is grounded on real structure, and is enforced by inexorable natural sanctions.

5. Good and evil are existential categories. It is good for an entity to exist in a condition of active realization. If its basic tendencies are hampered and frustrated, it exists in an evil condition.

Human nature includes the faculties of rational cognition and will, which enable the human individual to understand himself to some degree of clarity, and to direct his acts spontaneously from within. Such free self-direction is required for the authentic living of human life. In this sense, man is condemned to be free. Ethics is the study of this self-direction and how it should proceed. Since man is a finite entity included in the changing world of nature, the five ontological principles enumerated above apply to him. The first is too broad to have any special moral significance, though it underlies the rest. The remaining ones (2, 3, 4, and 5), however, entail three principles which are basically important for ethics.

1. From the second (2) it follows that the common traits of human nature, the tendencies determined by these traits, and the laws governing the fitting realization of these tendencies are the same for all men everywhere.

2. From the third and fourth (3 and 4), it follows that certain modes of action commonly called virtues or obligations must be pursued if frustration is to be avoided. These modes of action are not due to arbitrary decree, or preference, but are founded on human nature itself.

3. From the fifth (5) it follows that the good for man is the activation of his nature, the most complete and intensive living of a human life.

As we have observed, these ontological and moral theses have been defended throughout our cultural history by a large number of influential thinkers. They are collectively referred to as *the theory of natural law*. Let us now ask who first originated this theory? Who first developed it in a disciplined way? This must lead us to a new consideration of the thought of Plato and Aristotle.

CHAPTER FIVE

PLATO AS THE FOUNDER OF MORAL REALISM AND NATURAL-LAW PHILOSOPHY

S O FAR, in Part I we have studied certain modern criticisms of classical philosophy. In chapter 3, we discovered that some of these were based upon misunderstandings arising from subjectivist trends in recent thought. The radical opposition of such subjectivist philosophy to the realistic conception of natural law suggested that Plato and Aristotle may actually have founded this realistic moral theory. But before testing this hypothesis it was first necessary to examine the nature of moral realism as it has been manifested in the history of Western thought. Before we can ask intelligently whether Plato was the founder of natural-law philosophy, we must first know exactly what this philosophy is. As a result of our investigation of this question in the last chapter, we have concluded that the theory of natural law includes at least five ontological theses and three specifically ethical theses derived from these.

Any authentic moral realist must hold: (1) that the world is a nexus of interdependent tendential systems; (2) that each recurrent tendency is determined by a specific structure or form; (3) that the structure of substantial entities, like living things, determines essential tendencies shared by every member of the species; (4) that such tendencies must be activated according to a certain normal pattern or law; if (5) the good of that entity, its realization or completion, is to be achieved.

When these ontological principles are applied to human nature, three specifically ethical theses may be derived. These are: (1) the universality of moral or natural laws; (2) the existence of norms founded on nature; and (3) the good for man as the realization of human nature. Any thinker who explicitly and coherently defends these principles is a moral realist who belongs

134

to the tradition of natural-law philosophy. With these criteria in mind we are now in a position where we may intelligently inquire concerning the origin of this tradition. Did Plato belong to this tradition? Was he the first realistic thinker who attempted to think along these lines in a disciplined way?

Section I. STOICISM AS THE FIRST SOURCE OF NATURAL-LAW PHILOSOPHY

Most reference works suggest either that the doctrine was originated by the Stoics, or that its antecedents are vague and indeterminate. The modern idea that natural law is best expressed in Stoicism can be traced back to Samuel Pufendorf, the German codifier. He did not deny that the concept is found in Plato and Aristotle, but held that the Stoic version was much better and took pride in the thought that his teaching was "very close" to that of the Stoics.[1] According to the *Hastings Encyclopedia of Religion and Ethics*, a reference work now widely used by philosophers, it is stated under the heading "Natural Law" that: "The term 'law of nature' in its modern acceptation is seldom used by Plato and Aristotle; it was especially among the Stoics that it took a more prominent place, and here the idea of divine laws led to that of natural laws."[2]

Several points need to be noted about this statement. In the first place, it suggests the basic thesis that Plato and Aristotle had little to do with the original formulation of the theory of natural law, but that this must rather be attributed to the Stoics.[3] Two reasons for this widely held opinion are then indicated. One is repeated over and over with minor variations in many standard books and histories of the last century. This is the purely linguistic argument that "the term 'law of nature' in its modern acceptation is seldom used by Plato and Aristotle" —a philological consideration hardly relevant to the theory itself. Even though the *terms* used may be different, the *concept* could be present. The second is a theological point. It is implied that natural law is a theological rather than a philosophical conception, and that it was "the idea of divine laws which led to that of natural laws." In my opinion, these two suggested reasons are dubious and inconclusive, and fail to prove the basic

thesis, which is definitely false. The Stoics may have popularized the theory of natural law in an eclectic way;[4] but it was
originated by Plato and Aristotle.[5] Let us now review the two
arguments.

It is true that the linguistic *term* "law of nature" occurs only
rarely in the texts of Plato and Aristotle. In Plato it is found at
Gorgias 484 and *Timaeus* 83 E, though the phrase *agrapha nomi-
na* is used in this sense at *Laws* 793 B. Closely allied terms occur
in the Aristotelian texts at *De Caelo* 268 a 10, where the order
of beginning, middle, and end is referred to as one of the "laws
of nature"; at *Rhetoric* 1368 b 3 where *nomos idios* is contrasted
with *nomos koinos*, agreed to by all men; and at *Nicomachean
Ethics* V. 17, where *conventional justice* is contrasted with *natural justice* which is everywhere the same. Not only is the very
phrase itself found in both authors, but what is much more important, the concept, as we have defined it, is clearly developed
by both of them, and lies at the very root of their moral and
political doctrines.

The theological argument is equally dubious. It is true that
the medieval Church adopted this doctrine and emphatically
stressed its dependence upon the theory of a supreme lawgiver and the arguments of natural theology. But even if there
is such a connection, the theory of natural law depends on natural theology, not on revealed theology, a point which needs to
be stressed. Plato, Aristotle, and their Greek and Arabian followers worked out the theory of natural law without any special reference to Christian revelation, on strictly empirical
grounds connected with the analysis of human nature and its
essential tendencies towards realization. Furthermore, even in
post-medieval times, the possibility of defending this basic
moral conception without reference to theology has been admitted by well-known representatives of moral realism. Thus
Hugo Grotius in the sixteenth century in a famous passage of
his treatise *De Jure Belli et Pacis* maintained that the basic
principles of natural law would hold true even if it were granted
that God did not exist.[6] This is enough to cast grave doubt on
the argument that Plato and Aristotle could not have developed
the theory of natural law because it is a purely theological con-

ception. As a matter of fact, as we shall now attempt to show, they did develop it, and gave it the first precise and coherent philosophical formulation to be found in the history of Western thought.

As we have seen (chap. 4), the theory of natural law is basically ontological in character. Ethical categories are neither accepted as indefinable ultimate terms, nor are they given a purely psychological analysis and then left hanging. They are rather traced back to their ultimate roots in the existential structure of finite existence. Without this metaphysical underpinning, the theory is left without any solid foundation and withers away, to be replaced by relativistic points of view having a psychological or anthropological origin. Thus during the last century, with the decline of metaphysics, natural-law philosophy was also eclipsed. In addition to this ontological background, there are also certain distinctive ethical theses which are essential to this way of thought. Let us now turn to Plato and see if we can find these two kinds of doctrine, the ontological (Section II) and the more strictly ethical (Section III) in his writings.

Section II. THE ONTOLOGICAL FOUNDATIONS OF PLATONIC ETHICS

According to the analysis we have given, there are five ontological theses which are required by any articulate philosophy of natural law. These are: (1) the world is governed by a normative order embedded in the very being of its component entities; (2) each finite entity is marked by an intelligible structure distinguishing it from other entities, and determining its development in regular ways which may be expressed by a universal law; (3) the composite structure of any finite entity also includes an active factor of dynamism or tendency which urges it towards further existence not yet acquired; (4) when a concrete tendency is ordered to act in accordance with the law described under 2, this action is natural or right; and (5) good, in the most general sense, is the realization of tendency, evil the lack of fulfilment.

There are many ways in which we might show that these doctrines are to be found in the Platonic dialogues. We shall try to do this by analyzing the meanings of a single term *nature* (φύσις) which, together with various cognate forms, occurs ubiquitously in the works of Plato. This procedure is recommended by three reasons. First, it will save us time. Second, it will enable us to suggest more clearly the basic unity in which these different doctrines are held together. Finally, it will enable us to call attention to an aspect of Plato's thought which has been neglected by modern commentators, especially those in the Anglo-Saxon tradition.[7] We shall try to show that the word *nature* is used by Plato in all the five senses described above as: (1) the normative order of the world as a whole; (2) the determinate structure of a finite entity; (3) the dynamic tendency of such an existent entity; (4) the ordered process by which it attains some degree of fulfilment; and (5) the valuable or authentic condition of such fulfilment.

A. NATURE AS A NORMATIVE WORLD ORDER

The word *nature* is used throughout the dialogues in referring to the whole world of changing events, including the motions of the stars. Thus at the beginning of the *Protagoras*, Hippias is discoursing with his friends on astronomy and "about the world of nature."[8] A similar sense is found in the *Phaedo*[9] where the word refers simply to the world around us, or the general flux of world events. According to Plato, this flux of events is not without form or structure. Thus in an important passage of the *Parmenides*, it is said that "the ideas stand as models" not outside the flux but "in the world of nature."[10] Concrete changing things are modeled after structures which can be grasped by the mind. This participated structure, though incomplete, is nevertheless present in nature and normally governs the flux. In an interesting discussion of this statement, Constantine Ritter interprets it as a recognition of stable regularities or laws of change in nature.[11] Individual objects never perfectly exemplify a form. But they approximate it to various degrees in accordance with a law determined by structure.

Plato in his earlier dialogues often refers to the changing universe as an ordered whole or cosmos in which the different parts sustain each other in regular ways. Thus, we read in the *Gorgias*

that "friendship, orderliness, harmony, and justice hold together heaven and earth, and Gods and men, and because of this the
whole is called an order (κόσμος) and not a disordered chaos."[12]
In the *Laws* this cosmic order and its generative sources are
carefully examined, and constantly referred to by the term *nature* (φύσις). Book X of the *Laws* gives us the final and most explicit statement of Plato's theory of Natural Law. It contains a
complex argument for the priority of rational life over lifeless
matter as the first moving principle or nature of the cosmos. We
are told that the materialists wish to identify this principle
(φύσις) with earth, or air, or fire. But they do not use the term
rightly since as a matter of fact soul or life is the first moving
principle, and therefore "in a special sense exists by nature."[13]
This rational living principle of natural order is God. Moved by
the materialistic doctrine of might makes right, men commonly
say that law should have no regard for virtue, but only for power and its preservation. This is *held to be* "the definition of justice which is really founded on nature" (φύσει).[14]

But then, in conscious opposition to this physicalist conception of nature, Plato gives his own answer. "God, as the ancient saying has it, holding the beginning, the middle, and the
end of all beings, moves in a straight path according to nature
(κατὰ φύσιν), and justice always attends Him."[15] This cosmic
order of nature carries its own norms within it. That which follows these norms achieves some degree of fulfilment. That which
deviates is eliminated. In the case of men who are capable of
exercising choice in the matter, those who would be happy must
order their lives in accordance with natural law: those who seek
power in the madness of *hubris* are justly punished by frustration and destruction.[16] Here is a clear expression of Plato's conception of a moral law founded on the very nature of things and
thus enforced by natural sanctions. Nature determines what
modes of being are good for a thing, whatever it may be, and
also their order of greater or lesser importance. Thus, wealth is
to be sought "only for the sake of the body, and the welfare of
the body for the sake of the soul; and this order of subordination exists by nature."[17]

It is clear that Plato, like other philosophers of natural law, regards the world as a vast complex of diverse entities, whose transformations are subject to a cosmic law. So far as the law is obeyed, these entities sustain one another, and each achieves some measure of existential fulfilment. Disobedience is inexorably punished in the long run by privation and destruction. This order has been established by a living intelligence. But this intelligence has not proceeded arbitrarily, nor has it imposed an alien law on lawless entities. It has rather inserted this law into the original existential structure of the thing. Hence, it is a natural law, not capriciously imposed, but united with the very nature of each entity.

This gives rise to further questions about this existential nature. Let us see how Plato answers them.

B. NATURE AS THE EIDETIC STRUCTURE
OF CONCRETE ENTITIES

According to Plato, the concrete objects of the surrounding world are composite. Each of them results from a mixture of something vague and indefinite (ἄπειρον) with something fixed and determinate (πέρας).[18] The word nature (φύσις) is often used throughout the dialogues in referring to this definite structure which determines each thing to be of a certain kind, and distinguishes it from other kinds. In this sense, *nature* is equivalent to the essential form (εἶδος or ἰδέα), which makes each concrete entity *what it is*. This structure underlies and determines the dynamism and activity of the thing.

Thus, we are told in the *Phaedrus*[19] that the rhetorician who desires to influence the soul must first apprehend the soul itself as clearly as possible and find out whether it is one or many. Such a clear apprehension and exact description of structure— "this as we say is to reveal the nature."[20] In the *Republic*[21] the question is raised as to whether the painter attempts to represent each thing as it is "in its very nature" (ἐν τῇ φύσει) or in its pure structure. If so, he would be a scientist or a philosopher. But this is not the case. The purpose of the artist is different. He is trying to represent the concrete existent with all its individual qualities and peculiar accidents. Here *nature* is being used to refer to the pure form, or *idea*, as Plato calls it. Individual entities only imitate or participate in these forms which are never perfectly present. But the finest examples of concrete things come sufficiently close so that they may suggest their archetypes to the discerning intellect.

Thus, in the myth of the *Phaedrus*, when the charioteer sees a very beautiful object, he is reminded of "the nature of the beautiful,"[22] the pure idea of beauty itself. In the *Philebus* (25 A) we are told that when we see the similarities of those existential factors which are subject to more or less, we gather them all together and impress on them the seal of a single nature (φύσιν).[23] There are many other instances of such usage in the dialogues.[24]

Nature in this sense means the essential whatness of a thing, the structure which determines it, and distinguishes it from other entities. But this is only one factor in the composite existence of finite things. What else is present? We must now examine the answer Plato gives to this question.

C. NATURE AS FORMALLY DETERMINED TENDENCY

It is quite clear that Plato often uses nature in a wider sense to include something more than the form or essence (οὐσία) of a concrete thing. Thus he says in the *Phaedrus* that the rhetorician who wishes to learn how to act on the soul must "exactly reveal the essence of its nature"[25] which implies that the nature includes *other* structural factors than form. There are many other places where he refers to the composite nature of an entity, as at *Republic* 495 A where he speaks definitely of "the parts of the philosophic nature." What are the other parts? A key to the answer is indicated by Plato's habit of connecting change (γένεσις) with nature (φύσις) as at *Laws* 892 C and 942 E 1. The formal nature of a concrete thing determines it to change and to interact with other entities in certain appropriate ways.

As we have seen, no doctrine is more essential to the philosophy of natural law than that of the unfinished or tendential character of finite existence. There is hardly a page in Plato which does not either explicitly express or imply this doctrine. It is perhaps most strikingly asserted in a well-known passage of the *Phaedo* (75) which has attracted the attention of many commentators.[26]

Pure forms such as equality and justice are never wholly present in the concrete beings which only partake of them. Nevertheless, the forms are somehow *partially* present in their imitations, seeking and tending to perfect themselves so far as possible.[27] This thought is also expressed at Republic 473 A, where it is said that concrete practice always tends to the truth but always falls short of it. The imperfect forms of actual entities are ever striving to complete themselves. The word *nature* is often used not only for structure but also for the dynamic tendencies determined by this structure. Thus in the interesting passage of the *Phaedrus* to which we have already referred, Plato tells us that in studying any nature (φύσις), we must first try to understand its pure eidetic structure (εἴδη) and then the active and passive powers determined by this structure, how it acts and how it suffers "by nature."[28] Such a natural tendency may be thwarted and distorted, but it cannot be wholly eliminated, for as we are told in the *Timaeus*[29] what is, for example, contracted against nature (παρὰ φύσιν) fights to free itself from obstruction in accordance with nature (κατὰ φύσιν). The nature of every being disposes or fits it for certain acts which fulfil this nature. Thus, justice is defined in the *Republic* as rendering to every man his due, or enabling him to practice "that for which his nature is best fitted."[30] In this more inclusive sense, the nature of any entity refers not only to its essential structure, but to the active dispositions and tendencies determined by this structure.[31]

Since the world is not a chaos, subrational tendencies are fulfilled for the most part, though there are always exceptions. Plato sometimes uses the word *nature* to refer to these regular sequences determined by recurrent tendencies. Thus, monstrous births are not natural, but that a horse should generate a horse is according to nature.[32] Human tendencies, however, do not work in this automatic way. They are subject to spontaneous rational control, which may obstruct or distort the basic tendencies of nature through ignorance or intemperance. Nevertheless, these basic tendencies cannot be entirely eliminated.

As opposed to incidental desires, there are certain necessary needs as for food and drink which must be realized to some degree if human life is to be lived at all. They cannot be escaped. Also if pursued under rational control, they are not only apparently but really beneficial. We pursue such tendencies by "*a necessity of nature.*"[33] The same distinction plays an important role in the argument of the *Phaedo*, which is often interpreted as advocating the most extreme and unqualified asceticism. This, however, is not the case. The philosopher does not despise material things as such, but only "in so far as there is no great necessity of having them" (*Phaedo* 64 E 1; cf. E 5, 67 A 3–4, and 83 B 7). There are also other natural propensities which cannot be altogether rooted out.

The most important of these by far is the cognitive urge. This tendency, of course, may be terribly neglected and distorted. Nevertheless, it cannot be completely eliminated from any human life. "By its very nature (φύσει) every human soul beholds real being."[34] Reason is clearly the most accurate and comprehensive of all our cognitive faculties. Ordinarily it is suppressed or weakened by neglect. Nevertheless by nature it is the ruling faculty. Reason alone can lead us to the human good.

But how? What is the right way? And how is it determined? Let us see how Plato answers these questions.

D. NATURE AS THE CORRECT ORDERING
OF INCIPIENT TENDENCY

Virtue (ἀρετή) for Plato is a universal ontological category by no means restricted to man. At *Laws* 903 B we are told that all things are ordered to the preservation and excellence (ἀρετή) of the whole. When "each entity so far as possible suffers and does what is fitting," this is its virtue or excellence.[35] What is this more exactly?

We have already called attention to the tendential character of all finite existence. Each being is incomplete and tending towards its fulfilment or good. But this fulfilment cannot be achieved in an instant. It can be attained only in time through a succession of acts ordered in accordance with natural law. This law is enforced by inexorable natural sanctions.[36] In so far as the *initial* tendencies are feeble or misdirected, the fulfilment will not be achieved. "The vices of injustice, pride, and intemperance destroy us."[37] The properly ordered tendencies of virtue lead to safety and well-being. Hence, virtue is defined in the *Meno* as "the power of attaining what is good."[38] But "the virtue of an entity, instrument, nonliving body, soul, or any living creature does not happen by luck, but by the arrangement, and order, and art which is infused into each of them."[39]

Virtue is the initial ordering and directing of tendencies in such a way that they may achieve the fulfilment of the entity in question. Noncognitive beings for the most part have been endowed with properly ordered initial tendencies by the causes of nature. Their virtues are automatic. But this is not the case with man. Human agents have been given rational powers of self-direction. They must order their initial tendencies by habits which are largely under their own control. Thus, the *Republic* refers to the individual virtues as "forms and habits."[40] When these habits are rightly ordered, they can attain human fulfilment and are the salvation of man. What is the standard of rightness? Does Plato use the word *nature* when speaking of virtue in this normative sense? The answer is most emphatically *yes*.

The mode of ordering initial tendencies which is fitting (πρέπον), proper (προσῆκον), and right (ὀρθόν)[41] is one which agrees with the needs of nature. Hence, at both the subhuman level and the human level those virtuous acts which ought to take place are constantly described as being in accordance with nature (κατὰ φύσιν), each nature having its own proper virtue. Thus, we are told that "the first shoot of any plant being well advanced at the very beginning towards the virtue of its own nature has an advantage on reaching maturity, and this is true of other plants, of wild and tame animals, and of man."[42]

In the case of man, certain of his tendencies are more important than others, goods of the body being subordinate to goods of the soul, and all to the supreme virtue of wisdom. This is not an arbitrary order but one which has been determined by nature (φύσει).[43] Right action is described as agreeing with nature. The ideal community controlled by genuine wisdom is referred to as "a city which would be established *in accordance with nature.*"[44] This notion is applied not only to the ordering of essential phases of conduct, but also to less serious matters.

Thus, in the *Cratylus* we are told that there is "a correct and *natural* way" of giving names.[45] Certain sayings of Homer are referred to in the *Laws* as "according to God and *according to nature.*"[46] Even drinking, it is said, should be rightly ordered "*in accordance with nature.*"[47] The influence of reason must penetrate into the incipient phases of all human tendencies, ordering them into a coherent pattern of action which is capable of fulfilling our many-sided human nature. Such ordered action is Plato's conception of human virtue, which has not only the desire to achieve the good (all men have this), but the actual power of achieving it.[48]

What, then, is the relation of virtue to goodness? For Plato, they are evidently closely connected. The good is virtuous—certainly impossible without virtue—and virtue is good, the most important good of all. And yet there is a distinction between the two. How does Plato conceive of the relation between them? Perhaps his use of the term *nature* may help us to shed some light on this important question.

E. NATURE AS EXISTENTIAL FULFILMENT

For Plato, goodness or value is an ontological category applying to all existence, and by no means restricted to man. Its primary mark is sufficiency. The good, we are told, "is sufficient and complete and such as to be sought by all plants and animals which could live in this way all their lives."[49] It is important to notice here that the goodness of living creatures is not a fixed state ever to be finally reached, for their life is a process. Such a fixed state would be death. The good of a finite creature is rather a way of life, penetrating through the whole of the process. Plato apparently conceives of this kind of value as an ordering of the process in which each earlier stage leads to the next with a minimum of distortion and privation, so that the whole sequence—beginning, middle, and end especially, expresses most authentically the complete nature of the entity in question. At any given stage of development the more it has fulfilled its capacities, and the less it needs from the outside, the better. Goodness is the realization of tendency.

God alone is perfect and complete. He "lacks no perfection of beauty or virtue."[50] All finite entities are limited. But limitation is not the same as evil for Plato. Evil is not mere lack, but the lack of something obtainable which is required by the finite nature. There are several passages in the *Laws* which in some translations easily give the impression that Plato is asserting the radical evil of human nature itself. But when read more carefully, these passages may be seen to contain important qualifications which are inconsistent with such an interpretation. Two of them (691 C and 713 C) assert the limitation of human nature in its inability to bear supreme power without falling into pride. Two others (854 A and 875 B) deal with the weakness of human nature which subjects us to temptations of avarice and selfishness. But it is never asserted that this weakness can never be overcome. No matter how distorted the tendencies of an entity may later become, its original nature for the most part has all that is required. Nowhere is there any blanket condemnation of human nature as such. There is no reason in human nature itself why men should not realize its capacities and thus turn themselves into "a form and likeness of God."[51]

Value is the fulfilment of natural tendency. Evil is the unnecessary obstruction and frustration of such tendency. It is always described in negative, or rather privative, terms. Thus, injustice puts a man at war with himself and makes it "impossible for him to do anything."[52] Groups of thieves and brigands are able to act in so far as they maintain some honor among themselves. But "if they become *perfectly* unjust, they are *perfectly* unable to act."[53] Evil is always the privation of some good. The possession of money and material things is a good. The corresponding evil is poverty. Health is the good of the body. Its evil is disease and deformity. Virtue is the health of the soul. Vice is injustice and the lack of knowledge.[54] Good and evil are existential categories. To exist in a condition of realization and fulfilment is good. Evil is nonexistence and destruction.[55]

If an entity is to be in a sound condition it must realize its existential capacities. But this is not all. The realization must

fit the peculiar nature of the thing. What is good for one type is
not necessarily good for another. This is the second major characteristic of all goodness. It is not any fulfilment, but that which
is proper and adapted to the entity. Thus, at *Republic* 586 C,
Plato tells us "that is best for each entity which is most peculiar
to it."[56] In the *Timaeus* he says that there is only one way to exercise therapy over any being. That is "to give it the nurture
and motions which are proper to it."[57] Here again, nature is the
standard. The good is what is really natural. Plato makes his
meaning clear by two further uses of the term—the first negative, the second positive.

We must not confuse what is good with our own opinions and
wishes. We are in no position to legislate what is really good and
bad. This humanistic pride is a delusion of utilitarianism. It is
nature that first legislates independent of all arbitrary human
decree. Hence, throughout the dialogues this word is used to
suggest what is really sound and healthy as opposed to our subjective opinions and desires. The pragmatic followers of Protagoras are ready to grant with respect to what is merely advan-
tageous for a state, that one counselor may be better than another. But when it comes to the ultimate questions concerning
goodness and justice they collapse into relativism and stubbornly assert that "no one of these has by nature an essence of its
own, but that the common opinion of men is true when it is
adopted, and remains true as long as it is held."[58] In the *Cratylus*[59] Plato writes: "actions are performed according to their real
nature, and not according to our opinion." In these and many
other passages the word nature (φύσις) is used in a realistic
sense, to mean what actually exists as opposed to our subjective
opinions and desires. Real goodness has nothing to do with our
wishes. In so far as it ever exists, it really exists in nature, independently of what we think, and according to nature, not our
desire.

How, then, may we determine the real nature of an entity?
Plato again suggests his answer to this question by another usage of the term (φύσις). In the *Philebus* (44 E), he tells us that
"if we wish to discover the nature (φύσις) of any form—the
hard for instance—we should look at the hardest, rather than

the least hard."[60] All changing things are incomplete and tendential. To find out what is at the root of their tendencies, therefore, we should look at those examples which are "most extreme
and most intense."[61] Human nature will be observed at its best
in those individuals who have pushed their capacities to the
very breaking point. Here we shall find the most complete and
authentic human life. But we must be on our guard against fic-
tion and pretense. We must penetrate through outward display
to what is really there *in nature*, looking for situations in which
the tendency is able to display itself in act spontaneously, from
the agent himself.

Thus, if we are interested in finding out whether an individual
"really and not fictively respects justice, and really hates injustice . . ."[62] we must put him in a situation where his habits have
free play. We must observe how he deals with slaves, how he
treats the helpless under his charge. In such situations, his real
nature will be revealed. If he is just to those having no power
over him, this is more likely to be a genuine manifestation of his
nature, springing spontaneously from within, rather than a
mere response to external pressures. Finally, if any authentic
fulfilment is to be achieved, persistent concentration and order
will be required. Hence, random variety and lawlessness are not
the soul "in her truest nature."[63] These are all marks of goodness. Genuine fulfilment can be attained only with intensive effort, arising spontaneously from within, and consistently ordered to a coherent objective.

In the light of this analysis, we may attempt to cast some
light on Plato's conception of the intimate relation between virtue and goodness. On the one hand, they are distinct, and yet
on the other hand, so closely fused together that he often seems
to speak of them as though they were one. The meaning of this
should now be intelligible. Good and evil are not to be analyzed
in terms of formal structure (properties and qualities) alone.
They are rather dynamic modes of existence with a temporal
history. Thus, human good and evil begin as incipient tendencies and "spring from the soul . . . flowing out from thence . . ."
into fulfilment or deprivation.[64] The right ordering of these first
tendencies in accordance with nature is virtue—the chief cause
of good.

But *goodness* is fulfilment—the actual *being*[65] and full *posses-sion*[66] of realization. Virtue is the chief cause of good. But owing to the limitations of human nature, other good things like health of body, physical strength, and money are also required for the fullest realization.[67] The lack of such good things can keep us from happiness, and if sufficiently extreme may even lead to misery.[68] But the virtues are higher in the order of na-ture. Hence, to lack these is an even greater misery, disease of the soul itself, the inner, moving principle. To do injustice is worse than to suffer it. Virtue is the inner power to act and exist in accordance with nature. Finite goodness is the actualizing of this power, with the aid and support of other external forces. Hence, virtue is included within goodness as its most essential part, as a power is included in its realization.

In terms of subjective experience, the feelings of obligation and oughtness belong to the earlier stages of the human act. They are associated with virtue. The feelings of satisfaction and fulfilment belong to the final stages. They are associated with goodness.[69] But the latter if really natural and genuine cannot occur without the former.

Section III. The Concept of Nature ($\phi \acute{v} \sigma \iota s$) in Plato's Philosophy

We have now completed this study of the ontological presup-positions of Platonic ethics which are suggested by five distinct senses of the word *nature*. These senses are widely expressed in the dialogues, as well as in the later literature of realistic ethics, and even in the common language of our own time. To the atomistic mind, with an exclusive interest in logical separation and analysis, these distinct meanings given to a single word will be regarded as a manifestation of intellectual irresponsibility. Professor Lovejoy has so regarded them in his *Essays in the His-tory of Ideas*.[70] But the philosopher, interested in understanding the basic structure of the changing world, will view it in a differ-ent light. He will see in it an attempt to suggest the underlying unity of this composite structure, quite possibly verifiable by empirical evidence. Unless the universe is actually a chaos of separate logical atoms, to understand it adequately we need not only narrow concepts to express its distinguishable phases **but** also broad concepts to express the ways in which these are connected.

The word *nature* as used by Plato is certainly such a concept, one of the widest and richest in his whole vocabulary, and one of those which he most constantly employs. In this respect at least, he is a founder of the realistic tradition of natural-law philosophy. I believe that the results of our analysis, if not mistaken, indicate a connection far deeper than one of mere terminology. There are definite Platonic doctrines which are essential to any ethics of natural law. I shall now try to show this in summarizing our results.

As we have seen, Plato uses the word *nature* in referring to the whole world order of mutually supporting forces and tendencies. Some such view as this is a necessary presupposition of any realistic ethics which holds that moral norms are not man-made constructions. Whatever else they may be, norms are certainly principles of order. Hence those who believe that the real world is a chaos of disconnected atoms must hold that norms are arbitrary human constructions.

Plato also held that the changing entities of the world have structure, and often uses the word *nature* in a second sense in referring to this form or *eidos* of an individual thing. Nature in this sense is imperfect and incomplete, but it lies at the root of every concrete being, determining its characteristic modes of action. He tells us that the pure forms partake of the good. From this it follows that the imperfect natures of concrete things are also good. Norms are not invented by man. They are rather found embedded in the natures of things.

But the good itself lies beyond all form and essence.[71] Perhaps the most plausible interpretation of this obscure statement that has yet been made is that of Mr. G. C. Field who suggests that the imperfect forms of the natural world are tending or striving to complete themselves. This completion of being, which lies ever beyond them, is what is meant by good.[72] Whether or not this is the real meaning of this passage, we have shown that it is certainly the meaning of many others. The concrete forms are all tending to realize or complete themselves so far as this is possible.

In fact, Plato often uses the word *nature* in a third sense to mean not only the concrete *eidos* but the tending or striving which this determines in every actual entity. This conception is also necessary for any realistic ethics, since if reality were not tendential, but finally fixed and finished, ethics itself would have no meaning. It is a practical science concerned with the direction of active tendencies towards possible goods. Without a ubiquitous factor of unfinished tendency, ethics would be impossible and absurd.

Plato asserts that virtue is the fitting direction of these tendencies towards their natural fulfilment. Virtue is a general ontological category, for each thing has its own peculiar law of sound development. In man, however, it takes on a new importance because of his rational power of guiding incipient action into alternative channels. Unless he first understands the law of his own nature, he will misuse this power and act in vicious and destructive ways. Plato does not refer to this moral law as a law of nature, but he does come very close to it. His usual formula is by nature, or according to nature (κατὰ φύσιν). All virtuous action must be according to nature. This is a fourth related meaning of the term *phusis*—the rules or law according to which virtuous action must be directed. It is by no means accidental that the word *nature* is used in this connection, for in Plato's opinion such rules must be founded on, and derived from the actual nature, factually found in man.

The good of any finite entity towards which in a basic sense it must be necessarily striving is the fulfilment peculiar to its nature. Thus, the good for man is the authentic living of a genuine human life. The word *nature* is finally used in a fifth sense to refer to such authentic examples of existence, realized to a pre-eminent degree. This conception also is required by any realistic ethics. Such an ethics must hold that existence is radically good—that evil is privation. If so, the supreme value for any entity is to avoid frustration and realize all its natural capacities to the highest possible degree.

The commonly accepted opinion at the present time is that natural-law philosophy began with the Stoics. In the light of this examination of the Platonic ontology, I believe that I am justified in saying that this is a profound mistake. The unusual, but correct statement of Professor Solmsen,[73] "it is evident that the Stoics are greatly in his debt," is not only true, but an understatement. Similar ontological doctrines were held by all the important later representatives of realistic philosophy from Aristotle to Aquinas and Hooker. Nor is this to be understood as a sheer historical accident. As we have tried to show, these doctrines are not a mere jumble of disconnected concepts. They constitute a coherent theory of interconnected parts capable of accounting for wide areas of empirical fact accessible to all.

Section IV. DERIVED MORAL PRINCIPLES

So far, our study of Plato's realistic ethics has focused primarily on its ontological presuppositions. These presuppositions are really required by any ethics of natural law. But many defenders of such a theory have left them undeveloped. In order to give a further test to our thesis that Plato must be regarded as the founder of this tradition, we shall now turn to the Platonic ethics as such. Of course this can be only artificially separated from his ontology. From Plato's point of view, ethics results from an application of general metaphysical principles to the human situation. In considering the Platonic ontology, we have already outlined the ethical view it supplies.

Hence, in dealing with his ethics we may be very brief, merely referring to certain specifically ethical passages which show that Plato was aware of the basic moral implications of his ontology. We shall find that his ethics is clearly characterized by three doctrines which are opposed to modern utilitarianism and intuitionism but which are essential to any realistic ethics and which, as we have seen, are found in all the major representatives of the natural-law tradition.

A. THE UNIVERSALITY OF NATURAL LAW

We have already touched on this topic in our consideration of Popper's attack on Plato as a racialist (chap. 1, pp. 25 ff.). As we saw, there is no textual evidence to verify this accusation. It is quite clear that according to Plato, human nature and its essential tendencies are shared in common by all men. To confirm this statement, we may turn to certain myths of creation not yet examined where we find uniformly clear-cut assertions of the unity of mankind. Thus in the *Timaeus*[74] all souls are said to have been made according to one formula, and the myth of the *Politicus*[75] speaks of the whole human flock and of one divine shepherd.

Turning now from the myths to other passages, we find in the *Meno*[76] that virtue is applied equally to men and women in general—to young and old, to bond and free, and finally to "all human creatures." Plato's discussions of virtue, of philosophy, of law, and of the soul are uniformly permeated with a universal feeling. Thus, the philosopher-king thesis of the *Republic*[77] asserts that unless philosophers are kings, there will be no end of troubles for all of mankind. The *Republic* claims to be not merely a Hellenic ideal, but one for man in general, barbarian as well as Greek.[78] The subject of the *Phaedo* is not the soul of Greeks or Persians but the soul of man. The unwritten laws of nature[79] hold universally and underlie the written positive laws of every genuinely human community.

B. NORMS GROUNDED ON NATURE

There are a great many passages which we might select to show that Plato's conception of virtuous action is founded on his conception of human nature. We shall have to be content with brief comments on a few typical quotations.

Let us turn first of all to the discussion of virtue in general, at the end of the First Book of the *Republic*.[80] Here, Plato makes it quite clear that, for him, virtue is a general ontological category. Each thing has a certain nature which determines it to a certain function (ἔργον). This is true of the different organs of the human body. The *ergon* of the eyes is to see, that of the ears to hear. Living entities, like a horse, have a certain *ergon*. Even inorganic things are determined to act in certain ways. When any kind of thing performs its natural *ergon* well, without obstruction and interference, this is virtue (ἀρετή). The human soul, the animating principle of the human body, is no exception. It has a certain nature which determines it to certain modes of action, its *ergon*, which it alone can perform, such as managing and deliberating, which are specifically mentioned. The effective performance of these natural functions is virtue: their warping and distortion is vice.

Each individual person owes it to the nature he possesses to act in those virtuous ways which fulfil it.[81] Acts which warp and violate the nature of man and his essential tendencies are unfitting, inappropriate. This is the Platonic conception of duty or obligation. Since virtuous, dutiful action fulfils our nature, it is, of course, absurd to speak of any natural opposition between duty and interest. Thus, when Thrasymachus defines justice as the interest of the stronger, Socrates does not question the general form of this definition.[82] Justice is the interest of the stronger, for justice alone can realize human life which requires rational co-operation. The real question is: what *is* the interest of the stronger? Thrasymachus' superman is perhaps mistaken in his view of human nature and the acts which it requires.

Human society also is based upon nature. It arises not from any arbitrary convention or compact, but from basic needs. Without social co-operation, the infant cannot be nurtured and educated, nor can our manifold basic needs be fulfilled. The real creator of the city is our human need,[83] a phrase repeated in practically the same words by Hooker and other defenders of natural law. Later on, these common human needs were referred to as human rights, in distinction from incidental appetites. Plato does not use this terminology. But the concept is clearly and unambiguously stated.

C. THE GOOD FOR MAN AS THE REALIZATION OF HUMAN NATURE

Original nature is in a state of deficiency or need. Hence, Plato thinks of the human good as the fulfilment of such need. Whatever other characteristics may belong to it, the good is always complete or sufficient. Thus at *Philebus* 60 C, he says: "whatever living being possesses the good always, altogether, and in all ways has no further need of anything, but is completely sufficient";[84] and again at 61 A the good is said to be needless or complete.[85]

Living entities are always complex. There are certain subordinate parts with subordinate functions, and higher parts with primary or ruling functions. To reach and to maintain the condition of goodness or sufficiency, each part must perform its natural function. When insubordination and conflict arise, no part can properly perform its *ergon*, and the entity remains in a deprived or evil state. Moral vice or disorder is thus analogous to disease in the body, an analogy of which Plato makes constant use, together with most defenders of natural-law philosophy down to the present day. All of these theses are clearly exemplified and explicitly stated in an interesting passage at the end of the Fourth Book of the *Republic*.[86]

Certain parts of the body as well as certain parts of that by which we live (the soul) are ordered in a certain way, being thus by nature.[87] Justice and injustice in the soul are analogous to health and disease in the body. "To produce health is to establish that condition in which the physical organs rule over one another and are ruled by one another in accordance with nature (κατὰ φύσιν), while to cause disease is to establish that condition in which the different parts of the body rule over one another and are ruled by one another against nature (παρὰ φύσιν). . . . And is it not likewise the production of justice in the soul to establish that condition in which the different faculties of the soul rule over one another and are ruled by one another in accordance with nature (κατὰ φύσιν), while injustice is to establish that condition in which they rule and are ruled against nature (παρὰ φύσιν)?"[88]

Virtue is the natural functioning or health of the different faculties of the soul; vice an unnatural, disordered functioning, or disease. At 445 B we are told that the very nature (φύσις) of that by which we live is disordered and corrupted by vice. This comparison of virtue with health is of constant occurrence in the dialogues, as for example at *Gorgias* 478 and 503. Human nature is active or tendential. The good for man in general is the realization of his nature.

The texts show that Plato held firmly to three basic tenets of the philosophy of natural law: first, that the general pattern of virtuous action required for this is the same for all men everywhere; second, that certain virtuous modes of action are founded on human nature just as the healthy functioning of the body is founded on its physical structure; and third, that the end of man is the realization or completion of this nature. Some vague conception of moral law is doubtless as old as man himself. But in the West at least, Plato was the first philosopher to work out an exact and coherent theory of natural law.

Let us now turn to Aristotle. What does he say about the ontological and moral principles we have been considering? Is he a moral realist as we have defined this term? Granted that the words law of nature are rarely found in the Aristotelian texts, what of the concept? Can it be found in the structure of his thought, though expressed in other language? We shall consider these questions in the following chapter.

CHAPTER SIX

THE ARISTOTELIAN THEORY OF
NATURAL LAW

THE principles of natural law which underlie the Aristotelian practical philosophy have often been slurred over by
such modern commentators as Ross, who never even mentions them in his book.[1] Others have seriously distorted them.
Thus, Nicolai Hartmann has recently used Aristotle in his attempt to defend an ethics of abstract essences, based on an
extreme ontological dualism of fact versus value.[2] Prichard, on
the other hand, after a minute study of the *Nicomachean Ethics*,
without regard to the *Physics* and *Metaphysics*, finally persuades
himself that *agathon*, for Aristotle, means no more than what is
productive of happiness or pleasure.[3]

I think it can be shown from the texts that such interpretations are inadequate and distorted. The textual evidence is
abundant and clear. As has often been pointed out by careful
critics, Aristotle's *Ethics* cannot be understood except by plac-
ing it within the framework of his metaphysics and philosophy
of nature, where the notions of natural form or structure, and
the actualization of potential or incomplete being play a crucially important role. The Aristotelian ethics is an application of
general ontological principles to the peculiar nature of man. In
studying these, we shall become aware of their moral implications. Hence our consideration of Aristotle's ethics may be very
brief. We need only comment on certain passages which show
Aristotle also recognized the three basic principles which, as we
have noted, are held in common by all authentic representatives
of moral realism: (1) the universality of moral law; (2) norms
grounded on nature; and (3) the good for man as realization of
human nature.

Let us now turn to the ontological presuppositions of the
Aristotelian ethics. As in the case of Plato, we shall find it con-

venient to examine them in the light of five different meanings which Aristotle also recognizes in the term *nature* (φύσις). A casual glance at the great Bonitz Index will convince even the most casual student that this is a key term of Aristotelian philosophy. As we shall now try to show, it serves here as in Plato to unify the same basic ontological conceptions. After examining these foundational principles, we shall then turn our attention to the Aristotelian ethics as such.

Section I. THE ONTOLOGICAL FOUNDATIONS OF ARISTOTELIAN ETHICS

A nonsubjectivist or realistic ethics must show that norms are not imposed by human interest or arbitrary decree but are actually founded on the independent existence of things. If then, as we believe, Aristotle is to be regarded as one of the founders of natural-law philosophy, we must be able to show that his basic moral categories are derived from ontological structure. This we shall now attempt to do by examining his use of the term *nature*, which we have seen to be of crucial importance in following the thought of Plato. Was Aristotle a follower of his master in this respect? Did he also use this pivotal concept as a means of unifying norms with factual existence? Did he employ this term in the five ways we have noted to be characteristic of Platonic usage as referring to: (1) the world as a normative order; (2) the definite structure of a finite entity; (3) its dynamic tendencies; (4) the correct ordering of these tendencies; and finally, (5) the good condition of existential fulfilment? Let us now examine these questions one by one.

A. NATURE AS NORMATIVE WORLD ORDER

Aristotle habitually uses the word *nature* (φύσις) in referring to the changing universe as a whole. Thus, in the *Physics* he speaks of the principles selected by certain of his predecessors to explain "the nature of all being."[4] And in the *Metaphysics* he mentions the recurrent prejudice of scientists who become so obsessed with those material things which are the proper object of their study that they unfortunately come to think that they are "dealing with the whole of nature and being."[5] The world of

nature includes not only the motions of material things but also
man and his mental acts, as well as the first unchanging source
of change.[6]

This vast realm of ceaseless transformation and evolution is
not a random chaos. Our empirical observations do not extend
very far. But they indicate conclusively that these changes are
subject to a cosmic order. Though here and there we may find
striking exceptions, for the most part "nature does nothing in
vain, nor does it omit anything really necessary."[7] Working always in orderly ways, "nature ever tends towards the best of
what is possible."[8] If we examine these changes from a long-
range point of view, we discover anti-chance and orderly procedure "in all the works of nature."[9] The forms of human art are
not mere arbitrary inventions. "The resulting end of the generations and combinations of nature is the basic form of the beautiful,"[10] and the highest manifestations of human art are modeled
after these.

"The nature of the whole universe"[11] is compared to an army
made up of independent individuals whose activities are nevertheless "ordered together somehow for a common end."[12] They
are like the members of a single household each of whom contributes something towards the good of all. The subordinate participants in this ordered life, the animals and children, like the
natural elements, make a necessary contribution in a largely
unconscious way by random coming and going. But the more
mature members, understanding what is required of them, are
bound by the moral law.[13]

We have chosen only a few examples. But this conception of
nature as a vast field of ordered existence literally permeated
with norms is found throughout the writings of Aristotle, stated
of course in his own peculiar way. But it is essentially the same
conception as that of Plato—one which, as we have seen, is
necessarily presupposed by any nonsubjectivistic moral theory.

B. NATURE AS THE EIDETIC STRUCTURE
OF FINITE ENTITIES

According to Aristotle, each individual substance has an indwelling structure (μορφή) of its own. This determines the mat-

ter out of which the substance has been generated to be something of a certain kind. It also determines the powers and tendencies of the substance, since "in the order of nature from qualitatively similar things, similar occurrences flow."[14] As a possible object of knowledge, this structure is called an *eidos* (εἶδος).

The concrete substances of nature, including man, which have come into existence by an evolutionary process, also embody the matter out of which they have come. Since this matter is a necessary aspect of the constitution of any changing entity, it is also called *nature* (φύσις). But the form which makes this into the kind of thing it is, is more important. Hence, in the first and strictest sense, *nature* means definite structure.[15] Thus, the wood which is only potentially a bed does not become actually a bed until it receives this form in act.[16] *Nature* is used in this sense throughout the Aristotelian texts. When describing the process of vital generation in the *Metaphysics*, Aristotle points out that what is generated has a certain form (εἶδος) as well as that which generates it—"the so-called eidetic nature."[17] In the *Generation of Animals*, he states that of the two structural phases of any evolutionary being (matter and form), "the eidetic nature should (by nature) rule over the other."[18]

Many distinct phases are held together in the being of a natural or changing entity. The word *nature* is used to indicate the unity of this complex constitution. But the most essential and primary phase is the determinate form which makes the thing what it is. Nature (φύσις), for Aristotle, means this determinate structure which lies at the root of all the resulting powers and activities of the entity. It is to these that we must now turn.

C. NATURE AS FORMALLY DETERMINED TENDENCY

Aristotle is primarily a philosopher of change and evolution. According to him, all the entities which we directly experience, including ourselves, are in a ceaseless process of transformation. A natural entity is one which is tending or moving towards something. As he states specifically in the *Physics*, "all the beings of nature seem to have in themselves a source of movement or rest."[19] What is this indwelling source? This question cannot be given a *simple* answer. That which is absolutely simple cannot change. Whatever else change may be, it is certainly something complex, with several sources.[20] To regard it as though it were simple—as a unitary "event" or point instant—is to destroy it. Change is something composite. What, then, are its sources?

One of these is something incomplete, for change is never finished, but always on the way towards something beyond. Aristotle calls this factor potency (δύναμις). But it is never absolutely indeterminate. It is moving in one way rather than in another, towards some determinate goal. What is responsible for this definite factor in change? Aristotle gives his answer while discussing the different meanings of the term *nature* in Book V of the *Metaphysics* (the so-called Book of Definitions). "The source of change," he says, "in all natural entities is essence (or form)."[21] In the case of substantial change, the most radical kind of transformation, the form is present only potentially. But in the case of accidental changes of a single substance, this form is actually present, determining the tendency to proceed in a certain direction towards further fulfilment.

Aristotle constantly uses the word *nature* (φύσις) in this richer, derived sense when he refers to the definite forces and powers of the actual world. Thus in the treatise on the *Generation of Animals* he says that nature is "the active tendency" of a thing,[22] and then continues "this is the *nature* of each entity that works within plants and in all animals."[23] This notion is well illustrated in his doctrine concerning the human soul, the essence or structure of the whole living body,[24] and the ground of its being.[25] But the soul is also the source of movement and tendency,[26] of locomotion,[27] of growth,[28] of nutrition and reproduction,[29] and, indeed, of all the vital powers.[30]

It is because of this fact—similar forms determine similar tendencies[31]—that scientific induction is possible and future events predictable. Except in case of a peculiar coincidence involving the counteracting tendencies of an extraneous factor, similar entities, *for the most part* act in similar ways. Aristotle's formula here, *for the most part*, was also used by Plato.[32]

It is extremely important, of course, that natural tendencies should be properly directed during their early stages. In non-cognitive beings, this direction for the most part occurs automatically by the simple presence of the form. But in man, who is capable of rational self-direction, this does not automatically occur. The form of human nature is, of course, present in every human individual, as well as the vague urge towards realization. But the proper direction of this complex initial tendency into proper fields of action is left to human cognition. Unless the cognitive faculties provide this proper guidance, human life falls into chaos. But what is meant by "proper" in this connection? What is the real moral standard? Let us now consider Aristotle's answer to this question.

D. NATURE AS THE CORRECT ORDERING
OF INCIPIENT TENDENCY

So far, we have been merely describing observable facts. Nature is a vast order of interconnected changing things. Each entity is marked by a formal nature of its own, which determines its natural tendencies. This may be a rough description. But it is one which is certainly verified by the data of experience. These are facts. But what about norms? We now tend to think of norms and values as being radically separated from facts. Is there any evidence that Aristotle disagreed with this modern conception? As in the case of Plato, the answer is emphatically *yes!* How, then, did he conceive of this connection between norms and facts? Let us now ask this question of the texts. Once again, they tell us that the word *nature* (φύσις) plays a crucially important role in the Aristotelian answer.

The term *virtue* (ἀρετή) is clearly a normative word expressing both obligation and value for Aristotle. Thus, he says in the *Nicomachean Ethics* that "the virtue of man" is that "incipient active tendency (ἕξις) by which a man becomes good and by which he performs his proper function well."[33] But it is not man alone who possesses virtues. A body also has its virtue. Horses and other animals have their appropriate virtues.[34] The eye has its proper virtue.[35] In fact, "the virtue of anything whatsoever is what brings it into well-being, and makes it perform its function well."[36] Virtue or its opposite is necessarily connected with this tendential structure. When the tendency is properly directed to its natural fulfilment, this is virtue. Hence, it is not surprising that vice or evil action is described as "against nature,"[37] whereas virtue, "the direction of tendencies towards their proper activities, is according to nature."[38]

In the first, initial stages when tendencies are very weak, they are in an indeterminate state of potency. They may either proceed to full realization or be crushed by violent action from the outside. Such violence is exceptional and against nature ($\pi\alpha\rho\grave{\alpha}$ $\phi\acute{v}\sigma\iota\nu$). Human tendency is subject to an even higher degree of indeterminacy, since it is open to rational direction. It is not only capable of being distorted and crushed by external violence. It is also capable of being internally ordered by choice either towards its natural end or in the opposite way. The doctor, for example, may use his knowledge either to cure or to kill the patient.[39] Hence, it is peculiarly important to establish rational control over such tendencies in their early stages. This guidance of incipient power is virtue, "a first step towards completion," as Aristotle calls it.[40] But even though we possess the virtue, this is only a firmly directed tendency or habit ($\check{\epsilon}\xi\iota\varsigma$) still far from the final goal.[41]

This goal is the final value. Virtues are the inner powers that enable substantial entities to attain this goal. Hence, virtue is defined in terms of goodness. But how is this ultimate normative term defined? Is there any evidence to show that this also is grounded in observable facts of nature? According to Aristotle's theory there is. Let us now briefly examine this theory.

E. NATURE AS EXISTENTIAL FULFILMENT

The good is "that to which all things tend."[42] What is this? An answer is given in the *Metaphysics*. "The end is an act (ergon), and the act is an activity or a being in act ($\dot{\epsilon}\nu\acute{\epsilon}\rho\gamma\epsilon\iota\alpha$). Thus, the name *activity* is derived from act and points to complete actuality."[43] The end of an instrumental process, like weaving or building, lies beyond the process. We build only for the sake of the finished dwelling which will exist after the process is over. If life were like this, we should reach the end only when dead. But this is an error. Life is not a kinetic process in which something is turned into something else not there to begin with. It is rather the activation or fulfilment of something already in act that remains in its fulfilment.[44] Hence, the value of life lies in the very living. It is not a fixed quality or property but a certain kind of life,[45] a tendency already partly in act which sustains itself and realizes itself in acts of completion.

Hence, we can see why questions of right and wrong, and good and bad, do not apply to the abstract structures of mathematics and other formal disciplines.[46] Such entities have no act of existing. They do not tend to anything beyond. Each of them is a mere possibility—just what it is and nothing more. Hence, the nonmetaphysical atomistic intellect, prepared to see only the abstract forms into which it analyzes things, and blind to the synthetic acts of existing which hold them together in actuality, cannot grasp the basic moral categories. It will either attempt to identify them with some fixed structure which has no existential tendency, and is therefore irrelevant to value, or, dimly sensing the failure of this enterprise, it will assert that value is ineffable and thus abandon the quest. Goodness cannot be separated from the concrete. It is not a logical essence divorced from the actual world of action and becoming, but an *existential* category—a mode of tending and existing which permeates every phase of an actual moving entity. What sort of a mode is this? Is it ineffable and indescribable? Or can it be truly described and characterized?

Aristotle's answer is clear. The good can be truly characterized. But, like other basic ontological structures, it is too broad in scope to be univocally defined. Since it is a concrete existential category, belonging to the individual entity as it exists in nature, it must vary from individual to individual. There will be no *single* abstract good in general in which all good things participate, as all triangles participate in a single form of triangularity. This would turn goodness into an abstract essence. But rather "each entity tends towards its own peculiar good."[47] Nevertheless, this does not mean that goodness cannot be truly characterized in terms of a proportional similarity. Even though A be quite distinct from B, and A's good different from B's, we may still observe that A's good is to A as B's good is to B.[48] So a true description of goodness is still possible. But what form more exactly will this description take? How is A's good related to A?

If our eyes are not closed to the omnipresent datum of existence, we shall be able to understand the Aristotelian answer. An entity is good if it has completeness or self-sufficiency (τὸ αὔταρχες). By this we mean "that which alone by itself makes life desirable and lacking in nothing."[49] To be in a sound condition, an entity must maintain its existence intact and complete this existence by further activity.[50] To be in an unsound or evil condition, an entity must be in a state of need or lack, or finally lose such existence as it has. Evil is always described in negative terms. It is "privation" and "perversion."[51] Like goodness, "it cannot exist in abstraction apart from bad things."[52] Goodness is the fulfilment of existential tendency; evil the privation of such fulfilment. But how can we tell the sort of completion that is required? What is the ultimate standard of goodness?

This standard is necessarily connected with the tendential structure of changing beings. All the phases of this complex structure are held together in an underlying unity suggested by the term nature (φύσις). Goodness itself is also a necessary phase of this structure, its phase of completion. All the entities of the world of nature are changing and tending towards something beyond. These tendencies are observable. But we cannot observe a potency or tendency without at the same time grasping something of the final value which *would* fulfil this tendency, even though it is not now present. The tendency is founded on the structure of the thing, its essence (οὐσία). Hence, goodness itself, the ultimate norm, is founded on nature. It is nature in final act or fulfilment. "The changing entity is constantly passing or growing from something into something else. Let us now ask not from what but into what is it growing? This is its final form or nature (φύσις)."[53]

Nature is constantly tending to grow into itself, to become what it really is. Its norms are embedded in its very being. Extrinsic norms arbitrarily imposed on it from the outside can only distort and corrupt it. Nature is not only the form and the ordered tendency. It is also the "end *and* final value."[54]

Section II. THE CONCEPT OF NATURE (φύσις)
IN ARISTOTELIAN PHILOSOPHY

In opposition to subjectivistic types of ethical theory like hedonism, utilitarianism, and Kantianism, which assert that being is indifferent to value, and that norms are arbitrary human constructions, realistic ethics holds that being is not neutral to value but contains its own norms and laws which operate apart from all human enactment. Since the real entities of experience are involved in a continuous process of change and evolution, these norms, if they exist, must be observed in the complex structure of change. The word *nature*, therefore, or its cognate forms, meaning growth or process, must play a significant role in the development of any nonconstructionist ethics. For any such theory, nature, the realm of change, must be a normative term. The only alternative is to make man the supreme legislator of values. We have already noted in the last chapter that these ontological doctrines, characteristic of realistic moral theory, are found in the writings of Plato. Unless our preceding analysis is basically in error, the same doctrines are also to be found in Aristotle's writings.

For him, too, existence is not neutral to value. The changing things of the real world which, except for the most extreme subjectivist, exist independent of all human desire and decree operate according to norms which are founded on their inmost structure. Hence, for him also, *nature* is a normative term. We have discovered that, like Plato, he uses this word to express the underlying unity which holds together the important distinguishable phases of existential structure. We have found, in fact, that he recognizes in this unity all the five aspects distinguished by Plato.

Thus, he uses the term *nature* to refer to the whole cosmic order of change and evolution. He thinks of this order in pluralistic terms. It is made up of a vast variety of individual substances whose manifold tendencies and acts sustain and depend upon one another. Hence, the sources of this order must be found in the concrete being. Aristotle identifies the primary source with its formal structure (μορφή) which makes this entity into the kind that it is, and determines its active and passive tendencies. With rigorous consistency, he uses the word *nature* for this individual form, since it is responsible for the regular laws that govern the cosmic order as a whole.

He also uses the same term appropriately for the tendencies determined by this structure. Unless similar structures determined similar tendencies, the universe would collapse into chaos, and science as well as human life would be impossible. When these tendencies are temporally ordered, during their incipient phases, in ways which are maximally appropriate for achieving fulfilment, they are in a sound or virtuous state. But these normative orders are in no sense arbitrarily imposed from the outside. They are required by the existential structure of the thing itself. This ontological requiredness lies at the root of those moral experiences which we call obligation and oughtness.

Aristotle is often criticized for having neglected these moral feelings. If by neglect we mean the failure to believe in norms as totally inexplicable essences entirely divorced from reality, the charge may perhaps be defended. But they are clearly recognized by Aristotle as well as Plato and constantly expressed in such concepts as virtue (ἀρετή), fitting (πρέπον), appropriate (προσῆκον), etc., and finally natural (κατὰ φύσιν). The great difference between these thinkers and modern ethicists is that Plato and Aristotle refuse to leave these notions wholly unanalyzed and unexplained.

The word *nature* is also used to signify the existential fulfilment of an entity, which constitutes its goodness so far as this is achieved. These five existential factors are essentially connected. One cannot exist without the others. Hence, a broad and flexible term was needed to express this unity. For Plato and Aristotle the word *nature* (φύσις) met this need. Their linguistic usage has since been followed by realistic moral philosophers in the West, and for this reason realistic ethics came to be known as the theory of natural law.

The Aristotelian ontology of changing being is very close to that of Plato. It is more articulate and contains many further distinctions and refinements. The clarification of the difference between movement (κίνησις), which brings each structure from

potency into act, and activity (ἐνέργεια), which brings something already actual (in first act) into fulfilment, is a significant
contribution to the theory of tendency which is based on acute
phenomenological observation.[55] Aristotle's recognition of the
fact that the potency-act relation is analogical is an even more
important refinement of Platonic doctrine which cannot otherwise be defended against the charge of equivocation. But in
spite of these and many other developments, the Aristotelian
theory of nature is closely parallel to that of Plato.

For Aristotle, ontology is normative, and ethics is founda-
tionally ontological. So the two overlap, as they must in any
realistic theory. So far, our attention has been focused primarily
on the ontological foundations. Let us now turn to the ethics itself. Does it reveal the characteristic structure of natural-law
philosophy?

Section III. DERIVED MORAL PRINCIPLES

The Aristotelian ethics is an application of general ontological
principles to the peculiar nature of man. In studying these, we
have already become aware of their moral implications. Hence,
our consideration of Aristotle's ethics as such may be very brief.
We need only comment on certain passages which show that he
also recognized the three basic principles which, as we have
noted, are held in common by all authentic representatives of
moral realism: (a) the universality of moral law; (b) norms
grounded on nature; and (c) the good for man as realization of
human nature.

A. THE UNIVERSALITY OF MORAL LAW

There is no more trace of any doctrine of racialism or of innate
natural differences between groups of men in Aristotle than in
Plato. Human nature is everywhere and necessarily one. Like
Plato, Aristotle never writes on a special kind of soul, but on the
human soul in general; not on ethics for Greeks alone, but on
human ethics in general. There are, of course, indefinitely variable instances, but moral relativism arises from a nominalistic
incapacity to discern the basic similarities underlying the differences. Courage is concretely expressed in many ways, but

courage itself is always one. "To things just and lawful, justice is related as the universal to its particular; for just acts are many, but the justice that is predicated of them is one, since it is universal."[56]

According to the *Politics*,[57] ". . . it is evident that the same life is best for each individual, for communities, and for mankind collectively." In chapter 7 of Book V of the *Nicomachean Ethics*, as we have already noted, natural justice is clearly distinguished from *legal* justice (later called positive law). "Of political justice (πολιτικοῦ δικαίου), which includes all the virtues, part is natural (φυσικόν), part legal (νομικόν)—natural, that which everywhere has the same force and does not exist by people's thinking this or that; legal, that which is indifferent (by nature) but once laid down is not indifferent, e.g., that a prisoner's ransom shall be a mina." Natural law is abstract and universal. It always requires further positive determinations relative to the particular circumstances. Such positive law is variable. It may, of course, be contrary to natural law. This is always vicious, and punished by natural sanctions.

". . . The things which are just not by nature but by human enactment are not everywhere the same, since constitutions also are not the same, but there is only one which is everywhere by nature (κατὰ φύσιν) the best."[58] Human individuals share a common human nature. The universal end of man, the fulfilment of the common needs of this nature, is always and everywhere the same. The moral principles, or virtues, which must be obeyed if this end is to be achieved are also universal and morally binding on all men.

B. NORMS GROUNDED ON NATURE

According to Aristotle, every finite entity possesses a formal structure or nature which marks it off from other kinds of entity and makes it essentially what it is. This nature is not merely a determining *formal* cause, but an efficient and final cause as well. Hence, the repeated remark that in all subrational entities the formal, efficient, and final causes coincide.[59] In the Second Book of the *Physics* nature is defined as an intrinsic cause of motion or rest.[60] Each thing tends to act in accordance with its structure (μορφή). The world is through and through tendential. When such an essential tendency is realized, the act is said to be according to nature.[61] This dynamic ontology corresponds point for point with that of Plato, as does also its ethical application. It is Plato made more exact and explicit.

We are not born with those rational habits or virtues whose actualization constitutes the good life. On the other hand, character, or second nature, is no arbitrary creation. If the habits, which it is in our power to choose and form, conflict with the essential tendencies of our first nature, we fall into misery and vice. Hence, as Aristotle says,[62] "neither by nature (φύσει), then, nor contrary to nature (παρὰ φύσιν) do the virtues arise in us; rather we are by nature adapted to receive them. . . ." Nowhere has the central concept of natural law been more lucidly stated.

Following Plato, practical science is held to be related to the soul as medical science is related to the body. Normative principles are founded on theoretical truths. ". . . Clearly the student of politics must know the facts about soul, as the man who is to heal the eyes or the body as a whole must know about the eyes or the body. . . ."[63]

The soul is divided into three major parts whose essential tendencies must be fulfilled if human life is to be lived. First, there is the nutritive soul which requires therapeutic discipline for the proper provision of food, clothing, shelter, and other material artifacts. Second, there is the animal soul with its appetites for sensible objects, which requires the moral guidance of practical reason and moral virtue. Finally, there is the rational soul—the most distinctive human possession—which requires education if it is to provide that insight into man and nature without which human life sinks into a purposeless routine, and human culture into chaos and disintegration.

Aristotle also follows Plato in rejecting any conventionalist theory of the origin of society. "The family is the association (κοινωνία) established by nature (κατὰ φύσιν) for the supply of men's everyday wants."[64] Then, "when several families are united, and the association aims at something more than the supply of daily needs, the first society to be formed is the village." Finally, when several villages are united in a single community large enough to be nearly or quite self-sufficing, the political society comes into existence. In summarizing this view,[65] we are told that political society (πόλις) "originates in the bare needs of life (τοῦ ξῆν ἕνεκα), and continues for the sake of living well (τοῦ εὖ ξῆν)." Man, possessing speech and the means of rational communication, is a political animal. He can realize his nature only by political co-operation. Hence, the community is "natural (φύσει)" to man, for only thus can he attain his end, and "what each thing is when fully developed, we call its nature (φύσιν)."[66]

Here, we find, implicitly indicated, the four basic types of human right or need on which the recent United Nations Declaration is based: first, the right to material artifacts; second, the right to exercise practical reason and choice in the guidance of individual and social life; third, the right to education; and fourth, the duty of every individual to contribute to communal action and his right to participate fairly in the fruits of such action. For Aristotle, like Plato, these normative principles of natural law are founded on the factual structure of human nature.

C. THE GOOD FOR MAN AS THE REALIZATION
OF HUMAN NATURE

In stating his conception of the human good, Aristotle again uses almost the same words as Plato. We need note only a few passages from the *Politics*, *Ethics*, and *Metaphysics* to confirm this. In the *Politics*,[67] he says "the final cause and end of a thing is the best, and to be self-sufficing (αὐτάρχεια) is the end and the best." The good for man is the activation of the basic tendencies which belong to us by nature, to lack nothing really required. In the *Nicomachean Ethics*[68] "the final good is thought to be self-sufficient (αὔταρχες)," and "the self-sufficient we now define as that which makes life desirable and lacking in nothing."[69] Goodness is thus the fulfilment or completion of our natural powers and capacities. According to the *Metaphysics*,[70] excellence (ἀρετή) is a "completion (τελείωσις)," and "things which have attained their end, this being good, are called complete (τέλεια);

for things are complete in virtue of having attained their end."[71]
The good for man is to live a genuinely and completely human
life.

Section IV. THE THEORY OF NATURAL LAW AND ITS HISTORY

We may summarize our conclusions concerning natural-law
philosophy under two headings: (1) the ontological and moral
principles of natural-law philosophy; and (2) the origin and history of natural-law philosophy.

1. *The ontological and moral principles of natural-law philosophy.*—Under the first, we must note the following characteristics of all genuine natural-law philosophy. It is interested in
clarifying basic moral concepts such as good and evil, obligation
and vice. Since such concepts can be clarified only by referring
them to the most universal concepts of existence, this philosophy must be unreservedly ontological in character. It must be
concerned with the nature of existence in general, for it is only
in the light of such basic analysis that the moral structure of
human life can be more clearly understood. The empirical evidence conclusively indicates that a vast variety of distinct entities exist. Hence, this mode of philosophy is always pluralistic.
The world is constituted by a number of distinct contingent existences, each one depending upon others for its being and
activation.

Since the evidence of experience shows that the world is not
a blind chaos, but that many contingent entities, with the support of others, for the most part achieve some degree of activation, all realistic philosophers of natural law have recognized a
universal order of nature. Since it is very difficult to account for
such an order in terms of chance or blind spontaneity, most realistic thinkers have defended the theory of the primacy of life and
mind over lifeless matter in the universe. But with or without
this thesis, all of them have recognized the existence of a universal natural law or regularity, controlling the shifting episodes of
the world-process. Without such an order, science, of course, as
we know it now would be impossible.

All realistic thinkers have been interested in value, and have defended the reality of value. Hence, they have all rejected the theories that value is nonexistent or divorced from existence in a separate realm. For them, existence is basically or naturally good, and what is peculiarly valuable is the completion or fulfilment of this existence. Hence, they all reject the age-old separation of a realm of value from the realm of being and insist that genuine norms are founded upon the facts of existence. Norms are not imposed upon existence from the outside. Certainly they are not arbitrarily constructed by human preference. They are rather discovered in the facts themselves. Being itself contains its own norms. How is this to be explained?

The empirical evidence shows that the objects of experience are in a constant condition of change. This points to an answer—the active tendential nature of all finite existence. Each entity in nature has a certain determinate structure which distinguishes it from other entities. But by itself, such a conceivable structure is a bare possibility. In addition to this structure, each actual entity has something else—the act of existing—which separates it from the nothingness of bare possibility and enables it to move and energize. When a determinate structure of such and such a kind is given this act of existing, it determines it to further tendencies and acts which fulfil the original nature. This is true of everything observed in the universe. Every quality or character that we ever know is tending or acting to something beyond itself, and every tendency is of a certain character or kind. Every property is *dispositional*. No fact is ever fixed or finished. The whole world of nature is active and tendential.

This rejection of logical atomism or essentialism is common to all realistic philosophers of natural law. It alone makes possible for them an existential explanation of the categories of obligation, good and evil. Obligation, of course, takes a peculiar form in the life of man. But each kind of entity has its own peculiar tendencies and modes of fulfilling its being. Hence, it is rooted in the basic structure of all finite existence—the urge of every limited being to realize itself in further acts adapted and appropriate to its nature. When such obligations conflict, as they often do, there is obstruction and frustration. But for the most part, essential tendencies achieve some degree of mutual support and realization, or the universe would collapse into chaos. *For the most part,* finite entities act in accordance with the laws of nature, and science is therefore possible. To act in this way is *right* for any entity—its nature is fulfilled. To be frustrated or deprived of the further existence it requires is wrong. To exist in such an incomplete and obstructed condition is evil. The being is not really and authentically as it should be; not completely itself. On the other hand, to exist in the full realization of its capacities and tendencies is good, to be as it should be, completely and authentically itself.

Man is no exception to these basic ontological principles, for he is a finite existent. In so far as they apply to him, we may summarize them conveniently with this background in mind under the three distinct headings with which we have now become familiar.

First, since there are certain common or essential traits shared by all men in so far as they are men, the sound condition will also share certain common features, and the rules of action required for its attainment will be universally valid for all men everywhere. They are at least dimly recognized by all as the moral law and have been called the law of nature, or the natural law.

Second, the universal norms of human action, the moral laws, are founded on the structure of man. Modes of action which fulfil his nature are right; those which destroy or frustrate his nature are wrong.

Third, and finally, the good for man is the realization of his nature. To be in a sound condition is to be living a genuinely human life, lacking in nothing which such a life requires.

2. *The origin and history of natural-law philosophy.*—The first disciplined formulation of this realistic moral philosophy was achieved in the thought of Plato and Aristotle. They differ concerning many applications of moral philosophy to special problems. In the field of epistemology, their differences are, no doubt, more basic. But so far as the fundamental concepts and principles of practical philosophy are concerned, they are in profound agreement. They proclaim that all human individuals share a common human nature, as well as common active tend-

encies founded on this nature. The good for any man, or any human society, is the completion of human existence, the living of human life in the concrete. In any given case, this must include the performance of many particular acts with peculiar features elicited by the unique history and circumstances of the individual or group. But if human life is to be lived at all, it must include certain acts which to some degree realize the essential tendencies of man, and which fall into a certain universal pattern. This universal pattern of action which is always required, everywhere, for the attainment of the human end is the moral law, or natural law, as it came to be called.

This conception has played a crucially important role in the intellectual, political, and social history of the West. The Stoics popularized the theory and passed it on to the Roman jurists, who gave it at least a verbal recognition and actually used it to perform certain subordinate functions in the formulation of the Roman Law in the first centuries A.D.[72] In the Middle Ages it was united with similar conceptions of a universal moral law known to all men, independently developed in the Judaeo-Christian tradition. In this setting, it became the foundation on which scholastic ethics and Canon Law were based.

The early thinkers of the Reformation were led to ignore it, or even to deny it, by their anti-intellectualism and moral pessimism, but it was kept alive by Suarez, Hooker, and others, who used it to criticize authoritarianism and political tyranny. Later on, thinkers like Locke and Paine used it in formulating those political principles which played an important role in the American and French revolutions. In the comparatively peaceful period of the nineteenth century, it was again almost completely eclipsed by historicism and moral relativism. But now once again, in a time of troubles and unrest, it is being revived, as it always must be revived when men are led to think with radical seriousness about the foundations of human life and culture. The most noteworthy expression of this recent revival is the United Nations Universal Declaration of Human Rights which, in addition to the political rights recognized by the eighteenth-century formularies, also recognizes social, cultural, and economic rights—and duties as well.

The dim and hazy notion of a universal moral law is probably as old as man himself. But so far as Western philosophy is concerned, Plato and Aristotle were the first to give this conception a thoroughly coherent and disciplined formulation. They are the founders of natural-law philosophy.

This type of ethical theory differs sharply from the three kinds of moral view which have been most influential in the history of modern philosophy. It differs from Kant, and every type of dualist or conventionalist ethics, in holding that norms are not isolated from factual existence and that normative principles must be discovered in an empirical study of nature, rather than laid down by the action of a constructive human mind.

It differs from every type of consistent, utilitarian ethics in sharply distinguishing those freely chosen, deliberate modes of action which can be rationally justified as essential needs of man from incidental interests and raw appetites.

It also differs from the idealistic ethics of eudaemonism, as it is now often called, and of self-realization, clearly summarized by Bradley in the famous formula *my station and its duties*. As over against this glorification of the concrete historical process, a sophisticated version of might makes right, the philosophy of natural law defends the rational dignity of the human individual and his right and duty to criticize by word and deed any existent institution or social structure in terms of those universal moral principles which can be apprehended by the individual intellect alone.

This realistic and rationalistic conception has been interpreted and developed in many different ways throughout the long course of Western history. Some of these interpretations have been sound and fruitful, others unsound and distorted. But it received its first articulate and responsible philosophical formulation in the thought of Plato and Aristotle. In view of the significant role it has played in our cultural history, its worldwide revival at the present time, and the crucial function it must perform if the social and political problems now confronting us are ever to be solved, I earnestly hope that philosophers and classicists will turn their attention to this living concept as well as to the texts of those Greek authors where it received its first disciplined and philosophical expression. Such study may help to dispel the confusion into which academic ethics has fallen and may serve to strengthen moral sanity where it still exists.

Let us now take this advice seriously ourselves and in Part III bring this theory to bear on certain basic problems which lie at the heart of contemporary moral argument.

PART III

NATURAL LAW AND SOME PROBLEMS
OF CONTEMPORARY ETHICS

CHAPTER SEVEN

TENDENCY AS THE ONTOLOGICAL
GROUND OF ETHICS*

WE HAVE now completed a survey of the origin and history of natural-law ethics in Western thought. One essential phase of this realistic mode of philosophizing is its attempt to find firm ontological foundations for ethics. This recognition of metaphysics as the basic empirical discipline was characteristic of its founders as well as all its major representatives. No revival of authentic, realistic philosophy is possible without a revival of metaphysics. Is such a revival possible?

Metaphysics is commonly regarded as a chaos of abstract speculations quite remote from the immediate data of concrete experience. Hence, the most influential objection raised against it is that its concepts and theorems, having no empirical reference, are unverifiable and therefore meaningless.

As a matter of fact, it provides us with the only possible instruments by which we may hope to grasp the immediate data of experience in their full concreteness. Of all the philosophical disciplines, it is the most eminently empirical and closest to the brute facts as they are actually given. Not only do its basic concepts and theorems refer to evident data of experience—not only are they directly verifiable and meaningful—but without unambiguous reference to these foundational meanings, the basic concepts and theorems of all other disciplines lapse into vagueness, unintelligibility, and meaninglessness.

These are strong assertions. Nevertheless, they are true. To manifest their truth exhaustively, it would be necessary to examine the basic concepts of physical science such as energy,

<hr>

* The substance of this chapter was read at the third annual meeting of the Metaphysical Society of America at Yale University, March 22, 1952, and published in the *Journal of Philosophy*, Vol. XLIX, No. 14 (July 3, 1952), under the title "Tendency: Ontological Ground of Ethics."

change, and quantity, those of the sciences of man such as rationality, communication, purpose, etc., and those like truth, induction, validity, and beauty which underlie the subordinate philosophical disciplines of epistemology, logic, and aesthetics. We cannot now undertake this formidable task—even if we restrict it to the philosophical disciplines. We shall have to pass over other illustrations and focus our attention on the discipline of ethics in our attempt to show how the clarification of its basic concepts must depend on ontological description and analysis.

Section I. FOUNDATIONAL CONFUSION AND REDUCTIONISM IN RECENT ETHICAL THEORY

The modern analytic approach to ethics has raised questions of a peculiarly basic character which penetrate to the foundations of moral theory. Can goodness be defined or characterized in any intelligible way? Is it properly regarded as a quality or property? What is the nature of moral obligation and oughtness? Is it another peculiar property entirely divorced from value, or in some way dependent upon it and deducible from it? How is the subjective urgency of this phenomenon to be explained? Is it a noncognitive desire, or is it intimately related to some form of cognition? Finally, what in general is the relation of theoretical cognition to moral practice? What is meant by moral reasonableness and moral justification?

These important questions have been pressed with a new rigor and force. But no answer yet proposed by intuitionists, naturalists, or noncognitivists has met with much success. Each school seems stronger on destructive criticism of alien points of view than on constructive elaboration and defense of its own. The forms of debate have become somewhat stereotyped, and areas of agreement even at the phenomenological level seem to be diminishing rather than widening. Certain interesting suggestions concerning the need for a new approach have been made by participants in the debate. Two of these are in my opinion of special significance.

The first calls attention to the predominance of linguistic and logical analysis in recent ethical argument, and recommends a return to phenomenological description and analysis. Thus, Professor A. I. Melden says that "it is not the logical analysis of concepts, but the discrimination of the factors involved in the empirical fact of moral response that is required."[1]

The second goes even farther in the same direction. It calls our attention to the rich array of variegated fact that is involved in the concrete ethical situation and the need for larger perspectives to take account of all this relevant material. Thus Professor W. K. Frankena in a penetrating review of recent trends in ethical theory says, "We may elect to call this enlarged conception of method analytical philosophy, as in fact we have been doing; but only if we do so can we claim that analytical philosophy suffices for ethical theory, and, if we do so, the line between it and a minimal speculative philosophy becomes rather thin and shadowy."[2] Frankena also points out how recent criticism has revealed certain weaknesses in the more extreme versions of the opposed doctrines and urges the need for a broader mediating approach which may avoid the major difficulties now clearly revealed in each of them: broadly speaking, these are the failures of intuitionism to justify its peculiar properties and intuitions by a reasonable ontology and epistemology; of naturalism to account for obligation; and of noncognitivism to give an adequate explanation of practical reason and moral justification.

It is also significant that many thinkers of divergent schools agree that basic moral categories such as goodness, so far as they can be defined at all, must be identified with fixed, determinate qualities or properties of some kind. But this metaphysical assumption seems to lead only to reductionism, eclectic pluralism, or the dubious doctrine of indefinability. Can it be that a more basic existential category is being forgotten and ignored?

Let us select two pairs of related concepts, the ought and the good, existence and value, which are worthy of a brief glance. No recent school seems to have been able to focus the relation which holds the members of each pair together. Hence, one must be reduced to the other, or the two must be separated by a yawning chasm with paradoxical results in each case which have been often emphasized. Either reductionism or disintegration. This is the price we pay for a neglect of the concrete data and those ontological concepts by which alone they may be coherently understood.

Thus, if we attempt to reduce oughtness to the good conceived as a hedonic quality, difficulties arise concerning the intrinsic goodness of virtuous acts, and that peculiar binding power which the ought exerts upon the individual agent. On the other hand, if we separate the ought from factual value as two insular essences totally divorced from each other, we are forced to say that what we ought to do is not good, and the good is not what we ought to do. If they have nothing in common, how, then, can we weigh them against one another and compare them, as we must do in any serious process of deliberation? Moral law is then left with no factual foundation whatsoever, and moral justification seems meaningless.

In the case of goodness and existence as they are now ordinarily conceived, we are confronted with a similar dilemma. If goodness is reduced to existence in the sense of finished fact, then what is, is right, and ethics in general disappears. On the other hand, if we follow Kant and his influential followers in radically separating the two, value is left without any ground and collapses into a human construction or, if we are consistent, into nonbeing, nothing.

We may seek a refuge in the notion of indefinability or ineffability. But granted that this notion can be freed from difficulties, it offers no refuge for anyone who still conceives of ethics as an intelligible discipline. A supposed discipline whose basic concepts are ineffable and uncharacterizable cannot be anything but vague and ambiguous. It will be a house built on rotten foundations.

If metaphysics is not judged a priori to be impossible, there may be an escape from these problems and dilemmas. A neglect of the metaphysics of ethics is common to the modern schools. Nowhere is moral analysis brought into any disciplined relation with a critical analysis of being. I shall now attempt to suggest the outlines of such an analysis. For the most part, I shall follow patterns of thought already developed in the great classics of realistic ontology we have studied. But here and there I shall introduce modifications and corrections which, I believe, are essential for the purpose in hand.

In chapter 8, we shall bring our analysis to bear on the moral problems to which we have referred, the nature of value, obligation, and justification, and the relation of these to one another. Now, however, we shall turn our attention to the basic category of *active tendency* which is involved in every phase of moral reality. A clarification of this foundational concept is, therefore, a precondition for any adequate approach to the foundational problems of contemporary ethics.

Before beginning this ontological analysis, however, we must say a few words on the realistic conception of metaphysics as an "empirical" discipline and its relation to phenomenology. These matters are now widely misunderstood and require a preliminary explanation.

Section II. METAPHYSICAL PROTOCOLS AND PHENOMENOLOGY

The theories of any responsible noetic discipline capable of inspiring the respect of careful investigators must be confirmed by empirical data. Otherwise we have only idle speculation—not science. If metaphysics is to be revived and pursued once more as a science, we must first show that there are data not belonging to the restricted sciences—metaphysical protocols. There are such protocols, and it is of the first importance that all of us who are interested in the survival of philosophy should reflect on this, and emphasize it in our teaching and writing. The most basic of these is *being*, the proper object of metaphysics as an empirical discipline. In what sense is this a brute datum, and how is it to be distinguished from the data of the other empirical sciences?

A brute datum of science has at least three definable characteristics. (1) It must be thrust before the cognitive faculties with an external constraint which rules out subjective inference and interpretation. (2) To have any confirming power it must be structuralized; no intelligible theory can be verified by an ineffable datum, if there is any such thing. (3) It must be accessible to different observers at different times working under somewhat divergent conditions. Do existential data meet these evidential criteria?

(1) The existence of something now before me calls forth a *categorical* assent. I may not be sure just what it is, but that it is, is indubitable. It is highly improbable that any man has ever been able to doubt his own existence while consciously existing in an enveloping world of actual entities. (2) These existential data are structuralized. Among the more evident of these structures is that of existential plurality, both in space and in time. As we shall see, active tendency and dependency are in certain cases given with a high degree of clarity and cognitive constraint. (3) Without these data there would be no human experience at all. Hence, they are accessible always to any human observer, under all conditions in which any observation is possible. We must, therefore, conclude that these are immediate data with a high degree of confirming power. But are they not covered by other disciplines?

Here we must note three striking characteristics which sharply distinguish them from the data of the restricted sciences. They are pervasive, nonquantitative, and very rich in scope. Scientific data, on the other hand, are restricted, primarily quantitative, and abstract. In trying to grasp the determining characteristics of philosophic data, special instruments and machines will not help us. These data are presented to the scientist in the laboratory, and when he is walking home on the street. Measuring techniques are absolutely useless, for these inescapable, primordial data include much more than quantity.

But if these data are distinct from those of the restricted sciences, if they are certain, richly structuralized, and easily accessible to all, why then is it that they are so generally discounted and ignored, and that philosophy, the discipline whose function it is to study them, is in such a relatively backward and chaotic state? An answer to these crucial questions is suggested by the very reasons presented by those antiphilosophical philosophers who disparage all data not accessible to the "exact" quantitative methods of the "sciences." What are these reasons?

In the first place, it is said that data of everyday experience are crude and inexact. By this, it is meant that they are quali- tative and relational rather than quantitative and, therefore, subject to the "exact" measuring techniques of "science." This, of course, must be granted. But because they cannot be dealt with by one method does not imply that they cannot be dealt with by any other. Even though they cannot be exactly meas- ured, they may perhaps be accurately described and analyzed. Different kinds of data are apprehended in different ways, and each discipline must develop its own standard of exactitude.

Second, it is said that these data are confused and vague. I have heard positivistic philosophers sometimes use the word "sloppy" in this connection, and other terms with even more in- vidious connotations when speaking of everyday experience. What they mean is that the world of everyday experience is filled with a very rich and variegated content, and that it also fades away into obscure lacunae and dim horizons where, with- out patient examination and analysis, nothing can be clearly grasped, and sometimes not even then. These facts also must be admitted. But they hardly justify the proposed inference that this vast field of data should be neglected and the structures underlying them dismissed as insignificant. It is certainly true that the range of a concept such as existence is so broad that it cannot be covered by any univocal definition. In this sense, it must be vague and confused. But this does not mean that it can- not be grasped at all, as for example by analogy (cf. chap. 6, sec. V), and that we must abandon the attempt to understand the basic structure of experience.

A third objection takes the form of pointing derisively at the chaos of opposed theories and opinions still prevailing in the field of philosophy, and contrasting this with the accepted dis- proof of scientific theories and the consequent steady advance of science. These facts also must be granted. But do they indi- cate the unimportance of these data? Careful analysis will hard- ly support such a conclusion. Philosophical data are not acces- sible only to a few selected experts with special machines in iso- lated laboratories. They are accessible to all men everywhere. There is no human being, no matter how dull or careless he may be in his intellectual operations, who does not form opinions about these data. Without some opinion of this sort, no human life can be humanly lived. Is it any wonder, then, that the field is beset by a chaos of conflicting points of view?

Human life can certainly be lived without any knowledge of theoretical physics, for example. Its data now are extremely abstract and remote, quite inaccessible to the layman. Hence, they can be left to specialists, and the science is free to develop in abstract peace with steady progress. But what if these data were accessible to all? What if they were so basic and important as to obtrude upon the serious interest of the common man, so that he found himself forced to hold opinions about them and to defend these opinions as a part of his daily life? The field would soon be plunged into chaos and confusion. This would, no doubt, complicate the task of the physicist. But it would hardly indicate the triviality of his subject, unless we were ready to accept the dubious thesis of the universal madness of mankind. The physicist would still try to proceed in spite of the chaos, attempting to advance his subject in disciplined ways and to surmount the difficulties. Surely, then, the universal concern of men for philosophy, and the inevitable resulting confusion, is no argument against its importance. Quite the reverse. It is rather an incitement to further effort and a challenge especially to those who have the opportunity for disciplined observation and analysis.

A fourth objection is raised by those who regard pervasive philosophical data like existence and awareness as obvious. This, of course, is a recognition of the peculiar certainty that belongs to the apprehension of such data. The inference, however, that nothing further needs to be done by no means follows. This would follow only on the basis of that strange Cartesian assumption of the intellectualist that what we are most certain of in an existential sense is something eminently clear and precise. But this assumption is radically false.

What we are most certain of *as existing* is always at first vague and confused. The abstract structures and essences which we clearly and distinctly understand are less certainly existent. They may always turn out to be only possibilities. What we need is both clear knowledge and knowledge of existence. But we cannot get both without patient observation, analysis, and re-examination. The confused existential facts that are evident and obvious always turn out to be obscure and mysterious when they are subjected to patient analysis. As soon as we are certain that something is, there is sure to be work in store for us when we seek to discover precisely what it is. [The certainty of philosophical evidence, far from being a victory, is a challenge to further exact description and analysis.]

A final, fifth difficulty comes from those "empiricists" who complain that these ubiquitous and inescapable data are apt to turn out to be very *odd*. This also is quite true, and constitutes the final paradox. How strange to hear this from the lips of so many positivistic thinkers who pride themselves on their ruthless empiricism, which, of course, in this connection means precisely the opposite, a bigoted dogmatism which knows what the data must be without even examining them, and is ready to condemn anything not fitting their a priori theories as impossible or odd.

These objections of the so-called "empiricists," when carefully examined, confirm what we have said about the philosophic data. Of course, they are inexact, because they are more than merely quantitative. They are confused, because they are very fundamental and very rich, and require painstaking clarification and analysis. Of course, they call forth in every age a chaos of opposed opinions, because such analysis is very difficult and because they are of inescapable importance to every man, including scientists and even academic philosophers. Of course, they are obvious because their hazy objects are known with categorical certainty. And finally, like any data when carefully investigated, they are apt to turn out to be odd, because careful investigation of anything is rare and difficult and leads to conclusions quite at odds with our everyday expectations.

But if these pervasive and peculiar data cannot be investigated by the quantitative techniques of science, how, then, can they be investigated?

One way alone is possible—the method of phenomenological description. We must return to concrete experience itself, examine it carefully, separate what is incidental and transitory from the pervasive ontological data, and then use our reason to describe these data as they are given, refraining from all inference and interpretation. Only by the use of this method can we gain structuralized evidence capable of verifying our explanatory theories. Only then will a philosophical discipline be possible. Phenomenology and metaphysics go together. When men lose interest in the primordial data of everyday experience, metaphysics dies. Philosophy disintegrates into a chaos of partial abstractions and finally into linguistic analysis. When men return to the concrete and begin to wonder at its obscure depths and its rich profusion of qualitative structure, as in present-day Europe, metaphysics revives. If it is to live again in our own tradition, we must cultivate the discipline of phenomenology. This is a first priority. Before we speculate, let us first describe!

Section III. Essence and Existence: Essentialism vs. Existentialism

Let me give as an example an important discovery made in the past. Plurality is a primordial pervasive datum of experience. Thus, here and now as I look around me I find a voluminous multiplicity of divergent items, each marked off by something distinguishing it from the rest, geometric form, color pattern, and sound. This datum of existential multiplicity is indubitable. Even the most rigid monist must grant this in some sense as an original datum, no matter how much he is inclined to discount it because of his a priori acceptance of some explanatory theory. But let us postpone explanation for a moment, while we notice another important fact. These multiple items of my experience are also pervaded by something else which they seem to share in common. They all exist. In spite of their mutual exclusiveness, one exists as much as another. In this, each is similar to all the rest. All this is obvious, one may say. I believe that it is.

But it is also irreconcilable with the atomistic ontology of Lord Russell—and Hume—an a priori metaphysical assumption, never defended by reference to concrete evidence, but rather insinuated by a deceptive use of the term empiricism. This theory assumes that reality is composed of simple atomic units, into which we can analyze any existent entity. But the phenomenological datum of existent multiplicity, as we may call it, is absolutely incompatible with any such theory. How can a simple entity be both similar to, and distinct from, the very same entities? It cannot be. In order to explain this fact, we must infer an extraordinary ontological composition in the structure of even the most simple unit or impression.

It must have something in it, traditionally called *essence*, in virtue of which it is different from others, and something really distinct called *existence*, in virtue of which it is similar to them. Here is an ontological theory which can be verified by phenomenological data available to anyone. But what are these principles, essence and existence, which enter into the composition of any member of an actual set? How do they differ from each other? In our Western tradition, essentialist trends have been predominant.

Essentialist thought is pluralistic. Every object is analyzed into separate structural elements. The static order (the world at a moment) is viewed as a set of fixed, simple units, ideas, impressions, or atoms incidentally ordered by external relations which do not affect their inner core of determination. The dynamic order is similarly analyzed into a discontinuous succession of essences, each of which first appears and then disappears without trace. Essences do not act or tend to anything beyond. Hence, potency and causal efficacy are minimized, in spite of the evident facts of experience. Essences can be noted as they come. They cannot be explained. The law of sufficient reason is discounted or denied.

There is nothing there but finished facts or essences. Some vanish into nothing. Others emerge from nothing. So what? This fact of succession is no doubt very strange, but all facts are strange. Why is this any stranger than the others? If someone suggests to the essentialist thinker that something, an act of existing coming from nonexistence, is a contradiction, he pooh-poohs the idea. This attempt to demonstrate the principle of sufficient reason begs the question. Why should a bare essence (in itself nothing) come from anything or have a reason? It just comes. That is all. The task of science is merely to describe and to predict. It is never to explain.

To ask the question *why* is to fall into meaningless metaphysical tautologies. One essence cannot be explained by another. This is a contradiction. Each is just what it is. If you like, the essence *P* is explained by the essence *P*. No further explanation is possible. Unless existence is focused, this trend of essentialist thought is inevitable. The order of being is not clearly distinguished from the order of knowing, and metaphysics is reduced to logic, which becomes the central philosophic discipline. The act of existing is either ignored altogether, or, as in Hume,[3] identified with a clear and distinct essence or impression. Being is reduced to a discrete dust of essences which either lie side by side, or succeed one another in time. This essentialist pattern of thought has received divergent formulations in the West. But each of them gives us a world of static fixity in which nothing really moves or acts of itself.

In general, essence is that principle in a thing which determines it and marks it off from others. Existence is what separates it from nothing, and allies it to other existents. When we ask the question *ti esti, what is it?*, the answer is in terms of essence. Let us see if we can clarify the distinction between the two by contrasting them as they appear first in the static order resulting from a momentary cross section of the universe, second in the temporal order, and finally in the order of knowing.

In the static order, essence is what limits existence to this or that of a certain kind. There is nothing about existence as such which requires that it be restricted in this way. Essence limits and contracts. Existence realizes essence—completing or fulfilling it in a certain way. Essence separates one thing from another. Existence unites.

Turning now to the dynamic order, we find that essences are timeless and fixed. Each is simply what it is at one time as much as another. Change is irrelevant. Logical terms and principles are tenseless. But being, the term for existence, falls into tenses. Existence comes and goes. There is nothing about existence that pins it down to one essence alone. It may belong to one or to another, and thus may mediate between them. Hence, it is the principle to which we must ultimately trace the dynamism of experience. Furthermore, essences do not diffuse themselves and tend to anything beyond what they are. The number two as such does not tend to the number three. It remains just what it is. Hence, if the data show tendency, activity, or any mode of diffusiveness, this must be attributed to existence rather than to essence.

Turning now to the order of knowledge, we find differences which are equally striking. The essential quiddity or form of anything which marks it off from others is far more easily grasped by the human intellect than the indeterminate act of existing which in itself possesses no what, but which may be given to essences of radically different types. This is connected with another sharp difference. We can readily grasp essence without existence. Any single concept in fact does just this. But existence cannot be grasped without also apprehending an essence of some kind. If I am to think of existence, I must think of something (an essence) in the act of existing.

As a result of these differences, there has been a strongly marked tendency in the West towards a type of philosophy now called *essentialism*, and at present very influential, which either passes over existence altogether or tends to confuse it with the fixed essences which are so much more readily understood. This is balanced by an opposite tendency which has dominated oriental philosophy,[4] though not restricted to the East, which slurs over essence or confuses it with the vaguer datum of existence that pervades all things and binds them together into an existential unity.

But the metaphysical protocols of experience clearly manifest active tendency. I am directly presented with such tendencies within my being, and wherever I turn I find that they are either opposed or supported by alien tendencies arising in things outside of me. An essentialist ontology cannot account for this dynamism of nature. Something has been suppressed and sometimes completely lost from view. This is the act of existing. An essence is an intelligible determination which limits and restricts. But without existence it is a mere possibility, really nothing. An essence by itself does nothing and is nothing. Not to act is not to exist. To be is to be in act.

Section IV. ACTIVE TENDENCY AS AN
ONTOLOGICAL PRINCIPLE

This truth has been implicit in the tradition of realistic philosophy since the time of Plato, who actually suggested the definition we have just given in the *Sophist*.[5] But it has been obscured by the suppression of existence as against essence, and by a resulting failure to recognize active tendency as a third ontological principle correlated with essence and existence, and necessarily constitutive of any finite being. This thesis is confirmed by all the data to which we have access at the macroscopic level of everyday experience, where we never find abstract properties but always dispositional properties tending to act in certain ways. It is now also confirmed by recent evidence concerning the nature of microscopic and submicroscopic entities. The Cartesian idea of an inert matter incapable of action unless externally pushed or pulled has now passed into eclipse. Physical reality is no longer statically conceived as tiny billiard balls, but rather dynamically as fields of force or energy.

No doubt these tendential centers require external support. But they tend to act of themselves. It is understandable therefore that recent philosophy should be characterized by a marked emphasis on the active dynamism of nature and on such key concepts as creative evolution, emergent evolution, the creativity of Whitehead, and the creative freedom of Sartrian existentialism. According to this view, which I shall call *creativism*, finite entities are able to act creatively in the production of radically novel being completely discontinuous with what has gone before. In my opinion, this theory is closer to the truth than the opposite extreme, which I shall call *receptionism*, against which it is in part a reaction. But each of these extreme views is subject to certain difficulties which indicate that the truth lies in between. I shall now try to clarify this intermediate position by a brief criticism of these two opposed alternatives.

Unlike the extreme essentialist, the creationist is not prepared to abandon the principle of sufficient reason; he will not allow logical manipulations to distract him from asking the question *why*. Essences alone are clearly insufficient to account for the coming and going of essences. What will account for this coming and going? Within himself he directly feels tendencies forcing their way towards action on external things. He directly feels other tendencies in these things, either supporting or frustrating him.

Rightly recognizing such activity as present everywhere, he sets it up as an ontological principle required to account for the ubiquitous dynamism of nature. But he does not see that this must lead him to abandon the notion of finished fact. This fact is just what it is. Existence is not clearly seen as a distinct co-ordinate factor within this fact. Activity is viewed as a separate force which, once aroused, moves in from the outside first to annihilate the fact and then to create another new essence in its place. These are radical novelties absolutely discontinuous with what preceded them. To act is to create something new *ex nihilo*.

I believe that this view is close to the truth, far closer than its opposite, the receptionist view. But I think it is subject to certain weaknesses which make it incapable of withstanding a careful examination. The chief weakness is this.

The active tendencies of a finite being are derived from its act of existing which abstractly considered is indeterminate. But this act of existing is determined by the essence which exists. The active tendencies of the entity are similarly limited. They are tendencies of a certain kind. They can produce results of a similar nature, but not "creative" results completely divorced from the nature of the entity.

This ontological analysis is also born out by the facts of experience which show that similar entities act in similar ways. Otherwise, induction and science would be impossible. Purely creative action is not fit for a finite being.

Since the creationist theory does not agree with basic ontological data, nor with the data of any restricted science, as we should expect, I suggest that as empiricists we should abandon it. But this does not mean that we must accept the receptive theory of the later Aristotelian tradition.

This tradition recognizes the composite ontological structure of a finite entity as constituted by a fixed essence and an act of existing. But this act is often viewed in an essentialist manner as though it were fully finished and unable to act of itself. The law of sufficient reason is sometimes used (as by Gredt) to eliminate spontaneous tendency in a finite agent. Thus, it is held to be contradictory for a finite entity determined essentially as x and therefore *not* $-x^1$ to move actively to x^1. Such activity must not merely be sustained but actually inserted into the thing from an outside source.[6] Finite entities are thus frozen into a state of intrinsic immobility. Hence the theory of pre-motion of the human will which has led certain schools of Thomist thought to a most diluted view of human freedom.[7] If consistently developed, the theory would seem to imply a denial of intrinsic spontaneity in finite agents very close to occasionalism.

We may reduce this receptive view to two component theses: (1) no spontaneous act is performed in the agent of itself, but has to be inserted from the outside; and (2) no finite entity can of itself produce any new determination; at best it can only endure and preserve its preceding state. Neither of these theses is confirmed by sound ontological analysis, nor by the empirical facts.

1. The supposed ruling out of spontaneous action by reference to the principle of sufficient reason is based upon a tacit identification of existence with essence. For one essence x (let us say greenness) of itself to tend or move towards another x^1 (let us say redness) is, of course, a contradiction—impossible. Essences do not act or tend. But in each finite entity there is another existential principle which is diffusive and expansive. This act of existing is a sufficient ground for spontaneous tendencies towards further being. In fact, such tendencies are directly felt in ourselves and in many other entities which sustain or oppose our activities. They must be inferred as universally present in things to account for induction and the so-called laws of nature. To suppose that before I perform my acts they have to be inserted from the outside into an inert substance is to multiply entities without necessity.

2. The first act of existing is a separation from nothing. Furthermore, it is not restricted to the limits of any finite essence. Hence, as soon as it unites with such an essence, it transcends

these limits and tends towards further novel being. Active tendency is more than the fixed property or quality with which it is often identified in the Aristotelian tradition.[8] An existence completely restricted by its essence and unable to diffuse itself by action would be indistinguishable from an abstract essence, a pure possibility, timeless and self-enclosed. It would be a nonexistent existence, quite impossible.

This objection is also borne out by factual evidence. Every being we know not only preserves its own being but constantly tends towards further new determinations not in existence before. Inorganic things move to new positions; plants grow; desire moves animals to new satisfactions; and men pass on to further decisions and acts. The nouns by which we express essence are timeless. But the verb *to be*, and the other verbs which express modes of existing, are tensed. The world of nature is existential and historical. To be is to be in act, and this is to be active.

The receptionist theory also fails to agree with the data. It must be modified in two essential respects.

1. Active tendency is a third metaphysical principle co-ordinated with essence and existence, which necessarily results from them and enters into the constitution of any finite being. It is not the same as essence because it acts. It is not the same as existence because it presupposes something already existing which it tends to complete in fitting ways. It is not the same as this pre-existent entity constituted by essence and existence because it expands beyond towards further being not yet achieved. Existence is primarily responsible for this diffusive tendency and is closely similar to it. As existing separates something from nothing and gives it the act it can share in common with others, so activity separates something from privation and actually links it with others by either passion or action. Thus, existence is best understood as the source of activity, the first *act*. Existence is to nothingness as activity is to inaction. To be is to be in act, and for any finite entity to be in act is to tend towards further existence.

2. It follows from this that tendency in this sense cannot be restricted to a single univocal category as in certain branches of

the Aristotelian and Thomistic tradition.[9] The phenomena are too diverse to be brought under a concept with the same generic meaning. The magnet, the growing plant, the sensing animal, and the reflecting man are not all active in the same sense. This does not mean, however, that the term is equivocal. Like other ontological terms, including essence and existence, it is analogous in logical structure, and can be understood only by a proportional similarity. The attractive force of the magnet is to the magnet as growth is to the plant, sensing to the animal, and reflection to the man.

The essence of a thing separates and isolates it from other existences. By its existence it is allied to them. Activity is the gaining of further existence. By its activities, a finite entity emerges from its isolation and enters into relation with other beings, either passively receiving those influences to which it is actively open, or acting upon them in ways ultimately determined by its nature. All finite tendencies are partly passive. At the very least, they must be sustained. In addition, they are in part deflected by other alien tendencies.

There is no such thing as a purely passive or receptive entity. Here, the creationist view is correct. But neither is any finite action purely active or creative. At best it achieves more being, yes, but more being fit for its essence. Each finite entity by its act of existing transcends itself and tends towards further existence beyond what it already is. The tradition has been wrong in attempting to reduce this active tendency to the univocal categories of action and passion. It is rather a more pervasive structure like potency, act, and motion which run through different categories and must be analogously understood. Existence is necessarily diffusive. No finite entity can exist without expanding to further existence.

The observed facts are certainly in accordance with the theory we have defended. Wherever essence or structure is given concrete existence, it is found to be active and tendential. When the specific form is vague and thin (as in inorganic entities) the action is random and passively determined to a large degree from the outside. When it is definite and rich with intrinsic determinations, the action is more stable and immanent. When a vast profusion of rationally purified forms are cognitively present and open to flexible rearrangement, a new level of free spontaneity is attained. Even here at the level of man, action is never creative but limited by human nature. If it is to be justifiable and fitting, it must be in agreement with the human essence. "Creative action," which proceeds without regard to the moral law of nature, leads only to frustration and destruction.

Section V. A Dynamic View of Nature and Ethics

If the preceding analysis is not wholly mistaken, active tendency must be recognized as a third ontological category distinct from both essence and existence but equally wide in range. Wherever being is found, it is determinate. There is present a factor (*essence*) which marks it off from other entities and kinds. There is also present another factor (*existence*) which separates it from nothing and brings it into act. But in addition to these, there is a third factor which results necessarily from the union of the two. This is an active tendency which arises primarily from the act of existence but which is determined to proceed in a certain direction by the limiting essence. All being is vectorial and tendential, on the way towards further existence not yet possessed.

It is most important to realize that these three ontological phases must not be regarded as separate things or substances loosely associated together. They are not "things" at all but relational structures, each of which *is* only by virtue of the others. Existence is what it is because of the existence which brings it out of nothing. Tendency without the act of existing which urges it on, and the essence giving it a direction, is impossible. This analysis has an important bearing on the clarification of basic concepts in the philosophy of nature as well as those of philosophical anthropology and ethics, as we shall see in the next chapter.

We have already noted the emphasis on process, event, and active dynamism which is so characteristic of recent studies in the philosophy of nature which have grown out of the discoveries of modern natural science. This, of course, is in harmony with the tendential analysis of being we have suggested. The old idea of nature as static and inert, which stems from Descartes and his decadent scholastic antecedents, is now clearly outmoded. Nature contains sources of change and action within itself. But the far-reaching implications of this dynamizing of nature have only begun to be studied, as in Nicolai Hartmann's important work *Die Philosophie der Natur*.[10] At this place we may mention only a few suggestions.

The physical world cannot be defined exclusively in terms of extension and spatial structures as Descartes supposed. It is not only extended in space but also proceeding in time. This means that all the basic concepts of natural philosophy must be dynamized and temporalized.[11] The old idea of natural substance as something rigidly contained within geometrical bounds has been abandoned. It is no longer able to account for the empirical facts. Instead of this, we must learn to speak tendentially of energies, dynamic systems (Hartmann's *Gefüge*), and fields of force.[12] The whole notion of substance must be dynamized.

Instead of thinking of it merely as a static "form," ordering spatial parts into a geometrical shape or pattern, we must learn to think of it also as a center of dynamic tendencies capable of resisting opposed forces coming from the outside. The boundaries of such a dynamic system can no longer be conceived in purely geometrical terms but rather as a fluid equilibrium of contrary tendencies, ever unstable and ready for change.[13] A natural system ends where its tendencies can no longer act. It is destroyed when its dynamic tendencies are overcome by opposing forces, and its center of action absorbed into an alien energy continuum.

These suggestions of Hartmann are defensible and sound. But at more basic levels his rejection of realistic ontological analysis leads him into serious difficulties and antinomies. His peculiar conception of essence and existence (*Dasein* and *Sosein*) leads him finally to a Suarezian denial of the real distinction between the two, and finally to a denial of real possibility and potency in nature.[14] This rejection of basic ontological factors, which might make process and causation intelligible, forces him finally to the position that active tendency is an irreducible surd, completely ineffable, and not subject to any rational analysis.[15] This leads him at certain points to speak as though the flux of nature were a wholly indeterminate advance into creative novelty,[16] though at other points the facts constrain him to say that all natural change, no matter how indeterminate and vague, must possess a distinct direction.[17]

The realistic analysis we have suggested offers us a way out of these difficulties. What we have called essence, that which marks off one existence from others, must not be identified with formal structure alone. This distinguishes one kind from another. In addition, it also includes a factor of indeterminate potency which lies at the root of that individuation which distinguishes different examples of the same kind and which is found ubiquitously throughout nature. Hence, we need not deny real possibility and that factor of indeterminacy and existential incompleteness which underlies what we call disposition and change. Without this, we have no way of accounting for the continuity of process and must either reduce it to a mere succession of discontinuous forms or follow Hartmann in dismissing it as a completely unintelligible creation of radical novelty.

As we have seen, the realistic analysis enables us to avoid these impossible extremes. Process is neither a discontinuous succession of discrete forms nor a surd creation *ex nihilo*. It is rather the enduring expression of an imperfect tendency sustained by an act of existing and determined by formal structure. At the level of inorganic nature, this structure is realized in states, conditions, and dynamic systems which have only a precarious hold over fluid existence and whose tendential boundaries are vague and indefinite. It is at the level of living organisms that determinate systems with well-marked boundaries and an accentuated inner unity of action emerge from the flux of evolution. It is to such systems alone that the classical concept of substance in any sense legitimately applies.

But these are only suggestions. We are not attempting in this work to deal with the philosophy of nature as a whole. Our primary interest is in the field of anthropology and ethics. It is time for us now to turn our attention in this more specific direction.

At the beginning of this chapter, we referred to the attempts of contemporary schools of ethical thought to characterize the basic moral categories and to work out an intelligible account of their relations to one another. We also pointed out certain well-known difficulties into which these attempts have fallen and suggested that the most serious of these seem to be derived from an uncritical assumption essentialist ontology. All being is supposed to be made up of fixed essences, relations, or properties of some kind. If so, value and obligation must be defined in this way if they are to be defined at all. But no such definition, as we noted, seems to do justice to the actual facts.

The utilitarians, for example, have tried to define value univocally in terms of a fixed property—pleasure—or a fixed relation —satisfaction of interest. But there are many modes of existence which we recognize as valuable that do not fall within the scope of this limited conception. The intuitionists have tried to deal with obligation in a similar way, thinking of it as a peculiar property subsisting in a special realm of its own. But to intuit an abstract essence does not seem to be the same as to feel the existential pressure of an obligation. The definition does not fit the facts. Similarly, basic objections seem to apply to contemporary attempts to deal with moral justification. The naturalists have maintained that an act is justified if a great deal of pleasure results from it, but acts of desperate courage which turn out badly and the exact fulfilment of a difficult promise hardly seem to be justified in this way. The emotivists simply dismiss the phenomenon of justification as meaningless. But this seems to be a peculiarly high-handed procedure for thinkers who pride themselves on their empiricism.

In addition to the inadequacy of proposed definitions, we also called the attention of the reader to certain questions concerning the relation of existence to value and obligation which have never been satisfactorily answered by recent moralists. Here again, we have noted the manifestations of essentialist habits of thought. Indeed, if these three basic moral terms refer merely to three fixed and separate essences, each of which can be univocally defined, one of three things must happen. Either all three will be clearly defined as separate atomic entities admitting of no relational interdependence, or one will be reduced to another, or some will be regarded as ineffable and the whole attempt at intelligible characterization will be abandoned. As a matter of fact, we find every one of these alternatives defended in the contemporary literature. Yet *none* is very plausible. More arguments are raised and then opposed by counter arguments. But little progress seems to be made. Perhaps it is time to consider carefully the essentialist assumptions which underlie the whole debate.

In this chapter we have examined these assumptions and found them to be indefensible. We have suggested an alternative approach more in keeping with the classical realistic ontology and with the results of modern science. The central feature of this approach is the notion of *active tendency*. Being is not made up exclusively of fixed and static essences. It also contains an omnipresent factor of existential tendency. Can it be that the basic moral categories are existential, active, and dynamic? If so, the analysis we have just completed may be able to shed some light on certain unsolved problems in contemporary ethical theory. In the next and last chapter we shall bring this suggestion to a test.

CHAPTER EIGHT

NATURAL LAW AND CONTEMPORARY
ETHICS*

Iᴺ ᴘᴀʀᴛ ɪ of this work we made a study of the modern critics
of Plato. Certain misconceptions which we discovered in
these criticisms led us to the realistic conception of natural
law, long eclipsed by the idealistic trends of modern thought. In
Part II we made a more careful examination of this conception
and of its history in the West from the time of its first exact formulation in the thought of Plato and Aristotle to that of its
eclipse in the nineteenth century. In the last chapter, we presented an ontological analysis which attempts to embody the
major insights of this realistic tradition as well as to bring them
into line with the dynamic concepts of modern natural science.
In this same chapter we also referred to certain major problems
now confronting contemporary ethical theory. The time has
now come for us to apply our ontological analysis to these problems.

This final chapter will, therefore, be divided into five parts,
each devoted to a systematic analysis of a basic moral problem:
Section I, The Realistic Analysis of Value; Section II, The Nature of Obligation; Section III, Moral Justification; Section IV,
Existence, Value, and Obligation; Section V, Moral Realism
and the World of Today.

Section I. Tʜᴇ Rᴇᴀʟɪꜱᴛɪᴄ Aɴᴀʟʏꜱɪꜱ ᴏꜰ Vᴀʟᴜᴇ

A. REALISTIC ANALYSIS

At first glance, the recent attempts to analyze the notion of
goodness seem to present us with an array of opposed theories
which have nothing whatsoever in common. The naturalist
takes goodness to be a recurrent psychological property such as

* Most of this chapter was published as an article entitled "Natural Law and Contemporary Ethics" in *Ethics* (October, 1952).

pleasure or satisfaction, or a recurrent psychological relational structure such as object of interest or desire. The nonnaturalist, on the other hand, defends the view that goodness is a peculiar irreducible property which cannot be sensed but is rather grasped by intuition.

Diverse as these theories are, they nevertheless share something in common. All of them conceive of goodness as a fixed determinate property or relation which is either present or absent. The realist questions this ontological assumption that being consists exclusively of fixed determinate properties or relations. Existence, for example, which pertains to both properties and relations, cannot correctly be conceived as either one or the other. Goodness also, which is closely related to existence as a mode of being, is radically misunderstood as something fixed and determinate. It must rather be conceived dynamically as an existential mode, the realization of natural tendency. On this view, the world is not made up of determinate structures alone but of determinate structures in an act of existing which they determine towards further appropriate acts of existing. When such a determinate tendency is impeded, this privative mode of existence is what is meant by *evil* in its most universal ontological sense.

Thus, it is in vain that we look for some peculiar quality or relation which we can exclusively identify with good or evil. Like the abstract objects of mathematics, such pure structures do not exist as such. Hence, they are neither good nor evil. Such a quest, if we stubbornly persist in it, must lead to the conclusion of G. E. Moore, still maintained by others, that this property, since it cannot be found or intelligibly characterized, must be indefinable or ineffable. This conclusion, however, is necessitated by a tacit assumption that being must be either a determinate property or a relation and by the ruling out of other alternatives. The realist holds that such assumptions are arbitrary, and actually in conflict with a wide array of empirical evidence, which shows that being is not only characterized by definite structure but by act and tendency as well.

As a matter of fact, we never find structure alone by itself without a corresponding active tendency, for if determinate structures did not act upon us in some way we should never be able to know them. The reason we cannot characterize value and disvalue as determinate properties is not because they are ineffable or indefinable properties but because they are not properties at all. They are rather existential categories or modes of existing. As such, they may include a qualitative phase but are not exhausted by it. They include much more.

No determinate structure can be given existence without determining active tendencies. When such a tendency is fulfilled in accordance with natural law, the entity is said to be in a stable, healthy, or sound condition—adjectives of value. When it is obstructed or distorted, the entity is said to be in an unstable, diseased, or unsound condition—adjectives of disvalue. Goodness and badness in their widest ontological sense are not phases of abstract structure but rather modes of existence, ways in which the existential tendencies determined by such structures are either fulfilled or barely sustained in a deprived, distorted state.

Abstract properties and relations as such have no tendencies. They are neither fulfilled nor thwarted, neither good nor evil—but simply what they are, logical possibilities that may or may not exist. In abstraction, they may be defined and contrasted. Existential categories cannot be defined and characterized in the same way, for they refer not merely to abstract possibilities but rather to modes in which such possibilities are actualized. This, however, does not mean that they are uncharacterizable and ineffable. They can be described and contrasted in intelligible ways that do justice to the empirical evidence.

B. ANSWER TO OBJECTIONS

Four objections come to mind, with which we shall attempt to deal briefly, with a view towards clarification of the theory.

1. This theory identifies goodness with existence, evil with privation or nonbeing. Hence, it cannot give an intelligible account of the factual existence of evil as a positive reality. In answer, we may point out that this theory does not identify value with existence but rather with the fulfilment of tendencies determined by the structure of the existent entity. Furthermore,

it does not identify evil with nonexistence but rather with a mode of existence in which natural tendencies are thwarted and deprived of realization. This distinction is perfectly intelligible and can be readily illustrated by empirical examples. The young plant whose leaves are withering for lack of light is not non-existent. It exists but in an unhealthy or privative mode. The lame man is not nonexistent. He exists but with a natural power partially unrealized. Similarly, the uneducated man exists but deprived of the activation of certain intellectual tendencies determined by his nature.

2. This view is metaphysical, and metaphysical entities are queer. Their natures are unobservable and unverifiable. Hence this theory is empirically meaningless, and any discussion of it can lead only to futile verbosity.

We agree that the theory is metaphysical if by this we mean the attempt to clarify the most basic concepts and theorems underlying all intelligible discourse. That the objects of such concepts and theorems are in no sense observed or verified, we must sharply deny. Existence certainly pertains to the most direct and evident data of experience, for a nonexistent datum is clearly impossible. Furthermore, every determinate structure which is empirically presented to us is fused with existential tendency. Every so-called property, for example, is a dispositional property.

This is very clear in the case of those like solubility and elasticity where the activity is more sharply discerned than the determining structure. It is less clear in those like the middle *c* sound and the color red. But reflection will show that these qualities also, when presented to us in the concrete, are fused with active tendencies. If the color red, for instance, were not acting on the light in a certain way, we should certainly never see it. No tendency is ever given to us without being a certain kind of tendency determined by some structure. It is equally true that no structure is ever actually present without fused activity of its kind. No biologist can understand the nature of any living species without also understanding the kind of activities required to realize it.

Once this is understood, it is possible to distinguish between the normal and the frustrated state. We have already given empirical examples of this basic distinction which underlies the whole procedure of every therapeutic art, including human medicine. In the light of all this, I think we must conclude that existence, tendency, and frustration are as directly observable and analyzable as any data of science.

3. The third objection is more basic, and runs as follows. Your whole theory is based upon the tacit assumption that existence itself is good at least in the sense that it is better to be than not to be. But this metaphysical assumption is unempirical, illicit, and even absurd. If existence as such were good, we should be satisfied with things as they already are, for surely they are. But this would be the end of aspiration and of ethics. What we strive for rather is what is not. Such a nonexistent value is the goal of our aspiration precisely when it does not exist. This is enough to show that a good thing is equally valuable whether it exists or not. Value is a certain property, or set of properties, entirely indifferent to existence. The two realms are separate and neutral to each other.

In answer, we may point out that this metaphysical objection is based upon the common assumption that existence is fully finished or complete. As we have already noted, this assumption is refuted by abundant empirical evidence. We are never satisfied with things as they already are because they are always tendentially incomplete. What is good is the fulfilment of being. We strive to complete our existence. The widespread idea that we strive for nonbeing (unless we are nihilists) is not only bad philosophy but bad phenomenology as well.

It is true that human aspiration aims at a goal that is at first only imagined and not yet fully actual. But what we strive for is precisely the realization of this ideal, whatever it may be. Suppose we could have all the most marvelous glories and perfections under the one condition that they would not exist but would remain mere possibilities. Would we be any better off? This is enough to show that value cannot be divorced from existence. The "realm" of value is very wide and very rich. But it is no richer than the realm of being, for beyond this realm lies only nothingness, not value.

4. Finally, it will be said that this analysis of goodness is far too universal. In ordinary usage, terms like value and disvalue are applied to man alone. When applied to animals, plants, and most of all to inorganic entities, they lose their peculiar and distinctive meaning and become equivocal. Subhuman entities have no intrinsic value in themselves but only an instrumental value in conditioning or aiding in the attainment of human good.

We must, of course, agree to the objection, so far as common usage is concerned. Intrinsic value is commonly conceived as pertaining peculiarly to human life. There are at least two reasons for this. The first is the fact that we happen to be human beings. As such, we have a more intimate access to, and certainly a more intensive concern for, our own human values than for those of nonhuman beings. This, I believe, takes us far in accounting for ordinary usage. In accepting it, however, with all its consequences, as the expression of a fully verified ontological principle, that all value is human value, we must be on our guard against the familiar anthropocentrism which is often responsible for such attitudes and which is usually revealed by a critical scrutiny of the relevant facts. Thus, we do judge animals and even plants to be in a sound or healthy condition, and there is no reason for not taking such judgments seriously as a recognition of intrinsic value of a low order. This brings us to the second reason.

From a purely unbiased theoretical point of view, I think there is good reason for holding that human values are actually of a higher order than those achieved by subhuman entities. On the basis of the analysis we have suggested, a value is an act. What, then, is meant by acts of a higher and lower order? Such acts may be compared with respect to essence, existence, and the union of the two. Thus, acts may differ in what we call quality (essence), spontaneity (existence), and scope (breadth of being). Each of these yields a criterion by which we judge the ontological height of an act.

The first concerns the essence or, as we say, the quality of the act. Every act is of a certain kind. Some of these kinds may be immediately discriminated as intrinsically higher or lower.

Thus, the deliberate act of keeping a promise is intrinsically better than a nonreflective act of eating or walking, and the intrinsic value pertaining to one act of the former kind will outweigh the values achieved by an indefinite number of the latter. Certain human acts are qualitatively better than any which can be performed by other observable entities.

But an act is not exhausted by its quality or kind. It is also the activity of an existing being. As we have already observed, an act which is frustrated or deprived of complete fulfilment is also deprived of value. It is less actual and therefore less good. But the active agent may also be more or less active and responsible for the act. This gives us a second criterion. An agent performing an act autonomously, out of himself, without external influence or constraint, is more active and, therefore, at a higher ontological level or mode than one performing a similar act as a result of alien pressure. Human persons are far more immanently active in this sense than other agents known to us.

In addition to the quality and existential mode of the action, there is a third criterion of ontological value we may call scope. The natural world is organized in such a way that acts of higher quality and spontaneity are always dependent on acts of lower quality and mode. The former are never found without the latter, but the latter can occur without the former. The plant's operations of nutrition and growth are founded on acts of the inorganic order. The sensory pursuit and avoidance of the animal are founded on nutrition and growth. The deliberate acts of man, in turn, are founded on animal behavior. Thus, the higher agent performs operations of a lower order as well as operations peculiar to its own type. Its activity is wider in scope. This is a third criterion.

These considerations lead to the following conclusion. Human actions are of peculiar importance for two kinds of reason. First, they are more important to us because we happen to be men and are thus more concerned with them. They are, in fact, ontologically more important than other natural modes of action because they are higher in quality, more immanent in mode, and wider in scope. There is no reason, however, for refusing to recognize the lower intrinsic values which are realized in the activities of subhuman forms of life and even in the still lower values of nonliving operations about which very little can be known except by analogy.

This must serve as a sample of major difficulties which must be met by such an ontological theory of value. On the other side, we must note at least three advantages possessed by this theory as over against current contenders in the field.

First, there is the fact that it enables us to present an intelligible characterization of value and disvalue which seems to be verified by evidence coming from many widely separated fields, running all the way from botany and zoology to the moral experience of men. The theory does not require us to think of value and disvalue as subsistent objects inhabiting a peculiar nonempirical realm. They are empirical facts—ontological facts —directly observed in the data of experience.

Second, the theory does not require us to dismiss values as indefinable or ineffable qualities or properties. They are existential structures which may be coherently and intelligibly characterized.

Finally, in the third place, this theory enables us to understand the thread of continuity and similarity that runs through the vast variety of goods of different kinds and orders. It is only by penetrating to the basic ontological level of existence and action that we may do this, for there is no single property or quality which even different human goods can have in common, to say nothing of nonhuman goods. What, for example, does the good of keeping a difficult promise have in common with the good of eating a steak? They have no specific property in common. The one is reflective, arduous, and painful, the other nonreflective, easily achieved, and enjoyable. Rational deliberation consists in the weighing of such wholly divergent goods against one another.

According to certain current deontological theories, they have nothing in common. Hence, rational deliberation is impossible. But we do deliberate. Hence, such theories must be in error. What, then, do such values have in common? Not pleasure—for the realizing of an obligation may be extremely unpleasant. The identification of goodness with any such univocal quality must result in the arbitrary dismissal of other goods with different properties. We thus seem faced with a dilemma—either the reductionism of some such theory as utilitarianism, or a deontological separation of the goods that must make deliberation unintelligible.

According to our theory, there is a possible way out through analogy, an existential relational similarity. The act of fulfilling a promise and the act of eating are both acts. Their qualities may be entirely diverse. Nevertheless, they may be analogously similar and comparable. As the act of keeping a promise is to a certain basic tendency of our nature (to rationally govern our behavior by consistent action to others), so is the act of eating to another tendency of lower quality. The two acts differ in intrinsic value. But they have an analogical similarity by which they may be compared and weighed against each other with reference to quality, mode, and scope. This is true even of the divergent values of different species. A fish is different from a man. But the activation (or good) of a fish is to the fish as the activation (or good) of a man is to the man.

There is, of course, no single univocal quality or property under which the different values can be subsumed to make a quantitative calculus possible. But an existential comparison is possible. Value is realization or activation of being. Deliberation brings the most basic ontological categories into play and depends more especially on our insight into the peculiar being of man.

Which course of action will realize the higher qualities of being? One act of genuine generosity may outweigh millions of units of animal satisfaction by its existential quality. What course of conduct will be the more immanent and active in the sense of emanating from the agent himself? One such spontaneous act may have an existential value that outweighs those achieved by many otherwise similar acts externally elicited by threat. By what mode of action will the essentially human be least inadequately expressed and revealed? Such questions as these reveal the criteria of quality, immanence, and scope which may guide us in that process of weighing and appraising different ways of existing which we call *deliberation*. Human existence is at stake. Ontological insight is required.

Section II. THE NATURE OF OBLIGATION

Obligation is a peculiar datum of human experience which includes a factor of apprehension together with a subjective feeling of urgent tendency towards what is apprehended. Both factors are required, each in union with the other. An unconscious compulsion is not an obligation. On the other hand, no judgment as such, even though it is concerned with the most lofty and appealing values, can establish an obligation unless it calls forth a peculiar feeling of oughtness and binds or obliges us to act.

A. REALISTIC ANALYSIS

The chief difficulty now confronting contemporary theories is that of giving an intelligible explanation of both factors in that peculiar union which constitutes an obligation. Naturalistic theories begin with the theoretical side and emphasize certain empirical facts of pleasure, or satisfaction, which may be expressed in judgments that such and such has pleased me or has pleased millions of people. But they fail to explain why such facts should in any sense give rise to the unique sense of necessitation or binding-to-action which characterizes the actual phenomenon. Most thinkers of this school now pride themselves on being empiricists, and by *empiricism* they mean an atomic theory of experienced data which rules out all dynamism and tendency and, therefore, makes any tendential connection between discrete data inconceivable. For such thinkers, obligation is a hard nut to crack.

The only sort of empirical judgment they can admit with any relevance to ethics is the sort we have mentioned, stating some psychological fact: that such and such has aroused interest before or has pleased vast multitudes of people. But because this is so, why should I be bound in any way? How does it follow that because others have been pleased I ought to be pleased? It certainly does not follow with any logical necessity from such facts as these. Nor would it seem to follow with any psychological necessity, since I may be different. No matter how many people have been pleased by something, it is not necessary that I must be pleased by it. Why, then, should the statement of any such law be binding upon me?

At best, it might lead to the prediction that it is highly probable I might be pleased. But when I really feel that I ought to do *x*, this is not equivalent to the assertion that it is likely that I shall do *x*, and the feelings that attend such an assertion. I often feel that I ought to do something which it is highly unlikely that I shall do. Sometimes I go on feeling that I ought to have done something which I actually did not do and now can never do. Oughtness cannot be reduced to probable expectation.

Neither can it be reduced to any feeling or judgment concerning subjective states or conditions already attained. This is notorious. Because I now feel some desire within me, it does not follow that I ought to be desiring this. Because I now feel pleasure, it does not follow that I ought to feel it.

Obligation seems to be some kind of necessity that obliges and binds. So some have assumed a type of necessary psychological law, like psychological egoism, which would explain why certain judgments such as *x is pleasing* would necessarily arouse subjective urgency of desire. Such a theory would seem to come closest to the actual phenomena, but is still far wide of the mark. Obligation does not necessitate in *this sense*, for people often do not fulfil their obligations, knowing that they do not. In addition to this, there are many insuperable difficulties in psychological hedonism as a theory of human motivation and in any similar theory.

Obligation cannot be reduced to the statement of a finished fact, nor to the expectation of a probable future fact, nor to the recognition of a necessary psychological law of sequence, involving specific objects of desire, if any such law exists. No atomic empiricist has yet suggested a plausible theory of obligation. And I believe it is possible to see, on the basis of such an analysis as we have given, that no such theory can possibly account for the facts.

Impressed by these difficulties, another school, the so-called intuitionists, have insisted that rightness or obligation is a simple, irreducible, and even indefinable quality, which is directly apprehended or intuited as belonging to certain acts and not to others. Acts of promise-keeping, for example, possess this peculiar, nonnatural property. Such an act is intuited to be right, irrespective of whether its consequences are hedonically attractive or unattractive. This kind of theory has shown a marked capacity to take account of certain unquestionable moral data and to reveal the weaknesses of naturalistic and utilitarian theories. But recent discussion has revealed serious weaknesses of its own.

For one thing, to call a property nonempirical or nonnatural is to give a purely negative definition which conveys a minimum of information about the property in question and leaves an indefinite number of alternatives open. But though the question has been pressed as to what this peculiar property is, the defenders of the theory have been unable to present us with any adequate answer. They have produced negative epithets, pointed at examples, and then sometimes fallen back on the last refuge of indefinability. But this is unsatisfactory. Essential ambiguity at such a basic level is bound to permeate the whole theory and fill it with vagueness and confusion.

This weakness has now brought forth a noncognitive or emotive theory of ethics which reduces the whole phenomenon of obligation to the subjective compulsion of raw appetite or desire. To feel obligation is simply to be bound by an urgent appetite for or against something. Once such a desire has arisen, it may be qualified and redirected by cognitive cognition of relevant facts. But its origin is independent of cognition. Ethical terms like good and bad, right and wrong, have no descriptive or cognitive meaning. They are rather to be understood expressively as manifestations of desire, and persuasively as its diffusive tendency. Such language may be good or bad, i.e., approved or disapproved by us. It is neither true nor false.

While this theory has performed an important function in bringing home to modern thought the existence of a noncognitive factor in all practical reflection, its extreme irrationalism has laid it open to serious charges of which we shall mention only two. The first is this. Why should the desiderative element in obligation be thought of as a blind eruption of arbitrary impulse and thus identified with raw appetite? Many facts seem incompatible with such a conclusion. Because I want something it does not follow that I *ought* to want it. There are many cases where obligation conflicts with blind impulse and raw desire.

In connection with this, many proponents of the theory concede that cognitive evidence may qualify and redirect desire once it has arisen. But if such evidence (true or false) may thus moderate desire, why can it not elicit and direct such active tendency in the first place, as the facts of moral experience seem so clearly to indicate? Thus, suddenly becoming aware of certain facts, expressed in certain judgments that are true or false, acute suffering before me, and powers at my command, I may suddenly experience a new sense of obligation having nothing to do with my raw appetites and even radically opposed to them.

The second objection is even more critical. Unless obligation is in some sense grounded on verifiable cognitive judgments that are true or false, moral justification is impossible. According to this theory, it is impossible. When a moral decision is questioned, all we can do is to reiterate some active propensity in expressive or persuasive language. Such questions, then, are out of place and even meaningless. But we all feel justified in raising such questions, and they are not adequately answered by emotive diatribes. They can be answered only by judgments that are true or false in the light of moral evidence. Sometimes we find that one act is more justifiable than another and may alter our behavior accordingly. Facts of this sort are ubiquitous and well-known. The theory cannot be reconciled with them. Hence, an empiricist must reject it.

Having noted these current moral theories and certain major difficulties confronted by them, let us now turn to moral realism. Can it shed any light on obligation? I think it can. But we shall have to be very brief in confining our attention to certain phases of the theory which are relevant to the issues we have raised.

The logical atomist regards goodness as a fixed determinate structure rather than as an existential category. We have noted some of the difficulties in this view. As the realist sees it, most of these difficulties with obligation are rooted in a similar atomistic tendency to conceive it as a property. No such determinate univ-ocal property is found. Hence, we are led to the dogma of in-definability. Reality is not made up of properties alone but of existent properties with active tendencies. Obligation is another existential category founded on this fact of tendency which can be intelligibly described and characterized.

Each entity necessarily tends to act in accordance with its structure. So close is this ontological connection that each may be inferred from the other. From observing a kind of action in its measurable effect, the physicist can infer something about the structure of the entity, and from his knowledge of structure he may predict a tendency. In concrete nature, one is never found without the other. A peculiar relation of fitness holds be-tween the two.

A similar relation of fitness holds between a tendency and its fulfilment, though this is not necessary. Many tendencies exist in a privative or unfulfilled state. But we cannot understand the tendency without also understanding something of the fitting fulfilment. As soon as a biologist grasps the nature of a mode of vital action, he also grasps what will complete such action—the sound or healthy condition. Two points need to be noted about such knowledge.

First, it does not necessarily involve any attribution of con-scious purpose or teleology to the tendency in question. A mete-orologist charts the course now required to complete the tenden-cies already observed in a storm without assuming any con-scious purpose in the weather. What underlies such lawful "pre-dictions" is merely a knowledge of the observed dispositions and their intrinsic readiness, barring external factors, for a certain mode of completion.

The second point to notice is that this relation of fitness can be read in two ways from tendency to fulfilment (goodness) or back from fulfilment to tendency (rightness). The former is less necessary than the latter but more factual in the sense of sheer thereness. The tendency requires its realization as something more, not yet included in itself. Such requiredness is not strictly necessary. The tendency may be warped or impeded. But the fulfilment entails the tendency as something included within itself. The tendency persists in its realizations. This is strictly necessary and binding.

The tendencies of inorganic things have such a low level of quality and so little existential autonomy and scope that we ignore their relatively slight intrinsic value but think of them rather in terms of the extrinsic value they may have in aiding or hindering other tendencies of a higher level. But in the case of subhuman living things, we refer to incipient tendencies by value terms like requirement or need, and to their fulfilment by others like normal, sound, or healthy. When we analyze the structure in this way, we are recognizing the existential category of goodness—realization of imperfect tendency. Furthermore, we sometimes argue back from the realization to what it requires of the incipient tendency and speak of a diseased or warped plant in terms of how it should have grown, or of a maimed animal in terms of what it ought to have done to avoid the injury. There is no implication of any conscious teleology in this. We are merely recognizing existential tendencies requiring further acts for their fitting realization in accordance with nature. This requiredness lies at the root of what we call *obligation*.

Human existence is constituted by diverse tendencies, some shared by every human individual and indispensable to human life, others peculiar to certain individuals or groups, and dispensable. The latter are commonly called *desires*, *interests*, or *compulsions*. The former are rightly distinguished as needs. They must be realized to some degree if human life is to be lived at all—for example, the need for food and the need for education. When clearly focused by rational insight, they are called *rights*.

They have a right to be realized not merely because someone, or a great number of men, happens to feel them, but because they are required by human nature itself and the cosmic causes of human nature. The rational recognition of such natural needs and their distinction from ephemeral desires is the first step in the transformation of raw appetite into moral obligation. These needs are felt by the individual as unfinished tendencies in himself and others.

Now no tendency can be clearly understood without some understanding of what it requires for its completion. As soon as we recognize a need, we also recognize the universal value that will satisfy the need. The apprehension of such universal values, not relative to the particular interests of this or that individual or group, but tendentially relative to human nature as such is the second step in the complex experience of moral obligation. At this stage, we have the felt urge of existential common tendencies and the rational insight into the nonexistent values required to complete them.

That which will complete an inchoate tendency is some form of activity, either individual or co-operative. Rights can be realized only by acts. Hence, from universal values satisfying human needs, certain modes of action necessarily involved in them may be strictly deduced. Such modes of action, always required for the realization of human rights, are right acts or universal duties of man. The recognition of such prima facie duties, as Ross has called them, is the third step in the structure of obligation. We now have felt propulsive urge, recognized as need, cognition of value satisfying the need, and deduction of necessary acts from the value.

The fourth step is the subsumption of the individual in a concrete situation under a universal conclusion of the preceding deductions. I vaguely feel the desire to learn the truth from others. I clearly and abstractly understand this as a necessary condition of human communication, without which human co-operation and life is impossible; I understand the nature of truth-telling from this. Finally, I realize that in the situation before me I can tell the truth; and subsuming myself under the generalization, I recognize that I ought to tell the truth here and now.

But the concrete situation is always very rich and confused. The needs of man are multifarious. The duty of telling the truth may not only conflict with certain subjective desires over which it should clearly take precedence. It may also conflict with other basic needs of man such as that of preserving life. In this case, I must weigh the values to be achieved by alternative courses of action against one another and attempt to devise creatively some unique course of action that will minimize the sacrifice of value. Such a weighing of divergent values is always involved in any serious process of deliberation.

It certainly has a quantitative aspect. Where conflicting values are on approximately the same qualitative level, this quantitative aspect may be decisive. But usually those of different qualitative levels are at stake. In this case, there is no univocal quality or property under which the different values can be subsumed to make a quantitative calculus possible. But an existential comparison is possible. Value is realization or activation of being. Deliberation brings the most basic ontological categories into play and depends more especially on our insight into the peculiar being of man. Existential insight is required. But the process is not purely theoretical.

Fused with it from beginning to end is the urge to activate our nature which permeates all the psychical and physical phases of our being. It is the feeling of this imperative urgency to act which lies at the root of obligation. This expansive tendency inheres in our very being. Hence, it is felt as something which obliges us or binds us to act—to become what we are. That which will complete or activate a tendency is good. If the tendency belongs to man as such, if it must be activated to some degree in any living of a genuine human life, then it is a universal and intrinsic good for man. As we gain further insight into these tendencies and their goals, our thought is able to pass from the goal to the acts which this goal strictly implies, and therefore demands from every man, and finally from us in the concrete. This feeling of deductive strengthening which obliges us is also expressed by the word *ought*.

Such is the theory of human obligation to which our analysis leads. Let us now compare it with other contemporary theories.

B. COMPARISON WITH OTHER THEORIES

The realist is able to see a certain truth both in the emotive theory which identifies obligation with the felt propulsive force of appetites and interests, and in the intuitive theory which identifies it with rationally apprehended values and duties. But neither theory is sufficient by itself. The emotive theory is right in calling attention to the felt propulsion of subjective desire which is the beginning of obligation and the propulsion of ought-ness which is its end. But something has happened in between. The urge of oughtness cannot be identified with the uncriticized propulsion of raw appetite. Certain crucially important phases of rational reflection and justification have been omitted. Raw desires that cannot withstand this reflective criticism are often condemned by the final *ought*. Hence, the emotive theory can offer no intelligible account of moral justification. The mere feeling of a subjective desire does not justify itself. This leads to an individual subjective relativism.

Those different forms of utilitarian ethics, now commonly referred to as *naturalism*, try to meet this objection by their interpretation of moral reflection as a statistical counting of raw appetites and a recommendation of that course of action which will satisfy *the most*. But this theory also enslaves obligation to raw desire in a way which cannot account for evident facts. If the felt desire of a single agent cannot justify itself, it is hard to see why the mere addition of a million more should provide us with the qualitative factor obviously lacking. Instead of an individual moral relativism, we are landed in a social subjective relativism.

If most of my contemporaries happen to delight in certain things, this *eo ipso* is supposed to place me under an obligation to maintain the status quo. Obligation often binds men to rebel against vast numbers of their contemporaries and to struggle for things that are displeasing to overwhelming majorities. Sometimes these rebellions have been justified. Moral issues cannot be decided by statistics. What is right has a certain moral content which is universal in a sense that quantities of raw appetite can never have. The moral ought is qualitatively distinct from uncriticized appetite. Its actual content is often quite different from that of desire.

Some difference is recognized even by the utilitarian theory. After deliberation, the moral naturalist is supposed to desire not only the raw satisfactions that he has sensuously experienced but the greatest satisfaction of the greatest number. This will include many pleasures which he has not directly experienced at all but to which he has access only through theoretical judgments that are probably true. But why should such descriptive judgments have any binding power over my motivation? This question must cause embarrassment to the modern naturalist because of his nominalistic theory of human motivation.

According to this view, human drives are directed only towards satisfactions that are concretely felt. But such satisfactions are also restricted to the individual who experiences them. Why, then, should I be moved by the pleasures of another which I have never experienced? Why should I be bound by pleasure in general, to which I have no direct empirical access? Why should I feel any obligation to act in accordance with principles of justice, demanding that each satisfaction count for one, when such principles are never sensed but apprehended only by universal concepts and judgments? Why should I be obliged to alter my raw appetites to subordinate certain ones to others in order to seek a harmony of interests or a greatest good of the greatest number which I am incapable of directly experiencing?

As a matter of evident fact, we do feel bound by these universal obligations which the universal hedonist or utilitarian recognizes. In order to account for this fact, we must abandon the so-called "empirical" theory of value. We must recognize certain "nonempirical" or nonnatural values which do not belong to the realm of "experience," as this is ordinarily conceived, but which are intuited by a nonsensuous cognitive faculty of some sort. The chief empirical argument against deontologism then breaks down. Why should we not be able to cognize other nonnatural values in addition to universal pleasure, why not a universal oughtness, etc.? As we see so clearly in Sidgwick, when the utilitarian gets this far he has already abandoned what is most distinctive in his theory and is far gone in the direction of intuitionism.

Intuitionism is correct in recognizing the apprehension of universal value. The compulsive push of raw appetite must be distinguished from the binding power of obligation. The former can exist without any factor of universal apprehension; the latter cannot. Only that which is recognized as binding upon *any* man can bind me morally with the force of obligation. But what is the nature of this binding power? Why should a descriptive judgment concerning some universal property hold *me* or oblige *me* as an existing individual in any way? What is the relation of this property to my individual subjective motives? When such questions are pressed, they reveal two weaknesses in the intuitionist theory.

The intuitionist rightly sees that the value intuitions underlying moral obligation cannot be identified with those individual occurrences which, according to the so-called *empiricist*, make up the whole of our natural experience. These values are universal and not yet actualized. But instead of challenging the a priori atomism which underlies this view of experience, he tacitly accepts it. Then he is forced to imagine another nonempirical realm of value properties or abstract essences cognized only by peculiar nonnatural intuitions. This radical dualism places him at once at a great disadvantage. If values are not facts, nor even essentially related to empirical facts, what then are they? Where are they? What evidence can be offered for such suppositious nonfactual entities? No convincing evidence has been found. This deontological conception plays into the hands of naturalism.

It also leads to a second and even more serious difficulty. Even supposing that such nonempirical value entities exist, why should the cognition of them have any binding power over the factual motivations of men, or even any relevance to us? Knowledge about such entities, if we could attain it, might be supposed to possess a certain abstract interest. But how could it possibly bind or oblige us to act? I believe that moral realism shows us a way by which such difficulties can be avoided.

1. As we have seen, tendencies are facts. It is true that the fulfilment of tendency, which we call *value*, is not yet a fact. In this sense, the intuitionist is right. Values are not finished facts, except when they are past. But we do not need to assume a separate realm for them, divorced from the real world of nature. As the completion of unfinished, temporal tendency, they are grounded on the dynamic structure of this world. No other world of subsistence is necessary. This is our answer to the first difficulty. Human value is the universal apprehension of a dynamic tendency as realized.

2. As to the second—why should such an apprehension have any binding force over me?—the answer lies in the fact that I am a dynamic tendential existent. I subjectively feel the urges to human completion in my being. Hence, the clear understanding of what must be done to realize these urges is bound to move me with the peculiar dynamic feeling of *ought*, though I need not act upon this feeling. I understand the universal nature of a tendency concretely felt in my being: I recognize the universal value which would realize it; I deduce certain acts required by such realization; I see that I can perform such acts; I have the feeling of *ought*, or obligation. If a certain tendential pattern is to be realized, such an act *ought* to be performed.

But why should it be? Here we confront the profound need for justification. Can this hypothetical premise be justified? Can we reverse the logical process and confirm it by evidence accessible to all?

If not, our basic moral choices are wholly arbitrary, and ethics as a responsible discipline is impossible. There can be no such thing as ethical argument but only persuasive and suggestive propaganda. As a matter of fact, we do ask for moral justification both from ourselves and from others. We do argue over the correctness and incorrectness of choice. This implies that modes of action may be based on mistaken factual premises and that certain obligations may be based on factual judgments capable of verification.

How is this possible? How can the *ought* be deduced from or inferred from the *is?* Can realism throw any light on this matter? We shall conclude this paper by attempting to indicate how various suggestions already made may be fitted into an affirmative answer to this question.

Section III. Moral Justification

It is clear that justification is in some sense a logical process. If one of my subjective tendencies or acts is to be justified, I must discover some universal evaluational premise based upon facts open to observation under which I can subsume my tendency or act. Two things about such a premise need to be especially emphasized. In the first place, it must be a universal principle evident to any unbiased observer. Unless I can explain my act to such an observer, I am not justified. In the second place, this principle must be relevant to my own subjective tendencies. Otherwise, it could not subsume my act or have any binding power over me.

Recent criticism has shown that current ethical doctrines are unable to provide us consistently with any principles of this sort and are thus unable to account for the phenomenon of justification. This is perhaps most clearly evident in the case of the so-called noncognitive school. According to it, even though moral attitudes may be incidentally modified by the influence of purely cognitive judgments of fact, such attitudes are primarily the result of subjective urges peculiar to individuals or groups and have nothing to do with any facts which can be expressed by universal theoretical judgments. For such thinkers, the theoretical justification of moral imperatives is obviously impossible. Their position is based upon an underlining of this divorce between the theoretical and the practical. There is no such thing as moral justification. This has to be interpreted as a mere propaganda device. Moral disagreement in a theoretical sense is impossible. Such argument has to be interpreted as a mere battle of emotive language. The trouble is that men do actually seek to justify themselves. They do disagree and argue, even about fundamental moral questions. These are stubborn facts which the theory does not explain.

The intuitionist view is very different. It also maintains that the ought is radically separated from the is. Rightness is the peculiar intuition of a nonnatural property that cannot be further explained or analyzed. Hence, justification in the ordinary sense of this word is impossible. The property is unique and indefinable. To intuit this property is to be already under obligation. If we ask why we ought to do something, the only answer that can be given is because you ought.

But if this ought is sharply separated from all natural properties, it is difficult to see how any intuition of it can have a binding power over factual desires. The theory is overly intellectualistic in that it pays no attention to this imperative aspect of obligation. Why should the cognition of an isolated property oblige me to act if it is wholly disconnected from existent psychological structure and tendency? If it is said that such an apprehension automatically calls forth a feeling of active urgency, this seems rather an *ad hoc* assumption than an intelligible explanation, especially since the property is only ostensively referred to and never coherently defined or characterized. The quest for moral justification is a stubborn moral fact. It is not satisfied by the sterile repetition of a tautology. Hence, the theory is not entirely satisfactory.

The naturalist does at least have a theory of justification. According to him, it is right to perform acts which have given pleasure or have satisfied the interests of large numbers of people in the past. But the theory is unsatisfactory for the reasons already mentioned. These are primarily two. First, it does not explain the universality of obligation. What I ought to do is what anyone in similar circumstances ought to do, not merely what those with special appetites would do. Why yield to such special influences? This requires justification. Until we reach principles that hold for all, we are not justified. Naturalistic reflection must fall short of such universality. Some people have been pleased with certain things. This is a special fact that cannot justify me. No matter how many more persons we add to the billion and the billion billion, the proposition remains particular. I am either universally justified or not at all.

In the second place, the universal propositions by which human acts are justified must be recognized as in some sense binding, obliging me to act. This implies some connection with urgent tendency. Since the proposition is universal, it must be connected with some characteristic of human nature which I share. But naturalistic theories recognize only particular appetites and pleasures directed to particular objects. Hence, they cannot explain how any universal proposition can have any close connection with appetite. There is no universal appetite.

A. REALISTIC ANALYSIS

How, then, is moral justification to be explained?

We cannot explain it without recognizing that certain moral premises must somehow be based upon facts. What kind of facts are these? And what is meant by "based upon"? According to realism, the chief difficulties we have with this question arise from our tendency to think of all facts as finished properties and to ignore their existential status.

Existence is dynamic, indeterminate, and incomplete. It is not a property but a structuralized activity. Such activities are a kind of fact. They can be observed and described by judgments that are true or false: human life needs material artifacts; technological endeavors need rational guidance; the child has cognitive faculties that need education. Value statements are founded on tendential facts of this sort. They do not merely state the observed fact. They go beyond it. But they are founded on the directly verifiable fact of tendency or need. The value or realization is required not merely by us but by the existent tendency for its completion. From a sound description and analysis of the given tendency we can infer the value founded upon it. This is why we do not say that moral principles are mere statements of fact but rather that they are founded on facts.

Universal tendencies like that of hunger, which are common to all men, will found universal values. So moral argument has a factual foundation. It may find support or fail to find it in descriptive judgments that are true or false. Suppose I have performed an act of type z and raise the question as to whether it is justified. If observable evidence shows y to be a universal need of man, and if z is reasonably inferred to be a value completing y, then it is justified.

So far, however, we have only a complex set of inductive and inferential procedures, leading to certain principles of value founded on observable fact. Why are such principles felt to be binding on me? This is the last thing to be explained. The answer should be clear from what we have already said. The factual needs which underlie the whole procedure are common to man. The values founded on them are universal. Hence, if I have made no mistake in my tendential analysis of human nature, and if I understand myself, I must exemplify the tendency and must feel it subjectively as an imperative urge to action. If I am confronted with such a principle, together with the implied acts it requires of me, and then feel no obligation, one of two things is true. Either the principle is not adequate grounded and therefore false, or I do not understand myself.

In the case of any deductive argument, we may pass from the premises to the conclusion, or in checking our steps, from the conclusion back to the premises, and the facts on which these premises are based. This is also true of moral reflection. In the process which leads to the sense of obligation, we pass from certain universal facts to premises based on these facts and then to certain deductive conclusions which state obligations. In trying to justify ourselves, we reverse this process. Here, we begin with a supposed obligation, a sense that we ought to do something which is subject to question and needs to be confirmed. In so far as this feeling is justified, we are able to pass back to certain values which require the acts, to certain needs which the values satisfy, and to factual evidence showing these needs to be essential rights of man.

To discover an obligation and to justify it are simply two ways of reading the same logical process which mutually confirm and illumine each other. But the evidence is very rich. The inferences are complex. Thus, in attempting to justify an obligation, we often discover new obligations, and in doing this we are led to a new process of justification. On the whole, it is clear that those most sensitive to obligations are better able to justify themselves and vice versa. The one process is the inverse of the other. Such is the realistic conception of justification.

B. ANSWER TO OBJECTIONS

In connection with possible difficulties, several points deserve special attention. We must note first of all that moral obligation is justified by certain facts expressible in universal judgments concerning human needs or rights. But these are facts of a peculiar kind, not finished and complete but dynamic and tendential. We may refer to them as tendential facts. The feeling of oughtness is such a tendential fact.

Second, we must emphasize the fact that such needs or rights must be realized to some degree in the living of human life. In this sense, they are common to all men and shared by the reflective agent himself—inherent in his being. Hence, the first premise of a deliberative process must not only express the factual existence of a human need but must also be felt as an active tendency in the reflective agent himself. If he does not actually feel it, then either he does not understand himself or the premise is not universal and therefore false. In so far as the premise is true and the agent is aware of the urgent desire within himself, we have that peculiar union of universal reflection and urgent tendency which distinguishes moral or practical reflection and runs through the whole process from beginning to end.

Finally, the premises are not particular. They state universal tendential facts which are common to man. Hence, the deductions from them are binding on any human being no matter what his special appetites and circumstances may be. They will hold true of any man so far as he is man. An influential view of human motivation holds that impulse can be called forth only by some individual object of sense or imagination. If this theory is true, men can never be moved by the universal apprehensions of reason. But the facts of obligation show definitely that they are so moved. Hence, this theory is false.

Human nature is incomplete and dynamic. From the very start it is characterized by a general drive to realize basic needs. This drive is always partially canalized into special appetites directed towards individual objects of sense. But it can also be moved by the universal apprehensions of discursive reflection. Such insights alone are capable of directing it towards that complete activation which is the natural end of man. These insights into natural rights and duties are the source of obligation and the basis of justification.

Such a realistic theory is not subject to some of the major objections which have recently been raised in the discussion of prevailing ethical theories. Unlike noncognitivism, it is able to explain how the ought is founded on a certain type of fact, tendential fact, and how moral justification is possible. Unlike intuitionism, it does not attempt to ward off all questions by the identification of good and right with simple, nonnatural, and even ineffable properties. Finally, unlike naturalism and utilitarianism, it is able to offer an intelligent account of universal moral principles grounded on observable fact (the fact of need), and to explain without internal inconsistency how the cognition of such principles may move rational appetite.

It can thus answer many difficulties which beset other current theories. But on the other hand, it has much in common with them. With noncognitivism it shares the view that moral reflection includes a nontheoretical factor of imperative desire, moving in the moral agent and binding him to act. With intuitionism it shares the view that such reflection also includes a cognitive factor of rational intuition or apprehension. Finally, with naturalism it holds that moral obligation is justified by certain observable, natural facts (needs) which may be described in propositions that are true.

Section IV. EXISTENCE, VALUE, AND OBLIGATION

I shall now attempt to show very briefly that such an analysis as we have suggested is capable of shedding light on the fundamental categories of ethics and of bringing supposedly isolated atomic concepts into a meaningful relational unity. Let us begin with value and existence. From an essentialist point of view which regards existence as something fixed and finished, value is something else quite separate. Value is what ought to be. And the ought implies a certain futurity and tension which cannot belong to a finished fact. Hence, value is thought of as a peculiar kind of quality or property dwelling in its own realm apart from actual existence. But if value is really separated from existence completely, how can it be anything at all? Surely, there is some relation between the two. What is this?

Our analysis suggests a reasonable answer to this fundamental question. Existence, as we have seen, is tendential. Value is the fulfilment of existential tendency. It is true that it cannot be identified with any finished fact except in so far as this includes fulfilment. But in the concrete, no facts are ever finished. They are incomplete and tendential. Hence the sense of futurity and tension that attaches to the concept of the *ought*.

How, then, is value related to that which exists at a given moment? That towards which an entity is essentially tending, which will realize its nature, is good for it. This is the relation of fitness. By value, we mean what is fit for a thing, what is due to its nature, the further existence that will complete its basic tendencies, and its incidental tendencies as well, so far as these do not conflict with the former.

Can value, then, be deduced from fact? If by deduction we mean the tautology of modern logic, the answer is of course *no*. The fitting fulfilment of a tendency is not the same as its incipient stages. A synthetic connection is involved. But if we mean by *synthetic* two separate items which merely succeed each other in time with no real bond between, the answer to this again is *no*. We cannot apprehend an incipient tendency with any degree of clarity without understanding something of the Gestalt determining it and its fitting fulfilment. Thus, a biologist cannot observe a fossil skeleton without understanding something of the fitting activities required to complete its tendencies, the requisite environment, etc.

The tendency is not an atomic essence which we first understand by itself alone and from which we then "infer" the completion as another separate entity. It is rather a relational activity which is either grasped all together with some degree of clarity or not at all. In apprehending a relation, we must apprehend something of its term; so in apprehending a tendency, we must grasp something of what it is tending towards. Thus, values are rightly said to be founded on facts.

Does this mean that value is to be identified with all existence, and that what is, is right? By no means. Existence is tendential. This tendency may proceed in a fitting manner towards its natural fulfilment. The entity is then said to be in a sound or correct condition. On the other hand, it may be warped and impeded and still go on existing. Such existence is said to be unsound and incorrect. Goodness, therefore, is not to be identified with any existent fact cut off from the future, nor with a nonexistent property cut off from all existence. It is an existential fulfilment, fit for, and thus founded on, the essence and its essential tendencies.

Let us now turn to goodness and obligation which are also commonly separated by contemporary schools of ethics. Thus, goodness is held to be an object of cognition with no binding power, while oughtness is a subjectively felt, compulsive tendency to act. Hence, they are divorced as though they were fixed essences like greenness and blueness, as though goodness ought not to be achieved, and as though doing what I ought to do were not good. Surely this is absurd. What, then, is the relation between the two?

The essential needs or tendencies of human nature may be objectively understood, together with the fitting values or realizations founded upon them. From these values certain modes of required action may then be strictly deduced and stated in the moral law of nature. In a given situation, I may see that such an act is possible for me. I will then experience that peculiar union of rational insight into the tendential nature of man and the law founded on this nature, together with subjectively felt tendency (for I myself am human) which constitutes what we call an obligation. If I have ever paid any attention to the factual tendencies of human nature, I must feel something of this sort. If I do not feel it in a given instance, either my analysis of the tendency is wrong or I do not understand myself.

Section V. MORAL REALISM AND THE WORLD OF TODAY

From this basic ontological point of view, I am not forced to reduce oughtness to goodness, goodness to oughtness, or goodness to existence. Neither am I forced to separate them into isolated atomic compartments. They may be fitted together as existential categories into a meaningful structure that corresponds with the data of moral experience. But this will require the abandonment of essentialist prejudices very dear to the modern mind.

The first of these is the doctrine that value, if it is anything at all, must be a peculiar quality or property. Such a view must lead either to a reductionist ethics like hedonism and utilitarianism, a chaotic view like recent moral pluralism so-called, or a flight to ineffability like that of G. E. Moore and the so-called intuitionists. These are striking examples of the terrible price that must be paid for the neglect of first philosophy. Basic concepts like goodness and rightness can be clarified only by ontological analysis. Unless they are so illumined they will either be reduced and distorted or fade into unintelligibility.

This is not only true of the foundational concepts of ethics but of those of the other disciplines as well. Philosophic data are more pervasive and richer than the abstract data of any of the more restricted sciences. Hence, the attempt to squeeze these data, with all their variegated content, into the limited perspectives of one science, or even of all the quantitative sciences, must always lead to reductive distortion of data, chaos, or unintelligibility.

The broad concepts of ontology alone are capable of opening up perspectives which can take account of all the immediate data of experience without incoherence. It is our primary duty at the present time to keep this perspective open, first of all by phenomenological description, then by careful analysis of the ontological data inaccessible to the restricted methods of what we now call *science*, and finally by the formulation of explanatory hypotheses which can be checked by these data. Unless we perform these arduous functions in a disciplined manner, authentic empiricism will vanish, to be replaced as it is now being replaced by linguistic analysis, or as it has already been replaced in many quarters by a spurious so-called empiricism which is only a deceptive disguise for a bigoted a priori dogmatism. Metaphysics is the foundational empirical discipline—the empirical science par excellence.

The great social and political struggles of our era have called forth widespread and intensive reflection on the nature of law and its foundations. As in the past, such reflection has led to a serious questioning of that positivistic legal theory which denies any natural foundations for prescriptive principles and reduces all law to the level of subjective human decree. In many law schools, an interest in moral realism and natural law is being revived. This interest is now shared by all those who have any living hope for the establishment of a world community without the use of military force. The realistic doctrine of natural law has received its most recent, and in certain ways its most adequate, political formulation in the United Nations Declaration of Human Rights. A covenant for the legal enforcement of these rights is now under consideration. Such a covenant would revolutionize international law and also modify the internal law of many countries, including our own.

These expressions of moral realism are widely discussed and debated throughout the world. Unfortunately, however, this world-wide interest has not penetrated to departments of philosophy and courses in ethics. The concepts of moral realism and natural law are hardly touched upon in current texts. If not entirely neglected, they are confused with other theories like utilitarianism, Kantianism, and intuitionism from which they are really quite distinct. Early versions are sometimes touched upon in historical contexts where they are deprived of that close study and disciplined criticism of which they are desperately in need.

This book is only a fragmentary introduction to the subject. We have had no time for the consideration of many objections which may be brought up. I have tried to show that the theory is radically distinct from others now familiar to us, that it is capable of coherent exposition, and that it is able to take account of many evident data of moral experience. To those ethical theorists who have become dissatisfied with the one-sided emphasis of current schools, this new doctrine may have an appeal as a broader mediating point of view. Others, dissatisfied with the recent emphasis on linguistic analysis may be interested in a doctrine which will certainly lead them to a close study of the phenomenology of moral experience—the final test for any empirical moral theory.

NOTES

NOTES TO INTRODUCTION

1. Cf. F. M. Cornford, *Plato's Cosmology* (New York: Harcourt, Brace and Co., Inc., 1937), pp. 1–8.

2. Warner Fite, *The Platonic Legend* (New York: Scribner's, 1934), p. 142.

3. *Ibid.*, p. 318.

4. R. H. S. Crossman, *Plato Today* (London: Allen and Unwin, 1937), pp. 296–97.

5. *Ibid.*, pp. 214–15.

6. K. R. Popper, *The Open Society and Its Enemies* (Princeton: Princeton University Press, 1950), p. 87. Cf. p. 166.

7. *Ibid.*, p. 189.

8. E. O. Sisson, *Proceedings and Addresses of the American Philosophical Association* (1939), p. 143.

NOTES TO CHAPTER 1

1. Popper, *The Open Society and Its Enemies*, pp. 184–95.

2. *Ibid.*, p. 180.

3. *Ibid.*

4. *Ibid.*, p. 185.

5. *Ibid.*, p. 127.

6. *Ibid.*, p. 185.

7. *Ibid.*, p. 127.

8. *Ibid.*

9. *Ibid.*, p. 429.

10. Unless specifically stated otherwise, all references to the works of Plato will be to the Loeb Classical Edition (Cambridge: Harvard University Press). *Apology* 23 A. Cf. 30–31.

11. *Apol.* 29 B, 39 A.

12. *Apol.* 30 A, 41 E.

13. *Apol.* 26 A.

14. *Apol.* 30 D.

15. *Apol.* 19 B–D.

16. Fite, *The Platonic Legend*, p. 299.

17. *Ibid.*, p. 305. Cf. p. 80.

18. Not by Fite, who refers to the *Republic* in this connection. Cf. p. 305. But the *Phaedo* offers more opportunities for one who wishes to confirm the common interpretation of Plato as a Manichaean dualist and unqualified body-hater. Cf. R. Niebuhr, *The Nature and Destiny of Man* (New York: Scribner's, 1941), I, 7, 31–33. Plato certainly follows Socrates in holding that the body is less important than the soul and naturally subordinate to it. The nature of the occasion itself elicits in the *Phaedo* a greater emphasis on this subordination than in the *Republic*. But there is no essential difference in doctrine.

19. As 66–67. Cf. 64 D–E, 82–83.

20. ὅτι μάλιστα μηδὲν ὁμιλῶμεν τῷ σώματι μηδὲ κοινωνῶμεν. . . .

21. *Phaedo* 64 B.

22. *Phaedo* 82 E 6–83 A 1.

23. Niebuhr, *The Nature and Destiny of Man*, I, 7. This charge is also made by Winspear, *The Genesis of Plato's Thought* (New York: Dryden Press, 1940), pp. 277–78, 214.

24. *Rep.* 485 B. Cf. 441 E ff.

25. *Philebus* 63 E ff.

26. Cf. *Laws* 863 B–864 B.

27. Crossman, *Plato Today*, pp. 275 ff.

28. *Ibid.*, p. 277.

29. *Ibid.*, p. 278.

30. *Ibid.* Cf. Niebuhr, *The Nature and Destiny of Man*, I, 227.

31. *Phaedo* 89 D ff.

32. Cf. *Rep.* 493 E 3 ff., *Gorgias* 471 E ff.

33. Cf. *Phaedrus* 276 D 3.

34. According to Niebuhr, "all human knowledge is tainted with an ideological taint. . . . It pretends to be final and ultimate knowledge." Niebuhr, *The Nature and Destiny of Man*, I, 194 ff.; II, 262. Cf. Niebuhr, *Christianity and Power Politics* (New York: Scribner's, 1940), pp. 113, 155.

35. "The democratic spirit, directly its ideas become accepted and established, is forced to escape from them and to find other and newer concepts with which to fulfill its task as the 'gadfly' of human lethargy." Crossman, *op. cit.*, p. 298. Crossman, however, is not consistent in his attribution of this undiluted negativism to Socrates. Cf. chap. 3, pp. 84 ff.

36. Fite, *op. cit.*, p. 146. The evidence offered for these extraordinary statements is a short passage (*Rep.* 386 B), where Plato deplores the terror and timidity inspired by popular views of the "underworld."

37. Crossman, *op. cit.*, pp. 217 ff., 237.

38. Popper, *op. cit.*, p. 163.

39. Popper is not the first to have suggested a bloodthirsty interpretation of this sort. Cf. Shorey, *Rep.*, note *ad loc.* and Winspear, *The Genesis of Plato's Thought*, p. 266. There is no ground for it in the text. If Plato had in mind the elimination of the total adult population, he could easily have said so; but he does not. Such an assertion would be out of keeping with the persuasive tenor of the context. What Plato says is not that the city will be wiped clean of men, but that "the city and the characters of men" will be wiped clean of prejudices and unsound attitudes. Cf. *Rep.* 429 D–430 B, where opinions are compared to dyes, the soul to

wool, and education to a coloring process. The wool needs to be carefully treated and prepared (not eliminated), so that it may become deeply and permanently colored. It is Socratic self-criticism that protects the soul from thinking it knows more than it actually does know, and thus prepares it for the deep reception and assimilation of truth. Cf. *Sophist* 230 B ff. Hence, this critical part of education is "the greatest and most efficacious of all purifications," μεγίστη καὶ κυριωτάτη τῶν καθαρσεών, *Sophist* 230 D 8. This is what Plato means by "cleaning the canvas."

40. A. J. Toynbee, *A Study of History* (New York: Oxford University Press, 1947), p. 540.

41. *Ibid.* Cf. p. 219.

42. *Ibid.*, pp. 219–20.

43. *Ibid.*, p. 542.

44. *Ibid.*, p. 543.

45. *Epistle* VII 331 D. Cf. *Crito* 51 C, *Laws* 717 B ff.

46. *Rep.* 387 B 5–7.

47. *Laws* 909 A.

48. *Politicus* 264 A.

49. *Politicus* 276 E.

50. *Rep.* 576 B 10.

51. *Phaedo* 66 C. Cf. *Rep.* 373 E.

52. *Rep.* 411 D 7–E 1.

53. Popper, *op. cit.*, pp. 162–63.

54. *Ibid.*, p. 413. Popper refers to *Timaeus* 51 D–E. This text never mentions the claim to special authority, nor exceptional *native* intelligence. The distinction between true opinion and knowledge is here explained in terms of four factors: first, opinion is produced by persuasion, knowledge by instruction and argument, referring not merely to authority but also to evidence; second, knowledge can give an explanation and a justification of itself by referring to evidence, but opinion cannot; third, knowledge is unshak-

able, while opinion is unstable; and fourth, knowledge is rarer than opinion because it is harder to attain. What Popper calls "intuitionism," the claim to a higher knowledge which can give no account of itself (cf. *Meno* 85 C ff., 97 E), far from being knowledge in Plato's sense, is precisely what he means by opinion.

55. *Ibid.*

56. Toynbee, *op. cit.*, p. 541.

57. *Philebus* 20 C–22 C.

58. A. E. Taylor, *Plato* (New York: Dial Press, 1936), pp. 2, 266, 295, 463.

59. Cornford, *Plato's Cosmology*, pp. 5 ff. For a fuller discussion of Plato as a practical philosopher, cf. J. D. Wild, *Plato's Theory of Man* (Cambridge: Harvard University Press, 1946), chap. 1.

60. *Rep.* 517 A.

61. Toynbee, *op. cit.*, p. 219. The philosopher also lives in the community. If he is unwilling to rule, he will be ruled by an inferior and must suffer the consequences (*Rep.* 347 C 1–5). By participating in government, the philosopher makes a contribution to "the common good" in which he also shares (*Rep.* 520 A1).

62. *Rep.* 352 E ff.

63. *Rep.* 357 A–358 A.

64. For Plato, cf. *Pol.* 271 E and the other myths of creation where *man* is always regarded in a unitarian manner. Cf. pp. 211 ff. For Toynbee, see *op. cit.*, pp. 242–43.

65. Cf. *Laws* 683 E ff. and Toynbee, *op. cit.*, pp. 51–60, 255–75.

66. Cf. The Myth of Er, *Rep.* 616 ff. Once the free choices are made, they are subject to the decrees of necessity. Cf. Toynbee, *op. cit.*, chaps. 16 and 18, especially pp. 307–9. Bad choices are punished by cultural breakdown and disintegration.

67. Cf. *Rep.* 427 D–434.

68. Cf. Toynbee, *op. cit.*, pp. 405–6.

69. *Ibid.*, chaps. 13–17. Cf. *Rep.* VIII.

70. *Laws* X, *Phaedo* 85 D 3–4.

71. Toynbee, *op. cit.*, pp. 495 ff., 524.

72. These antirational tendencies in Toynbee's thought are manifested in several characteristic but dubious doctrines: first, his view of society as a mere *coincidence* of individual fields of action (Toynbee, *op. cit.*, pp. 209 ff.); second, his idealization of "creation" and "change" without further qualification—surely all change, as such, is not good (pp. 62–67, 212 ff.).

Platonic philosophy, no doubt, lacks the fuller insight and inspiration for common action which has been often derived from high religion. But it can supply a more empirical and intelligible doctrine to replace these dubious, antirational elements in Toynbee's categorical scheme.

73. Cf. B. Bosanquet, *The Philosophical Theory of the State* (London: Macmillan and Co., 1930). For his totalitarian interpretation of Plato, cf. pp. 5–11, 208–9.

74. Popper, *op. cit.*, pp. 160, 219, 222. Cf. Winspear, *The Genesis of Plato's Thought*, pp. 225, 228, 263, 296, and Vlastos, "Slavery in Plato's Thought," *Philosophical Review*, L (1941), 303.

75. *Ibid.*, pp. 79 ff., 86, 102, 111, 112, 139, 220, 232.

76. *Laws* 716 C.

77. *Euthyd.* 290 C 1.

78. *Laws* 892 A, 896 C.

79. Cf. *Rep.* 544 E.

80. *Rep.* 544E

81. *Rep.* 497 C 8.

82. *Rep.* 545 D.

83. As Popper argues. Cf. Popper, *op. cit.*, pp. 79 ff.

84. The whole is distinct from *some* of its parts, but never from *all* of them. Hence, there is no difference between "whole" and "all of the parts." Cf. *Theaet.* 204 A 8–205 A 9.

85. The word κοινόν is often used for that co-operative activity of giving and receiving which constitutes the common good. *Rep.* 520 A 1. Cf. *Rep.* 369 B 5 ff., the realization of natural, common needs. There is no trace of any organic theory of the state.

86. *Rep.* 420 C–D.

87. *Rep.* 488.

88. Popper, *op. cit.*, pp. 37 ff., 67, 74, *et passim*.

89. *Ibid.*, pp. 41 ff.

90. Thus, at the beginning of Book VIII it is clearly stated that the subject to be discussed is not concrete human history as in *Laws* III, but forms or species of social order (544 A 3, εἴδη: cf. D 2, D 8), pure, unmixed justice and injustice (545 A 7). The discussion is not a statement of mixed fact (cf. *Phaedo* 103 B), but an analysis of pure forms and their ideal order. It is a hypothetical discussion of what would happen *if*, not a historical description. Cf. 545, 9–12.

91. This underlies the whole Platonic ethics, but is most clearly stated in the Myth of Er, *Rep.* 617 E.

92. This notion of a hypothetical moral law expressing what must happen *if* certain choices are made is seldom clearly focused in "naturalistic" ethical discussion. Thus, it is entirely absent from Popper's moral categories. For him a law is either a description of an observed sequence, admitting of no exceptions, or a norm expressing individual preference and sharply separated from fact. Cf. Popper, *op. cit.*, chap. 5.

93. *Rep.* 496 B.

94. *Rep.* 516 C ff.

95. As Popper holds. Cf. Popper, *op. cit.*, p. 41.

96. *Rep.* 472 E.

97. Cf. Fite, *op. cit.*, pp. 318 ff.

98. Cf. Popper, *op. cit.*, p. 103.

99. Cf. Toynbee, *op. cit.*, chap. 19.

100. *Rep.* 443 C–444 B. Cf. Adam, *Rep.*, note *ad loc.*

101. *Rep.* 619 B.

102. Toynbee, *op. cit.*, pp. 183–84.

103. Popper, *op. cit.*, p. 134.

104. *Ibid.*, p. 239, note 50.

105. Cf. *Laws* III. In this account of human history a strict philosophical neutrality between Greeks and barbarians is maintained. Cf. 699 E.

106. In commenting on the Myth of Metals at *Rep.* 414 C ff., Popper says: "These metals are hereditary, they are racial characteristics." Popper, *op. cit.*, p. 138. Cf. pp. 149–50. This, of course, is a *non sequitur*.

107. *Rep.* 503 B 6–E.

108. *Prot.* 361 A 7–C 2.

109. *Rep.* 519 A.

110. *Rep.* 412 E ff.

111. R. L. Nettleship, *Lectures on the Republic of Plato* (London: Macmillan and Co., 1937), p. 135, note 1.

112. Popper, *op. cit.*, p. 555.

113. *Rep.* 473 D.

114. K. R. Popper, *The Open Society and Its Enemies* (London: Routledge, 1945), I, 134–35. Cf. Amer. ed., pp. 149–50.

115. *Ibid.*, pp. 134.

116. Cf. *Laws* 693 A.

117. *Laws* 729 E–730 A.

118. Popper, *op. cit.* (Amer. ed.), pp. 70, 94, 112, 149.

119. *Ibid.*, p. 515.

120. A. E. Taylor, *Plato, the Man and His Work*, 3d ed. (London: Methuen, 1929), p. 271.

121. G. C. Field, *The Philosophy of Plato* (New York: Oxford University Press, 1949), pp. 89 ff.

122. W. C. Greene, *Moira* (Cam-

bridge: Harvard University Press, 1944), p. 238.

123. Winspear, *op. cit.*, p. 146.

124. Popper, *op. cit.* (Amer. ed.), pp. 95, 563.

125. On page 58 of the English edition (cf. Amer. ed., p. 70), Popper translates Antiphon (Diels, *Vorsokratiker*, 1922 ed., II, xxxvi, Fr. B, col. 2) as follows: "The nobly born we revere and adore; but not the lowly born. These are coarse habits. Our natural gifts are the same for all on all points whether we are Greeks or barbarians. . . . We all breathe the air through our mouth and nostrils." Popper is no doubt justified in referring to this as "equalitarian." But he also includes Antiphon in what he calls the "Athenian anti-slavery movement" (Eng. ed., p. 237), for which he gives no convincing evidence.

In the very next passage Antiphon seems to condemn all morality in any form, and on pages xxxii–xxxiii all prescriptions of law over eyes, ears, and desires. Popper refers to this as "utilitarian ethics" (Amer. ed., p. 70).

126. Wilamowitz - Moellendorff, *Platon*, 2d ed. (Berlin: Weidmann, 1920), p. 263.

127. Popper, *op. cit.* (Eng. ed.), pp. 113, 134, 162, 171, and notes 37, 47, 48 to chap. 8, pp. 234–37. Cf. Amer. ed., pp. 95, 151, 180, 560–64.

128. *Ibid.*, p. 162.

129. *Ibid.*, p. 236.

130. *Ibid.*

131. *Ibid.* (Amer. ed.), p. 149.

132. *Ibid.* (Eng. ed.), p. 250.

133. Popper's reasons for attributing the impressive array of liberal and humanitarian doctrines to Antisthenes are interesting. They will be exhaustively criticized by Levinson in his forthcoming book on Plato, soon to be published by the Harvard University Press. The following points made by him are of special importance.

In note 47 to chap. 8, p. 561, he sets forth the traditional view that the Cynic school came from Antisthenes and the Stoic school from the Cynics. Hence, the humanitarianism of Roman stoicism can be attributed to Antisthenes who, unlike Plato, the corrupter of Socratic teaching, derived it from his master, the humane Socrates. Cf. Eng. ed., pp. 207, 237, 250. Aside from other dubious assumptions, this, of course, ignores the many other channels through which ideas might pass from a single source and then later reunite.

Why are ideas like "the unity of mankind" and "the brotherhood" of all men attributed to Antisthenes? Antisthenes said there is one God by nature, many by convention. As Wilamowitz points out, this tells us very little until we know what he means by God. But, according to Popper, this affiliates him with the monism of Parmenides. This is confirmed by the fact that Antisthenes was a pupil of Gorgias, who was influenced by Zeno. Therefore, "Antisthenes was influenced by Parmenides," who elevated one God over many. So it is reasonable to suppose that Antisthenes elevated the one humanity over the many men "whom he *probably* considered as brothers, since equal in their distance from God" (Eng. ed., p. 234). In the text p. 162, the *probably* drops out, and Antisthenes is categorically asserted to be one of those "who developed . . . the creed of the universal empire of men."

134. *Ibid.* (Eng. ed.), pp. 82, 171, 262.

135. Cf. *Apol.* 22, *Gorg.* 515 ff.

136. *Apol.* 32 C.

137. *Crito* 53.

138. Cf. A. D. Winspear, *Who*

Was Socrates? (New York: Gordon Co., 1939), p. 24, and Winspear, *The Genesis of Plato's Thought*, pp. 213–14. Popper, *op. cit.*, pp. 41, 192–95.

139. *Prot.* 322 C.

140. Cf. Popper, *op. cit.* (Amer. ed.), pp. 39–40. (All later references will be to the Amer. ed.).

141. *Pol.* 273. Cf. *Laws* 677.

142. *Rep.* 617 E.

143. *Rep.* 617 E.

144. *Laws* III 694 ff.

145. "It [Book VIII] is intended to describe both the original course of development by which the main forms of constitutional decay were first generated and the typical course of social change." Cf. Popper, *op. cit.*, p. 42. Cf. also the note, p. 490, where this interpretation is defended as in accordance with "the whole spirit of Plato's logic," which demands that "the essence of a thing is to be understood by its original nature, i.e., by its historical origin."

This is certainly not Plato's view. The abstract essence must not be confused with *any* concrete exemplification whether first or last. Cf. *Phaedo* 103 B.

146. Popper, *op. cit.*, p. 39.

147. *Laws* 797 D.

148. Popper, *op. cit.*, chap. 9.

149. *Ibid.*, pp. 158, 160–61.

150. *Ibid.*, p. 155.

151. *Ibid.*, p. 156.

152. A citizen may use the gradual means of persuasion (piecemeal social engineering) to correct injustice in his country. Violence is *never* justified. Cf. *Crito* 51 B–C.

153. Cf. Winspear, *The Genesis of Plato's Thought*, p. 227, and Winspear, *Who Was Socrates?*, p. 24.

154. Popper, *op. cit.*, p. 169.

155. *Ibid.*

156. *Phaedrus* 249 A.

157. Popper, *op. cit.*, p. 218.

158. *Ibid.*

159. *Ibid.*, p. 211.

160. *Ibid.*, p. 189.

161. *Ibid.*, p. 67.

162. *Ibid.*, pp. 126 ff.

163. *Ibid.*, p. 195.

164. *Ibid.*, pp. 108 ff.

165. Cf. *ibid.*, especially chap. 4, text and notes, especially notes 3 and 11.

166. *Rep.* 425 B–427 A.

167. Fite, *op. cit.*, pp. 81–89.

168. "Never was a man more in earnest in his hostility towards the individual. . . . He hated the individual and his freedom . . ." (Popper, *op. cit.*, p. 103).

169. *Rep.* 496 E 4.

170. Cf. *Prot.* 329 A.

171. *Gorg.* 471 E ff.

172. Popper, *op. cit.*, pp. 184 ff.

NOTES TO CHAPTER 2

1. This common charge is made by Fite, Crossman, Popper, Toynbee, Winspear, and others.

2. Cf. *Menexenus* 238 C–D.

3. Winspear, *The Genesis of Plato's Thought*, pp. 168–70, and Popper, *The Open Society and Its Enemies*, pp. 189 ff.

4. *Apol.* 29 D. Cf. *Crito* 51.

5. *Epistle* VII 324 D–E.

6. *Epistle* VII 326 ff.

7. Cf. *Rep.* 518 B–D.

8. Fite, *The Platonic Legend*, p. 152.

9. Cf. Winspear, *The Genesis of Plato's Thought*, chaps. 10, 11, especially pp. 164, 223, 225, and Popper, *op. cit.*, pp. 189 ff. Winspear and Popper, however, differ radically on Socrates. For Winspear he was, like Plato, a reactionary enemy of democracy (cf. Winspear, *Who Was Socra-*

tes?), while for Popper he was a friend of the Periclean democracy and one of the great individualists of all times.

10. Cf. Crossman, *Plato Today* pp. 291 ff.

11. Cf. Popper, *op. cit.*, chap. 10.

12. *Ibid.*, p. 534, *et passim*.

13. Cf. Locke, who defines democracy in terms of majority rule. J. Locke, *A Second Treatise on Civil Government* (New York: Van Nostrand, 1947), chap. 10, "The Forms of a Commonwealth," pp. 141–42.

14. Fite, *op. cit.*, chap. 7.

15. *Ibid.*, pp. 134 ff. Cf. Vlastos, "Slavery in Plato's Thought," *Philosophical Review*, L (1941), 291–92. Hoernle refers to Plato's guardians as "a governing class" and "a selected élite." Hoernle, "Would Plato Have Approved of the National Socialist State?" *Philosophy*, XIII (1938), 172.

16. *Ibid.*, p. 152.

17. Crossman, *op. cit.*, pp. 265 ff.

18. Winspear, *The Genesis of Plato's Thought*, chap. 11.

19. Popper, *op. cit.*, p. 134.

20. *Ibid.*, p. 40.

21. *Ibid.*, p. 50.

22. *Ibid.*, p. 146.

23. *Ibid.*, p. 52.

24. *Ibid.*, pp. 50 ff., 148 ff. Crossman makes the same charge. Cf. Crossman, *op. cit.*, p. 132.

25. Hoernle's comparison of the *Republic* with the national socialist state is based on a relativism of this kind. Cf. Hoernle, *op. cit.*, pp. 168–69.

26. Cf. *Rep.* 369 B 5–6.

27. The guardians are referred to as: "Friends and supporters of whose freedom they had been the guardians," *Rep.* 547 C 1; "helpers of their fellow citizens," *Rep.* 417 B 1; "saviours and helpers," *Rep.* 463 B 1–2.

28. Popper, *op. cit.*, chap. 6. Vlas-

tos, *op. cit.*, p. 293, and Farrington, *Greek Science*, Penguin ed., I, 142, both preceded Popper in making this charge.

29. Otherwise, the selection of prospective guardians specifically referred to at *Rep.* 415 C 3 and 423 C 8 would be impossible. The early literary education (music and gymnastics) which continues to the age of twenty (*Rep.* 537 B) will also include mathematics and science, though taught in a "playful manner" quite distinct from the serious study of these subjects by the prospective guardians between the ages of 20 and 30. Cf. *Rep.* 536 E ff.

30. *Rep.* 422.

31. Crossman, *op. cit.*, p. 275.

32. Popper, *op. cit.*, pp. 136–41.

33. *Rep.* 382 A–C. Cf. 535 E.

34. *Rep.* 331 C.

35. Popper, *op. cit.*, pp. 138 ff. Cf. pp. 553–55.

36. *Ibid.*, p. 138.

37. *Ibid.*

38. *Rep.* 415 D 3. Cf. 414 E 2, 415 A 3 and A 8.

39. Crossman, *op. cit.*, p. 277.

40. Popper, *op. cit.*, p. 130.

41. *Theaet.* 189 E 4 ff.

42. *Rep.* III 412 D 7 ff.

43. *Rep.* 413 B 1–3.

44. Cf. Crossman, *op. cit.*, pp. 275 ff., and Popper, *op. cit.*, chap. 5. Cf. note 11, p. 580.

45. Crossman, *op. cit.*, chaps. 3–4, and Popper, *op. cit.*, pp. 130–31, 184–95.

46. Popper, *op. cit.*, pp. 598–603.

47. *Ibid.*, pp. 593, 603.

48. *Gorg.* 463 ff.

49. *Gorg.* 467–80.

50. *Rep.* 506 C ff.

51. *Gorg.* 495–503.

52. *Gorg.* 523 to end.

53. Praechter, *Die Philosophie des Altertums* (Berlin: E. S. Mittler, 1926), I, 336.

54. Fite, *The Platonic Legend*, p. 184.

55. *Ibid.*, pp. 189–90.

56. Niebuhr, *Nature and Destiny of Man*, I, 31–33.

57. *The Genesis of Plato's Thought*, p. 228.

58. *Ibid.*, p. 214.

59. *Plato Today*, p. 266.

60. *Ibid.*, pp. 266–67.

61. *Open Society* (Eng. ed.), pp. 61 ff.

62. *Ibid.*, pp. 61–62.

63. *Ibid.*, p. 64.

64. *Plato's Theology* (Ithaca: Cornell University Press, 1942), pp. 167 and 184.

65. H. Cairns, *Legal Philosophy from Plato to Hegel* (Baltimore: Johns Hopkins Press, 1949), p. 37.

NOTES TO CHAPTER 3

1. A view defended by Popper. Cf. *The Open Society and Its Enemies*, chap. 5.

2. Ethical terms, like *good* and *ought*, are often regarded as wholly beyond the range of rational analysis, as "ineffable," "unique," and "indefinable." From this point of view, any attempt to deal with them theoretically is a threat to the autonomy of ethics. Cf. pp. 85 ff. and 205 ff. for a further consideration of this difficulty.

3. *Nicomachean Ethics*, Book VI, 1139 b 3–4.

4. Cf. *infra*, pp. 91 ff.

5. I. Kant, *Fundamental Principles of the Metaphysic of Ethics*, Abbott tr. (10th ed.; New York: Longmans, 1929), pp. 78 ff.

6. *Ibid.*, pp. 71 ff.

7. R. B. Perry, *The General Theory of Value* (New York Longmans, 1926), chap. 5.

8. J. Bentham, *An Introduction to the Principles of Morals and Legislation* (London: W. Pickering, 1823), chap. 4.

9. F. H. Bradley, *Ethical Studies* (Oxford: Oxford University Press, 1927), Essay V.

10. Cf. C. L. Stevenson, "The Nature of Ethical Disagreement" in Feigl and Sellars, *Readings in Philosophical Analysis* (New York: Appleton, 1949), pp. 587 ff.

11. Winspear, *The Genesis of Plato's Thought*, p. 193.

12. *Ibid.*, p. 194.

13. Fite, *The Platonic Legend*, pp. 83 ff.

14. Cf. *Phaedo* 74 D 9, 75.

15. *Die Philosophie der Natur* (Berlin: de Gruyter, 1950), pp. 331 ff. and pp. 389–92. To hold that natural processes are structuralized is not to hold that they are determined by an intrinsic purpose. Thus, Aristotle makes it quite clear that in sub-human nature the final cause coincides with the *form* (cf. *Phys.* 198 a 25 and *De An.* 415 b 10 ff.).

In his polemic against formal structure Hartmann sometimes seems to speak as though process were a sheer indeterminate fluidity lacking form and therefore all intelligibility (*op. cit.*, p. 333). Such a view, if consistently defended, would make all analysis impossible.

So at other times we find Hartmann recognizing that "the causal process always has a determinate *direction*" (p. 333), and that a natural system (*das Gefüge*) must be defined as a relational complex "which has its own central determination" (p. 470). This, of course, is what has always been called formal structure. One can recognize such structure without reifying it into a subsistent entity which exists apart from process. Structure and flux are relational phases neither of which can exist apart from the other. A natural system is such a union of form and process, a "flowing form" (p. 390).

16. Most conditional propositions refer to such tendencies of something determinate towards a determination distinct from what it already is. Thus, for example, I may say that *if we prepare for war, there will be war; or if x has a certain disease, he will die.* The present difficulties into which the modern "logical" analysis of contrary-to-fact conditionals has fallen are due to the atomistic presuppositions of modern logic. An atomic fact either is or is not, and a proposition asserting it is, either true or false. But a tendency of A to B is a fact of a different kind. The tendency may exist if B does not, and even if neither A nor B exists in a given instance. Cf. Wild, "A Realistic Defense of Causal Efficacy," *Review of Metaphysics*, II, No. 8 (June, 1949), 1–14.

17. Similar natures must give rise to similar tendencies. This ontological principle lies at the root of the so-called "inductive" procedures of science.

18. Popper, *op. cit.*, pp. 73 ff.

19. *Ibid.*, p. 73.

20. *Ibid.*, p. 78.

21. *Ibid.*, pp. 206 ff.

22. *Ibid.*, chap. 11.

23. *Ibid.*, pp. 218 ff.

24. *Ibid.*, pp. 58–59.

25. *Ibid.*, p. 211.

26. *Ibid.*, pp. 211–12.

27. *Ibid.*, pp. 212–13.

28. This is also Plato's view in the later dialogues. Cf. *Theaet.* 186 C, and Farrington's comment *ad loc. Greek Science* (Penguin ed., 1949), I, 106–7.

29. Popper, *op. cit.*, p. 213.

30. *Ibid.*, pp. 213–17.

31. *Ibid.*, p. 214.

32. *Ibid.*

33. *Ibid.*, p. 215.

34. *Ibid.*, p. 207.

35. Popper omits this last step. But it is required if anything is to be demonstrated to be true.

36. Popper, *op. cit.*, pp. 65–66.

37. *Ibid.*, p. 65.

38. *Ibid.*, pp. 65–66.

39. This dualism has been thoroughly analyzed in an article by Henry Veatch, "Concerning the Distinction between Descriptive and Normative Science," *Phil. and Phen. Research*, VI (1945–46), 284 ff.

40. *Ibid.*, pp. 60–61.

41. *Ibid.*, pp. 58–60.

42. Fite, *op. cit.*, pp. 81–85.

43. Popper, *op. cit.*, chap. 5.

44. *Ibid.*, p. 60.

45. *Ibid.*, pp. 67 ff.

46. *Ibid.*, p. 58.

47. *Ibid.*, p. 59.

48. *Ibid.*

49. *Ibid.*

50. *Ibid.*, p. 64.

51. *Ibid.*, p. 61.

52. *Ibid.*, pp. 73–74.

53. *Ibid.*, p. 511, note 18.

54. *Pol.* 258 C.

55. *Pol.* 258 D 9.

56. *Nicomachean Ethics* 1139 b, 3–4.

57. *Nicomachean Ethics* 1140 a 24 ff., 1141 a 20 ff.

58. *Nicomachean Ethics* 1142 a 20 ff.

59. *Nicomachean Ethics* 1112 a 20 ff.

60. ἐπὶ τὸ πολύ: Aristotle *Physics* 196 B 11, *et passim.*

61. Cf. Aristotle's remarks on Antisthenes who apparently, like Popper, rejected the notion of real definition. Cf. Aristotle, *Metaphysics* 1024 b 32; 1043 b 24; and Popper, *op. cit.*, pp. 218, 636.

62. It is interesting to note that in his discussion of "metaphysical ethics," *Principia Ethica* (Cambridge, 1922), G. E. Moore takes no

cognizance of realism and fails to consider the views of Plato and Aristotle. They certainly attempted to clarify the meaning of basic ethical terms by ontological analysis. Hence, they must have committed "the naturalistic fallacy." But Aristotle, at least, certainly thought of metaphysics as an empirical discipline, whereas Moore thinks of it as being concerned exclusively with "supersensible" realities (p. 112).

63. Cf. Moore, *op. cit.*, chap. 1.

64. Popper, *op. cit.*, chap. 5, p. 512, note 18.

65. Essence is what makes a thing *what it is* and marks it off from other entities. Existence is what actualizes an essence in different modes and separates it from nothing.

66. Good in the broadest ontological sense is what we have in mind when we apply it to nonhuman animals and plants as an analogous term. The *human* good, its ethical sense, applies to man and is univocal, at least so far as *essential* goodness is concerned. The concrete realization of an individual, including all of his accidents, may be only analogous to that of another.

67. A basic source of confusion in the theory of definition is a neglect of the intentional or relational structure of all cognition as cognitive-act-in-relation-to-an-object. All cognition is of something. Regarded purely symbolically, the symbol of the *definiendum* differs from that of the *definiens*. From this point of view, the two are strictly different, and definition becomes a paradox, for we cannot see any unity. As a matter of fact, this unity lies in the intentional object. The object of *definiendum* and *definiens* is the same. The mode of apprehension differs.

68. Popper, *op. cit.*, p. 78.

69. Winspear, *The Genesis of Plato's Thought*, chap. 5.

70. *Ibid.*, chap. 4. A similar interpretation of Greek intellectual history is presented by Farrington, *Greek Science*, Penguin ed., I, 1949, pp. 38–63 and pp. 76–88.

71. *Ibid.*, pp. 105–11.

72. It is interesting to compare Winspear's interpretations of pre-Socratic philosophers with those of Popper. Heraclitus, for example, is classified by Winspear as a "materialist" and a "progressive philosopher" (*ibid.*, pp. 113, 126–30), and by Popper as an antidemocratic historicist and tribalist (Popper, *op. cit.*, chap. 2). For Winspear, Parmenides is a static, idealist conservative (*ibid.*, pp. 98–102), while for Popper he helped to inspire the democratic philosopher Antisthenes with a progressive faith in monotheism and universal human brotherhood (*ibid.*, p. 560, note 37).

73. Winspear, *Who Was Socrates?* p. 19. Cf. also: "To the idealists, concerned as they were to defend inequality and the rule of the few as just, justice became an eternal principle, a transcendent authority, a divine self, speaking through semidivine teachers and prophets. To the sophists, concerned to defend the right of democrats to overthrow the rule of a favored few, justice was a historical arrangement, relative to the growth of the society that produced it and claiming no greater validity than the sanction of custom and social agreement" (Winspear, *The Genesis of Plato's Thought*, p. 77).

74. Popper, *op. cit.*, p. 72.

75. Winspear, *The Genesis of Plato's Thought*, pp. 147 ff.

76. Popper, *op. cit.*, pp. 388 ff.

77. Cf. *ibid.*, pp. 65–66.

78. H. Kelsen, *Naturrechtslehre und das Rechtspositivismus* (Charlottenburg: Pan-Verlag Rolf Heise, 1928).

79. Cf. chap. 5, C, and chap. 6, B.

NOTES TO CHAPTER 4

1. *Hastings Encyclopedia of Religion and Ethics*, "Natural Law."

2. Diogenes Laertius, *Lives of Eminent Philosophers*, with Eng. tr. by R. D. Hicks (London: W. Heinemann, Loeb Classical Library, 1925), pp. 7, 140.

3. Von Arnim, *Stoicorum veterum fragmenta* (Leipzig: Teubner, 1903–24), II, 915.

4. *Ibid.*, I, 555.

5. *Ibid.*, II, 300.

6. *Ibid.*, pp. 308, 325.

7. *Ibid.*, I, 200, 201, and II, 263.

8. Cf. *Hermes* 51 (1916), pp. 598 ff.

9. According to Zeno, the supreme moral principle is ὁμολογουμένως τῇ φύσει ζῆν. Von Arnim, *Stoic. vet. fr.*, I, 179.

10. Seneca, *De vita beata* 8, 2, which is undoubtedly a statement of the ancient traditional doctrine.

11. *The Meditations of the Emperor Marcus Aurelius*, translated with Commentary by A. S. L. Farquharson (Oxford: Clarendon Press, 1944), Vol. I, Book VI, p. 38.

12. *Ibid.*, Vol. I, Book X, p. 2.

13. *Ibid.*, Book X, p. 38.

14. *Ibid.*, Book IV, p. 36.

15. *Ibid.*, Book XII, p. 32.

16. *Ibid.*, Book V, p. 3.

17. *Ibid.*, Book V, p. 16.

18. *Ibid.*, Book X, p. 15.

19. Cf. *Prima Secundae*, qu. 90–97.

20. *Ibid.*, Part I, qu. 47, art. 3.

21. "Nomen naturae videtur significare essentiam rei, secundum quod habet ordinem vel ordinationem ad propriam operationem rei." *Summa Theologica*, I, 29, art. 1, ad 4. Cf. I, 65, art. 3.

22. *Ibid.*, I, 48, art. 1. Cf. I, 5, art. 1, and 44, art. 4.

23. "Unde cum anima rationalis sit propria forma hominis, naturalis inclinatio inest cuilibet homini ad hoc quod agat secundum rationem; et hoc est agere secundum virtutem" (*ibid.*, I, 44, art. 3).

24. *Prima Secundae*, qu. 94, art. 2.

25. *Ibid.*, Part I, qu. 5, art. 3.

26. *Ibid.*, Part I, qu, 5, art, 3, ad 2.

27. R. Hooker, *The Laws of Ecclesiastical Polity* (Keble ed.; Oxford: Clarendon Press, 1865), I, 237.

28. *Ibid.*, p. 215.

29. *Ibid.*, p. 239.

30. *Ibid.*, p. 237.

31. *Ibid.*, p. 234.

32. *Ibid.*, p. 215.

33. Hugonis Grotii, *De Jure Belli et Pacis*, ed. Whewell (London: Cambridge University Press, 1853), Vol. I, *Prolegomena*, pp. xli–xlii.

34. "Ex principio aliquo intelligente extrinsico" (*ibid.*, p. xlii). Cf. *ab auctore naturae Deo*, Book I, p. 10.

35. "Nam ut esse rerum postquam sunt et qua sunt aliunde non pendet, ita et proprietates, quae esse illud necessario consequuntur . . ." (*ibid.*, Book I, p. 12).

36. "Est autem jus naturale adeo immutabile, et ne a Deo quidem mutari potest. . . . Sicut ergo ut bis duo non sint quatuor ne a Deo quidem potest effici, ita ne hoc quidem, ut quod intrinseca ratione malum est, malum non sit" (*ibid.*).

37. *Ibid.*, Book I, p. 29.

38. *Ibid.*

39. Grotii, *Prolegomena, op. cit.*, p. xli.

40. *Ibid.*, p. xliv.

41. *Ibid.*, Book I, p. 10.

42. *Ibid.*, Book I, p. 16.

43. *Ibid.*, Book I, p. 4.

44. *The Works of Tom Paine*, ed. Faner (New York: Citadel Press, 1945), I, 483.

45. *Ibid.*, II, 752.

46. *Ibid.*, I, 275.

47. *Ibid.*, I, 342.

48. *Ibid.*, I, 274.
49. *Ibid.*, I, 356.
50. *Ibid.*
51. *Ibid.*, I, 275.
52. *Ibid.*, p. 276.
53. Paine, *Rights of Man, op. cit.*, I, 316.
54. *Ibid*, I, 398.
55. *Ibid.*, p. 388.
56. *Ibid.*
57. Hobbes, *Leviathan* (Oxford: Clarendon Press, 1909), chap. xxxi.
58. *Ibid.*
59. *Ibid.*, chap. xiii.
60. *Ibid.*
61. *Ibid.*
62. *Ibid.*
63. Hobbes, *Elements of Philosophy* in *The English Works of Thomas Hobbes*, ed. Molesworth, I, 19–20.
64. Hobbes, *Elements of Philosophy*, chap. viii.
65. *An Answer to Bishop Bramhall*, ed. Molesworth, *Works*, IV, 309.
66. *Elements of Philosophy*, chap. xxvi.
67. *Leviathan*, chap. xxxi.
68. *Philosophical Rudiments*, ed. Molesworth, *Works*, II, 150.
69. *Leviathan*, chap. xiv.
70. *Philosophical Rudiments*, II, 186.

71. *Leviathan*, chap. xvii.
72. *Human Nature*, ed. Molesworth, *Works*, IV, 32.
73. Locke, *An Essay concerning Human Understanding*, Book IV, chap. 10.
74. *Ibid.*, Book II, chaps. 21, 26; Book IV.
75. Locke, *A Second Treatise on Civil Government*, chap. ii, p. 78.
76. *Ibid.*, chap. ix, p. 141.
77. *Essay*, Book III, chap. vi, sec. 9.
78. *Ibid.*, chap. vi, p. 44.
79. *Ibid.*, Book II, chap. xxvi.
80. *A Second Treatise on Civil Government*, chap. vi, sec. 89.
81. *Ibid.*, chap. ii, sec. 15, pp. 82–83.
82. Cf. Hooker, *Ecclesiastical Polity*, Book I, p. 10.
83. Locke, *A Second Treatise on Civil Government*, chap. ix, pp. 130 and 141.
84. *Ibid.*, secs. 129–30, pp. 140–41.
85. *Essay*, Book II, chap. xxviii, sec. 6.
86. *Ibid.*, Book I, chap. iii, sec. 4.
87. *Ibid.*, Book II, chap xxviii, sec. 7.
88. *Ibid.*, sec. 8.
89. *Ibid.*, chap. xxviii, sec. 5.

NOTES TO CHAPTER 5

1. "Ego Stoicorum sanae doctrinae proxime accedo": *Eris Scandica* (2d ed.; 1743), pp. 102–3. From this it was only a short step to the widely current view that the whole theory of natural law began with the Stoics. This theory is openly expressed or tacitly assumed by most histories of philosophy which are widely read at the present time.

2. *The Catholic Encyclopedia* in its account of natural law, though not so explicit, gives a similar impression. The views of Aquinas are presented, and the Stoics are mentioned. Plato and Aristotle are not even referred to, except for some disparaging remarks concerning incidental aspects of their moral theory.

3. Cf. G. H. Sabine, *A History of Political Theory* (New York: Holt, 1938), who says nothing of natural law in Plato and Aristotle, but first mentions this doctrine in connection with Cicero, p. 164. Cf. Dessoir, *Geschichte der Philosophie* (Berlin, 1929), p. 209, and Paul Barth, *Die Stoa* (Stuttgart: F. Frommann, 1908), p. 195, and Carlyle, *A History of Mediaeval Political Theory in the*

West (Edinburgh and London: W. Blackwood, 1930), I, 8.

4. Cf. J. Sauter, *Die Philosophischen Grundlagen des Naturrechts* (Vienna: Springer, 1932), pp. 44 ff.

5. ". . . the stoic theory is not so radically different from the classical Greek—from Plato's at any rate —as it is orthodox among historians of political theory to maintain" (G. P. Maguire, *Plato's Theory of Natural Law*, "Yale Classical Studies," X [1947], 178).

6. H. Grotius, *De Jure Belli et Pacis* (Whewell ed.; Cambridge: Cambridge University Press, 1853), *Proleg.*, sec. 11, Vol. I, p. xlvi. Cf. Book I, sec. 5: *Est autem jus naturale adeo immutabile, ut ne a Deo quidem mutari queat.*

7. "Modern students of Plato have largely ignored this (natural law) aspect of his thought" (Maguire, *op. cit.*, p. 152).

8. περὶ φύσεως. *Protagoras* 315 C 5.

9. *Phaedo* 103 B. Cf. *Republic* 515 B 5.

10. *Parmenides* 132 D: τὰ μὲν εἴδη ταῦτα ὥσπερ παραδείγματα ἑστάναι ἐν τῇ φύσει.

11. *Die Kerngedanken der Platonischen Philosophie* (München: Reinhardt, 1931), pp. 118 ff., 144, and 181 ff.

12. *Gorgias* 508 A. Maguire gives an illuminating interpretation of this passage, *op. cit.*, pp. 160–62.

13. εἶναι διαφερόντως φύσει. *Laws* 892 B–C.

14. *Laws* 714 C 3. Cf. 715 A.

15. *Ibid.*, 715 E 7.

16. *Ibid.*, 716 A.

17. πέφυκε. *Ibid.*, 870 B 4–5.

18. *Philebus* 25 D ff. Cf. *Timaeus* 50.

19. *Phaedrus* 271 A.

20. τοῦτο γὰρ φαμὲν φύσιν εἶναι δεικνύναι. *Ibid.*

21. *Rep.* 598 A 1.

22. τὴν τοῦ κάλλους φύσιν. *Phaedrus* 254 B.

23. *Phil.* 25 A.

24. Cf. *Rep.* 525 C and 597 D 3, *Sophist* 245 C, and *Cratylus* 387 A 1.

25. τὴν οὐσίαν δείξει ἀκριβῶς τῆς φύσεως. *Phaedrus* 270 E 3.

26. Cf A. Diès, *Autour de Platon* (Paris: G. Beauchesne, 1927), II, 594; C. Ritter, *Platon* (Munich: Beck, 1923), II, 74–75; and the interesting remarks of G. C. Field, *The Philosophy of Plato* (Oxford: University Press, 1949), p. 39.

27. *Phaedo* 75 B.

28. τῷ τί ποιεῖν αὐτὸ πέφυκεν ἢ τῷ τί παθεῖν ὑπὸ τοῦ. *Phaedrus* 270 D 6–7.

29. *Tim.* 62 B.

30. εἰς ὃ αὐτοῦ ἡ φύσις ἐπιτηδειοτάτη πεφυκυῖα εἴη. *Rep.* 433 A 6.

31. Cf. *Politicus* 264 A, *Crat.* 389 C 6–7, *Laws* 927 B 3, *Rep.* 490 A.

32. *Crat.* 393 C; cf. 394 D, and *Laws* 932 A 1.

33. Τῇ φύσει ἀνάγκη. *Rep.* 558 D–E. Cf. 554, 561 A–C, 572 C, 581 E, 586 A–B; *Phil.* 62 A, and *Laws* 782 D.

34. *Phaedrus* 249 E.

35. εἰς δύναμιν ἕκαστον τὸ προσῆκον πάσκει καὶ ποιεῖ. *Laws* 903 B 6–7.

36. Maguire refers to *Rep.* IX 517 A ff., 577 C, and 588 C ff. in this connection. As he says: "the pictures, especially in the *Republic*, of the unhappiness which flows from the disorderliness of the unjust Soul, inevitably remind us of another idea so common in later theorists—the *poenae naturales* which follow upon violations of the Natural Law" (Maguire, *op. cit.*, p. 159).

37. *Laws* 906 A 8.

38. δύναμις τοῦ πορίζεσθαι τἀγαθά. *Meno* 78 C 1.

248   NOTES TO PAGES 144−58

39. *Gorgias* 506 D 5.
40. *Rep.* 435 E 2: εἴδη τε καὶ ἤθη.
41. These normative terms occur constantly in the writings of Plato, expressing the general notion of obligation and oughtness.
42. *Laws* 765 E: πρὸς ἀρετην τῆς αὐτοῦ φύσεως. . . .
43. *Ibid.*, 631 D 1–2.
44. *Rep.* 428 E 9: κατὰ φύσιν.
45. *Crat.* 390 E ff. and 395 D 4: ὀρθῶς καὶ κατὰ φύσιν.
46. *Laws* 682 A: κατὰ φύσιν.
47. κατὰ φύσιν, *ibid.*, 642 A.
48. *Meno* 78 C 1.
49. *Phil.* 22 B: οἷσπερ δυνατὸν ἦν οὕτως ἀεὶ διὰ βίου ζῆν.
50. *Rep.* 381 C 2.
51. *Ibid.*, 501 B: θεοειδές τε καὶ θεοείκελον, cf. *Theaetetus* 176 C.
52. *Rep.* 352 A 6: ἀδύνατον αὐτὸν πράττειν.
53. *Ibid.*, 352 C 7.
54. *Gorgias* 477 B 2–C.
55. Cf. *Laws* 906 A.
56. *Rep.* 586 C: τὸ βέλτιστον ἑκάστω, τοῦτο καὶ οἰκειότατον.
57. *Tim.* 90 C 6: τὰς οἰκείας ἑκάστω τροφὰς καὶ κινήσεις ἀποδιδόναι.
58. *Theaet.* 172 B.
59. *Crat.* 387 A 1.
60. *Phil.* 44 E.
61. *Ibid.*, 45 A 2.
62. *Laws* 777 D 5.
63. *Rep.* 611 B 1: τῇ ἀληθεστάτῃ φύσει.
64. *Charmides* 156 E 6: πάντα γὰρ ἔφη ἐκ τῆς ψυχῆς ὡρμῆσθαι, καὶ τὰ κακὰ καὶ τὰ ἀγαθὰ τῷ σώματι καὶ

παντὶ τῷ ἀνθρώπῳ, καὶ ἐκεῖσθεν ἐπιρρεῖν. . . .
65. *Symposium* 206 A 6: καὶ εἶναι τὸ ἀγαθὸν αὐτοῖς ἐρῶσιν.
66. *Ibid.*, 205 A: κτήσει γάρ, ἔφη, ἀγαθῶν οἱ εὐδαίμονες εὐδαίμονες. . . .
67. *Laws* 631 B–E.
68. *Gorgias* 469 B 5–6.
69. *Ibid.*, 499 C 6 ff.
70. A. O. Lovejoy, *Essays in the History of Ideas* (Baltimore: Johns Hopkins Press, 1948), Essays V and XVI.
71. *Rep.* 509 B 6 ff.
72. G. C. Field, *op. cit.*, pp. 60–61.
73. *Plato's Theology* (Ithaca: Cornell University Press, 1942), p. 167; cf. p. 184.
74. *Timaeus* 69 C–D.
75. *Pol.* 268 D–274 E.
76. *Meno* 73 A–D.
77. *Rep.* 473 D.
78. *Ibid.*, 499 C.
79. *Laws* 793 B.
80. *Rep.* 353 ff.
81. The word χρή is often used in this connection, as at *Rep.* 331 C: "If one who has loaned us a weapon goes mad and demands it from us," then: οὔτε χρὴ τὰ τοιαῦτα ἀποδιδόναι— or as Shorey translates: "We ought not to return such things in that case."
82. *Rep.* 339 ff.
83. ἡμετέρα χρεία. *Ibid.*, 369 B.
84. ἱκανὸν τελεώτατον.
85. τέλεον.
86. *Rep.* 443 ff.
87. τοιούτου ὄντος φύσει. *Ibid.* 445 A 9.
88. *Ibid.*, 444 D 3.

NOTES TO CHAPTER 6

1. Sir W. D. Ross, *Aristotle* (New York: Scribner's, 1924).
2. N. Hartmann, *Ethics*, Coit tr. (New York: Macmillan, 1932), sec. 5.
3. H. A. Prichard, *Moral Obliga-*

tion (Oxford: Oxford University Press, 1949), chap 3, especially pp. 52–53.
4. *Physics* 189 a 27: τὴν τῶν ὄντων φύσιν.

5. *Metaphysics* 1005 a 33: περὶ τε τῆς ὅλης φύσεως σκοπεῖν καὶ περὶ τοῦ ὄντος.

6. Cf. *Meta*. xii. 10.

7. *De Anima* 432 b 21.

8. ἡ φύσις ἀεὶ ποιεῖ τῶν ἐνδεχομένων τὸ βέλτιστον; *De Caelo* 288 a 2. Cf. *Parts of Animals* 658 a 23; *Nicomachean Ethics* 1099 b 21, *et passim*.

9. *Parts of An.* 645 a 23: ἐν τοῖς τῆς φύσεως ἔργοις.

10. *Ibid.*, 645 a 25.

11. *Meta.* 1075 a 11: ἡ τοῦ ὅλου φύσις.

12. *Ibid.*, 1075 a 18: πρὸς μὲν γὰρ ἓν ἅπαντα συντέτακται. . . .

13. *Ibid.*, 1075 a 19.

14. *Rhetoric* 1360 a 5.

15. *Meta.* 1015 a 13; cf. *Phys.* 193 a 30 ff.

16. *Phys.* 193 b 1; cf. *Meta.* 1015 a 5.

17. *Meta.* 1032 a 24: ἡ κατὰ τὸ εἶδος λεγομένη φύσις.

18. *Generation of Animals* 770 b 16: ἡ κατὰ τὸ εἶδος φύσις.

19. *Phys.* 192 b 13: τὰ μὲν γὰρ φύσει ὄντα πάντα φαίνεται ἔχοντα ἐν ἑαυτοῖς ἀρχὴν κινήσεως καὶ στάσεως.

20. *Ibid.*, i. 7 ff.

21. *Meta.* v. 4, 1015 a 17: καὶ ἡ ἀρχὴ τῆς κινήσεως τῶν φύσει ὄντων αὕτη [οὐσία].

22. *Gen. of An.* 740 b 35: ἡ ποιοῦσα δύναμις.

23. *Ibid.*, 741 a 1. Cf. *Parts of An.* 658 a 23, 32; 659 b 35; *Eudemian Ethics* 1247 a 10, *et passim*.

24. *De An.* 415 b 11: ἡ οὐσία τῶν ἐμψύχων σωμάτων ἡ ψυχὴ αἰτία.

25. *Ibid.*, 415 b 12: τὸ γὰρ αἴτιον τοῦ εἶναι πᾶσιν ἡ οὐσία.

26. *Ibid.*, 415 b 10.

27. *Ibid.*, 415 b 21.

28. *Ibid.*, 415 b 23.

29. *Ibid.*, 416 a 19.

30. *Ibid.*, 413 b 11.

31. *Phys.* 198 b 35.

32. Cf. Plato, *Laws* 792 B 1, and 875 D 4.

33. *Nic. Eth.* 1106 a 22: ἕξις ἀφ' ἧς ἀγαθὸς ἄνθρωπος γίνεται καὶ ἀφ' ἧς εὖ τὸ ἑαυτοῦ ἔργον ἀποδώσει.

34. *Rhetoric* 1361 b 3.

35. *Nic. Eth.* 1106 a 14.

36. *Ibid.*, 1106 a 15: πᾶσα ἀρετή οὗ ἂν ᾖ ἀρετή, αὐτό τε εὖ ἔχον ἀποτελεῖ καὶ τὸ ἔργον αὐτοῦ εὖ ἀποδίδωσιν. . . .

37. *Phys.* 192 b: παρὰ φύσιν.

38. *Ibid.*, 255 a 29: κατὰ φύσιν.

39. *Meta.* 1048 a.

40. *Ibid.*, 1021 b 20: τελείωσις.

41. *Nic. Eth.* 1096 b 34.

42. *Ibid.*, 1094 a 3: οὗ πάντ' ἐφίεται.

43. *Meta.* 105 a: τὸ γὰρ ἔργον τέλος, ἡ δὲ ἐνέργεια τὸ ἔργον διὸ καὶ τοὔνομα ἐνέργεια λέγεται κατὰ τὸ ἔργον, καὶ συντείναι πρὸς τὴν ἐντελέχειαν.

44. Change is a passage from the *absence* to the *presence* of some character. This is not fulfilment—ἐνέργεια. Activity is the realization of a tendency already possessed in act. Thus, in order to think, we must have actual habits already formed within us. These are not eliminated but rather sustained and strengthened in the acts of their fulfilment. Hence, Aristotle refers to such activity as the "growth of an entity (not into something different but into its very self) and the fullness of realization": εἰς αὐτὸ γὰρ ἡ ἐπίδοσις καὶ εἰς ἐντελέχειαν; *De An.* 417 a 6. Happiness, the human good, is a self-sustaining activity of this kind. *Nic. Eth.* I. 10.

45. *Meta.* 1050 b 1: ζωὴ γὰρ ποιά τις ἐστίν.

46. *Ibid.*, 996 a 24.

47. *Nic. Eth.* 1218 a 32: ἕκαστον γὰρ ἰδίου ἀγαθοῦ ὀρέγεται.

48. *Ibid.*, 1096 b 28. Aristotle's remarks are often interpreted as a

complete rejection of the Platonic idea of the good. This, I believe, is a mistake. He also maintains that all good things share something in common, i.e., a proportional similarity. But without the notion of analogy, this Platonic conception cannot be adequately defended against the charge of equivocation.

49. *Ibid.*, 1097 b 15: τὸ δ᾽ αὔταρχες τίθεμεν ὃ μενοῦμενον αἱρετὸν ποιεῖ τὸν βίον καὶ μηδενὸς ἐνδεᾶ.

50. *De An.* 417 b 6; cf. *Meta.* 1050 a 34.

51. *Meta.* 1051 a 20–21: ἁμάρτημα and διαφθορά.

52. *Ibid.*, 1051 a 17.

53. *Phys.* 193 b 16: ἀλλὰ τὸ φυόμενον ἐκ τινὸς εἰς τὶ ἔρχεται, ἧ φύεται. εἰς τί οὖν φύεται; οὐκὶ ἐξ οὗ, ἀλλ᾽ εἰς ὅ. ἡ ἄρα μορφὴ φύσις.

54. *Ibid.*, 194 a 28: ἡ δὲ φύσις τέλος καὶ οὗ ἕνεκα.

55. *Meta.* 1048 a.

56. *Nic. Eth.* 1135 a 5.

57. *Politics* 1325 b 30.

58. *Nic. Eth.* 1135 a 2.

59. *Phys.* 198 a 25, *Meta.* 1044 a 36, *Pol.* 1252 b 30.

60. *Phys.* 192 b 22.

61. *Ibid.*, 192 b 35: κατὰ φύσιν.

62. *Nic. Eth.* 1103 a 24.

63. *Ibid.*, 1102 a 19.

64. *Pol.* 1252 b 12.

65. *Ibid.*, 1252 b 30.

66. *Ibid.*, 1252 b 33.

67. *Ibid.*, 1253 a 1.

68. *Nic. Eth.* 1097 a 14.

69. *Ibid.*, 1097 a 14.

70. *Meta.* 1021 b 21.

71. *Ibid.*, 1021 b 23.

72. Cf. E. Levy, "Natural Law in Roman Thought," *Studia et Documenta Historiae et Juris* (1949).

NOTES TO CHAPTER 7

1. A. I. Melden, "On the Method of Ethics," *Journal of Philosophy*, XLV (1948), 179.

2. W. K. Frankena, "Main Trends in Moral Philosophy at Mid-Century," *Philosophical Review* (January, 1951), p. 50.

3. Hume, *A Treatise on Human Nature* (London: Longmans, Green, 1878), Part II, sec. 6.

4. Cf. *Essays in* East-West *Philosophy*, edited by C. A. Moore (Honolulu: University of Hawaii Press, 1951), pp. 249–71.

5. Plato, *Sophist* 247 D–E.

6. Cf. Gredt, *Elementa Philosophiae Aristotelico-Thomisticae* (Herder, 1926), II 242–43.

7. *Ibid.*, 255 ff.

8. *Ibid.*, 155–56.

9. Thus, Gredt, following John of St. Thomas, defines *potentia* (which we have called tendency) as "an accident disposing the subject to operating or resisting," II, 155. He classifies this as a species of the univocal genus *quality*, and includes under it such diverse tendencies as nutrition, organic growth, intellectual, and voluntary power (p. 156).

10. Hartmann, *Die Philosophie der Natur* (Berlin: Walter de Gruyter & Co., 1950). This is certainly the most thoroughgoing and best informed treatise on the philosophy of nature which has been published for a long time.

11. Cf. Hartmann, *op. cit.*, pp. 216 ff.

12. *Ibid.*, Abschnitt IV, pp. 442 ff.

13. *Ibid.*, pp. 447–74.

14. Hartmann, *Grundlegung der Ontologie*, Westkulturverlag Anton Hain, Meisenheim, 1948, pp. 128–50; *Möglichkeit und Wirklichkeit*, 1949, chaps. 31–32; and *Phil. der Natur*, pp. 349, 367, and 375.

15. Hartmann, *Phil. der Natur*, pp. 329 and 391.

16. *Ibid.*, pp. 325 ff., 340.

17. *Ibid.*, pp. 311, 333, 383.

INDEX OF NAMES

INDEX OF SUBJECTS

255